Margaret,
daughter of Beatrice

by the same author

PRIVATE MEMBER:
A psychoanalytically orientated study
of contemporary politics

Margaret,
daughter of Beatrice

A Politician's Psycho-biography of
Margaret Thatcher

LEO ABSE

JONATHAN CAPE
THIRTY-TWO BEDFORD SQUARE LONDON

First published 1989
© Leo Abse 1989
Jonathan Cape Ltd, 32 Bedford Square, London WC1B 3SG

A CIP catalogue record for this book
is available from the British Library

ISBN 0-224-02726-3

Photoset in Linotron Bembo by
Rowland Phototypesetting Ltd
Bury St Edmunds, Suffolk
Printed in Great Britain by
Mackays of Chatham PLC

To my friends, John Denham, psychiatrist; Eva Rosenfeld,
psychoanalyst; Maurice Capel, philosopher; and
Tom Williams, Parliamentarian and judge.
In memoriam.

And to

Marjorie and Bathsheba in love.

The secret of the greatest fruitfulness and the greatest enjoyment of existence is: *to live dangerously*. Build your cities under Vesuvius! Send your ships into uncharted seas! Be robbers and conquerors – you lovers of knowledge!

NIETZSCHE

Contents

Acknowledgments

Responsibility for the contents and the blemishes of this book are mine, but responsibility for the book having been written must be shared by my historian son, Dr Tobias Abse. His refusal to allow me to grow my roses upon my retirement in 1987 from the Commons, and his provocations and persistent dialogues with me, ensured the completion of the essay. That he should have spared time for his incitements whilst heavily engaged in producing a book of his own was indeed selflessness.

I am also indebted to three of my friends. Michael Foot generously read early drafts of many of the chapters, and by his constructive criticism and encouragement spurred me on; Geoffrey Goodman, former industrial editor of the Mirror Group, gave me invaluable advice; and Dr Graham Little, Reader in Political Science at the University of Melbourne, defied geography and unstintingly put at my disposal his own researches into political leadership.

Barbara Kirton, my personal assistant and amanuensis during the whole of my professional and political life, has, in preparing the book for publication, yet again shown her forbearance and loyalty.

I must add that, without having been both a participant and observer at Westminster, I would not have presumed to embark upon this enterprise. That was possible because of the support of members of the Torfaen Labour Party and, over thirty years, of the electorate of the Eastern Valley of Gwent. This is their book as much as it is mine.

Apologia

IN the middle of August 1986 the Conservative Party Central Office made, with the concurrence of Margaret Thatcher, its fateful decision to contest the next election primarily on the basis of the Prime Minister's personality. The *Daily Telegraph*, then handmaiden of the Tory Party, unequivocally stated the rationale of the Tory strategists: 'They believe', we were informed, 'that on the basis of personality Mrs Thatcher wins hands down over her opponents.' Moreover, to indicate to the press and television that no antic was barred in pursuit of the tactic, the newspaper added, 'she is willing to respond to media interest whatever the situation.' And, lest there should be any doubts that there was a limit to her willingness to demean herself to retain power, the *Telegraph* summed up the new personality approach with this remark: 'Her run up a Cornwall beach being pulled along by a borrowed dog delighted her Party managers.' The campaign thus gloriously began.

Initially the Labour Party did not take up the challenge. We did not favour a personality contest – activists of my generation have sobering recollections of the disasters that befell the Party when it became besotted with its leadership. Although I may have fought more elections, local and national, than anyone now alive, my recollections go back even further than my first candidacy at twenty-one: as a lad I can recall my initial political disenchantment when I listened to my heroes, Ramsay MacDonald and Philip Snowden – upon whose charisma my Party had so much depended – savage their own past and Party. Many years later, in the election of 1970, I witnessed to my chagrin and unavailing protest, Wilson's vulgar, policyless, presidential campaign which goaded the electorate, repelled by the public display of such unjustified and limitless vanity, into a determined punitive attitude.

With such traumas as part of Labour's history, it was not surprising that the Party wished to avoid the personality duel the Conservatives were proposing. But the challenge was, in the event, not to be evaded. The provocations were to persist, and in the run up to the 1987 election, the attempted character assassination of Neil Kinnock overstepped all Parliamentary conventions. In the end the Speaker intervened to prevent well-publicised Early Day motions which criticised the Labour leader in unprecedented abusive terms being placed on the Parliamentary Order Paper. But the stage had been set; the election was to be fought in presidential terms and although the emergence of Neil Kinnock as a significant figure rocked the Conservatives the Tory strategists persisted in their tactic right up to polling day.

During the campaign, seeing the domineering Tory Party leader become the acquiescent photographic model shamelessly posing for the press photographers, Hugo Young acidly commented in the *Guardian*:[1]

A certain fastidiousness attends the matter of personality in politics. As well as the Tories' claim that the issues are what matter, there is Labour's pious contention that it is not discussing Mrs Thatcher personally but only the nature of Thatcherism: the consequences of the lady, they say, and not the untouchable subject of her persona.

These are pedantic pretences on both sides. And they are entirely misplaced. They pose a distinction without a difference. For although it may occasionally be right not to discuss the intellectual and moral weaknesses, the hypocrisy and the private character, of one politician or another, the only consequence of forswearing an analysis of Mrs Thatcher's personality would be grossly to misrepresent both the past and the future politics in this country.

I entirely endorse Young's view.

More, since Thatcher has asserted her intention to go on and on, and, at the Conservative Party Conference of 1987, indicated her intention to vie with Lord Liverpool's fifteen years' administration, her continuing challenge cannot be ignored. She put her personality under scrutiny during the 1987 election and she and her party managers cannot now demand that restraints be imposed on the exploration of her character.

Although Thatcher has so provocatively invited ripostes, there are others without such obvious vested interest who nevertheless will be squeamish and resist my justification for this essay, and will condemn the validity of its methodology. Political scientists in Britain have, for the most part, and with a discreditable display of pusillanimity, turned away from the guidelines set out by Harold Lasswell and those early twentieth-century political scientists, who sought to apply psychoanalysis to their disciplines. Many British political scientists have become tedious psephologists or, at best, makers of informed contributions that rarely match the perceptivity of our best political journalists.

When I have been invited to address the annual conference of the International Society of Political Psychology, I have noted the paucity of attenders from our universities, even when it is held in Britain. In the English-speaking world it is the antipodes, as in the University of Melbourne,[2] which practise the application of depth psychology to political science. Our home breed fights shy of such a bold manner of proceeding and richly deserves Trotsky's scorn for the 'pusillanimity of an historic fatalism which in all questions, whether concrete or private, passively seeks a solution in general laws, and leaves out of account the mainspring of all human decisions – the living and acting individual.'

The stark reality is that political science without biography is taxidermy; even as politics without personality is a myth. It is ironic that although almost every political-science undergraduate will have been taught that all political philosophies have been based on theories of human nature, he is nevertheless discouraged from responding to the challenge of Sir Isaiah Berlin's question. 'Who will deny', Berlin has asked, 'that political problems, e.g. about what men and groups should be or could do, depend logically and directly on what man's nature is taken to be?'

Too many of our political scientists compulsively distance themselves from living material. They lapse into reliance on a psephology which provides them with statistics; allows them to deal with the – often illusory – reality of aggregates; and protects them from their fears of the factual face to face encounter.[3] When the late Bob McKenzie, Professor of Politics at the London School of Economics and the most popular of television psephological pundits, was brought by a skilled television producer to be filmed participating in discussion with me at my dinner table, the production was a failure. McKenzie was a voyeur, relishing his forays into pornographic shows in Denmark and Holland, liking to view the displayed obscenities even as he enjoyed being viewed on TV, but never, never touching: not for nothing did he live in an isolated homestead. The intimacy of our dinner table, steadfastly maintained despite the intruding cameras, discomfited him. The meals my wife provides and the wines I pour at dinner parties are secularised versions of biblical feasts, unselfconsciously designed to bring communality, and the success of an evening is to be measured by how close we have brought people

3

together. This was anathema to McKenzie and in such an ambience he could not maintain his impeccable television standards: he botched the programme. His métier was in the impersonality of the studio, not the home; that evening he was but a caricature of so many political scientists desperately but vainly striving to obtain objectivity by ridding themselves of all affect. Seduced by the model of quantitative science, they are attracted to areas where the subject matter seems intrinsically amenable to quantification. By studying voting behaviour they exorcise their fears and reassure themselves that they remain in omnipotent control as they chatter of numbers and percentages, and comment on changes in numerical terms. Ignoring the infinite variations into the felt intensity of political attitudes[4] and their unconscious determinations, treating votes as numerical units, they imprudently claim that they are scientifically able to make valid numerical co-relations with independent factors like class and income. Such political 'scientists' will have no palate for this essay.

Nor, moreover, will many British psychoanalysts approve of this effort to plunder what they regard as their private domain. They too suffer from the cultural ambience of provincialism in which the Grantham woman and the late Alderman Roberts have so successfully enveloped Britain. Unlike the founding fathers of psychoanalysis who always yielded to the superb temptations of speculation, they seem fearful of applying their craft outside the consulting rooms: the hostile environment created by behaviourists and scoffing nihilists[5] – avoiding the painful insights that have to be faced through the calibrations by introspective work into personal resource – has done its destructive worst. Perhaps the British psychoanalysts' retreat to the consulting room, where nothing is overheard and the outside world banned, is also a shield, protecting them from the charges the French psychoanalyst Lacan made against the American practitioners, that they had become conformists in their society, turning psychoanalysis into adjustment therapy. The British psychoanalysts' stance certainly protects them from the countercharge made against Lacan's French followers that they have directed psychoanalysis towards literature and towards the social cultural function quite divorced from treatment.[6] Psychoanalysis is being played safe in Britain, too safe.

Yet if the younger psychoanalysts frankly accepted that the status of psychoanalysis as a natural or social science is problematic, but that it is unquestionably a form of hermeneutics they would be less timorous. The goal of natural science is the domination of nature by the use of scientific techniques, as the goal of those social scientists modelled on the natural sciences is prediction and control of human beings, seen as objects. The goal of psychoanalysis is not domination,

4

prediction or control, but understanding. That comes through methods that are essentially hermeneutic.[7] Moreover, if they accepted the view put by some American psychoanalysts[8] that the general metapsychological theories of psychoanalysis are metaphors, far from the realm of empirical testing, then British psychoanalysts may be less concerned with those who inappropriately apply the methodology of the natural or social sciences in assessing the validity of psychoanalytical findings. Freed from such constraints, they could break out of Hampstead and recapture some of the roving spirit that came out of Vienna.

Although there are exceptions,[9] for the most part British psychoanalysts seem embarrassed by the inheritance of social thought bequeathed them by Freud; his *Totem and Taboo*, *Leonardo*, *Civilisation and its Discontents* and *Moses* are not part of their mental climate. Clinical psychoanalysts set their boundaries, and the field is left open in Britain for an occasional lively but opportunistic political-scientist interloper from academe who – distanced from clinical work or from the heat and dust of political battle – brutally pillages Freud's social thought to justify an authoritarian conservatism.[10]

Of course, psychoanalysts, while acknowledging their diffidence towards Freud's social thought, could also plead they have Freud on their side in condemning an enterprise such as mine. In a letter written in 1922 he affirmed, 'In my opinion psychoanalysis should never be used as a weapon in literary or political polemics.' But his moral indignation was to overcome his scruple, and he fortunately failed to follow his own advice. His nostalgia for his first love, politics, was never dissipated, as indeed was made clear when his iconoclastic study (with the diplomat William Bullitt), of the egregious President Woodrow Wilson was released in 1967. His ambivalence to politics must, moreover, be seen not only in relation to a justifiable fear that the armoury of psychoanalysis may be abused; he was surely defending himself, too, from his youthful wishes to be lawyer and political leader – for in a sense Freud, happily for us, was a failed politician.

Some perceptive historians, re-examining the dreams of Freud[11] celebrated in his *Interpretation of Dreams*, have correctly divined that the setbacks he suffered in his political and professional ambitions when Vienna was destroying all his earlier liberal hopes, led him first to fantasise the triumph over politics, and then manifestly to make his fantasy a reality. He attempted to challenge the primacy of politics; his intellectual goal was to neutralise politics by reducing it almost to a psychological category.

Surely because of this and despite it, no science has the impress of politics upon it more than psychoanalysis: for Freud's work wasn't done in an insulated cell. He lived in the world of a grandiose but decaying empire even as we have done in Britain, and the congruences between the loss of national identity felt in Vienna and those felt now in Britain should prompt us to be keenly sensitive to the consequence of Freud battling for survival in his professional and personal life within a seething sea of almost continuous and dangerous political crises. Those turbulent waters overflowed both when he was young and when he was old – into his social life, into his home and into his consulting rooms.

The premonition that Victor Adler, Freud's fellow student at the University and the founder and leader of the Austrian Socialist Party, would succeed where Freud failed by becoming politician and psychiatrist, surely contributed, apart from usual youthful homosexual rivalry, to Freud's challenge of Adler to a duel;[12] and it is unlikely to have been an accident, but rather because of Freud's strivings to overcome posthumously his rival, that led him to the triumph of living his last days in Austria in the house at Berggasse which Adler had formerly occupied.[13] The significance of the acting out of Adler's son, Friedrich,[14] another dominant figure in the Austrian Socialist Party, who, in his authoritarian father's lifetime, displaced his Oedipal hatred by assassinating the reactionary Austrian premier, would not have escaped Freud, so keenly aware of his rival's temperament and career.

Meantime, there could have been few who understood the psychopathology of Otto Bauer,[15] who succeeded Victor Adler to the leadership of the Austrian Socialist Party and was to become Austria's Foreign Minister. Freud had not only treated his father and was aware of the bizarre family background but by unravelling the perplexities of Otto Bauer's sister discovered the aetiology of hysteria. Otto Bauer in exile was buried by Léon Blum, then the French prime minister, with all the ceremony of a state funeral, but it is impossible that Freud did not understand, fateful as it proved to Austrian democracy, the consequences of Bauer's hysterical personality which shaped his seductive and dangerous political style, combining as it did a militancy of language with an almost total absence of deeds.

There were, of course, others who were active in the Socialist Party who were well within Freud's orbit: the first woman analyst in the Vienna Psychoanalytical Society was the wife of the neo-Marxist theoretician, Rudolph Hilferding: the one-time President of the Psychoanalytical Society was Paul Federn, a committed member of the Socialist Party, and Theresa Schlesinger, a founder of the Austrian Socialist Party, and her father were warmly received at Freud's home.

And Freud's close friendship with Heinrich Braun could hardly have left him uninterested in the career of Heinrich's son, Otto, who became the Prussian prime minister.

The suggestion that Freud's social thought was cocooned from and indifferent to the turbulence of the party political strife surrounding him has no validity. Judging by Paul Federn's interview given to a Chicago newspaper in 1927, in which he gave a psychoanalytical interpretation of the serious riots in Vienna, there was no hesitation within Freud's most intimate circle in using psychoanalysis to evaluate contemporary political events. The British psychoanalysts who run away from applied psychoanalysis and eschew Freud's social thought evade the part the political ambience of the Austro-Hungarian Empire and the conduct of leading Viennese politicians had in shaping it: more, they fail to acknowledge sufficiently the impact on Freud of the turmoil around him.

It is not, for example, irrelevant to draw attention to the extraordinary series of assassinations and attempted assassinations of state leaders that took place from the year Freud completed his university studies until his first work related to mass psychology *Totem and Taboo*. Tsar Alexander; President Garfield; the French President, Carnot; the Bulgarian Premier, Stambuloff; the Irish Chief Secretary, Lord Cavendish; the Persian Shah, Nasr-el-Din; the Italian King, Umberto; the American President, McKinley; the Serbian King Alexander; the Portuguese King Carlos; the Spanish Premier, Canalegas; constitute by no means an exhaustive list of those slain. These events were more than suggestive to Freud of his vision of the theme of patricide via fraternity, and of mass movements reminiscent of the power struggles of the primal horde.[16] And clearly the war and the consequent disintegration of the Austro-Hungarian Empire prompted wide-sweeping revision of his conceptual system and produced his *Group Psychology and the Analysis of the Ego* in which he addressed the favourite question of philosophers since Hobbes and of sociologists since Durkheim: what holds society together? In writing such works he was pursuing his early interests which had led him to relieve the tedium of his military service by translating the essays of the most distinguished candidate ever to contest the Westminster constituency, John Stuart Mill.

Their lack of focus on Freud's social thought results too often in our psychoanalysts playing into the hands of those sociologists and social historians who seek to dismiss them as prisoners of what these arid academics see as the time-bound quality of Freud's world of ideas. The attempt is made to avoid the discomfort of Freud's penetration by suggesting that psychoanalysis is founded only on clinical material based on case studies of repressed and idle Jewish Viennese women living in a highly restricted, near decadent bourgeois world, and, consequently, that his findings have little contemporary relevance. The facts are otherwise: his consulting room was a cosmopolis in which a majority of patients conducted their analyses in English, and those analysed ranged from French princesses and German judges to American poets. It may suit some social historians and structural sociologists, in their private war against the mood-of-the-enlightenment historians and *littérateurs*, to affect man does not exist, only men. The fashion of treating history as a social science has focused attention in historical work on significant trends and broad interpretations: biographical detail is shortchanged. But Prosopography – the approach by the historian to the study of individual persons – personifies the abstract, gives it life, a face, a curriculum vitae.[17] Unfortunately, although its exponents may be vigorous in France,[18] there appear to be few echoes here. No one is gladly prepared to acknowledge the intractable; but human nature cannot be wished out of history or called peremptorily to submission. Yet, even when I have found in private discussion with a few of this generation's sociologists a grudging acknowledgment of the social forces operating upon Freud's metapsychology, they still claim that to view contemporary politics through the eyes of a nineteenth-century Viennese Jew is wholly anachronistic; of course it is not a view which I share. Events during the war took me on my final RAF posting to Vienna in 1945 and permitted me to hear the last whimpering of the Habsburg Empire. The Viennese were at last rid of their Jews, but they were still possessed with the same ugly, exculpatory hate which welcomed Hitler in and drove Freud out. And in 1986, more than forty years on, during their presidential election, I was present again in Vienna to see the same sickness leading to the election of Kurt Waldheim: the tainted, demonic forces at work which surrounded Freud in Vienna are certainly not spent. When during a broadcast I shared with Waldheim's daughter she assured me and the listeners I was wrong to accuse her father of war crimes and that some of her and her father's best friends were Jews – then I was painfully aware of how little had changed.

That does not mean I would ignore the social factors that have caused psychological changes in recent decades. Thanks to the generosity of my constituents, I was able to live at Westminster for thirty years and was thus given the opportunity to be responsible for more Private Members Acts – nearly all of which impinged on human relationships – than any Parliamentarian this century. I have always been profoundly conscious that I have been legislating on a moving staircase and that certain social factors, like the increased employment of mothers; the increase of one-parent families; the tendency of yuppie fathers to put work ambitions before family; the gender blurring within the increasingly democratic family with men and women abandoning the stereotype roles they formerly accepted, have all been determinants which have complex and delayed influences upon the psychology of the individual. But whatever the modifications, the bedrock remains. In any case, when one scrutinises the psychodynamics and psychopathology of an individual like Thatcher, the early formative and determinant influences are found to be remote from today's pronounced contemporary feminism; indeed in her case, they are not even to be found in the Edwardian era but rather – thanks to her intimidating, living-in grandmother – in the Victorian ethos. Ironically, Thatcher is closer to Freud's much abused feminine construct than most women who have reached pensionable age.

This apologia will doubtless leave unmoved most political scientists, British psychologists, sociologists and social historians – and certainly it would be resisted by conventional politicians. The protective armour of the practising politician, assuming the affectation of undiluted commitment to principle and community, and dismissing the *ad hominem* argument as a vulgar irrelevance in no way invalidating his manifestos, is paper thin. The conventional politician, always seeking to elevate his personal prejudices into principles, hates what he describes as the personalisation of politics. This type of politician strives to protect himself from anatomisation by evoking every man's fear that his private fortunes may be pried into. But politicians, having chosen to live on the public stage, cannot claim the same rights of privacy to which the citizen is well entitled. The politician in our more open society is fighting a losing battle when he attempts to invoke the canons of taste and etiquette to protect himself against those who will not accept the old boundaries beyond which enquiry into motivation was required to halt. The tired, formal pavane formerly so primly danced between politicians and the acquiescent establishment press is over. A prurient torrent, undirected and often only destructive, has burst through the protective barriers erected by yesterday's politicians; and since the mercenary press owners find there is money in filth, a popular press is now awash in scum and trivia. It is for the reader to judge whether this essay falls into the iconoclastic category I am castigating: the conventional politician will seek to persuade the reader that it does.

Yet those of my mind must persist. If Freud bursts through his canons to deplore Woodrow Wilson, how much more justified then are we who attempt to protect ourselves in an atomic age, and in a world so rent with the consequences of Hitler, Stalin and Mao, all of whose personal problems – acted out at a time of socially resonating conditions – became so catastrophically enmeshed, through symbolic resonance, in the public domain. It is too complacent and optimistic a view even when it is persuasively presented, as by Anthony Storr,[19] to suggest it is not the fact that politicians have a psychopathology which is important but what is important is the creative use they make of their psychopathology: it is, however, the malignant not the benign consequences of their psychopathology that the world has endured in my lifetime. Moreover, I do not believe it is sufficient simply for the armoury of psychoanalysis to be used to probe and open up the concealed psychotic elements in a society; it is too passive an approach to conclude that when a psychotic constellation of impulses, fantasies and defences dominates a group that the group then inevitably throws up leaders who best represent the psychotic elements.[20] Excellence in political leaders can quench those elements even as evil leaders can activate them. In some of my campaigns I have seen how, in bringing about a social reform, the educational debate on the issue can be a maturational experience for significant sections of a nation; even as primitive leadership can lead to a nation's emotional regression.

The political leader is all-important and needs, in the interests of the community, to be determinedly scrutinised. The psychoanalyst, jealous of his craft, who demurs by affirming that, even with the privileged access to the internal world which a patient allows to an analyst, unravelling infantile sources of current attitudes is complex and difficult,[21] is confusing an analysis with a psycho-biographical work. An analysis is essentially private and is undertaken to assist the patient: a psycho-biography, if necessarily more rough hewn and lacking the nuances of an analysis, can be a needed admonitory exercise, an attempt to alert an over-acquiescent public. There are timorous critics who will assert that such an exercise will inevitably lead to subjective assertions being used as indicative facts, but such criticism must be suffered stoically. These are the critics who too often fail to acknowledge that the research method adopted in so many branches of medical research, of identifying a possible pathogen and studying its possible effects prospectively, can lead to the original conjecture being validated.[22] This essay seeks to establish that there is no shortage of material in Thatcher's adult life to point unerringly at the pathogen she is carrying, of her aetiolated affectional bonds with her mother, and which in so many of her political stances is torridly displayed.

This, therefore, is not intended as a personal attack on Thatcher –

although it will be so interpreted. It is intended to draw attention to the unconscious forces which provide the dynamic, the pathology and the distortions of her political policies. Nietzsche (of whom Freud said,[23] 'He had a more penetrating knowledge of himself than any other man who ever lived or was ever likely to live') once declared: 'I never attack persons; I merely avail myself of the person as of a strong magnifying glass that allows one to make visible a general but creeping and elusive calamity.'[24] I do not presumptuously claim the purity of Nietzsche, but in this little contribution I have tried to be mindful of his tocsin.

1

Tory MPs in the Crèche

IN a rare glimpse of his fantasy life Edward Heath once provided an explicit and sad corroboration of his difficulties in enjoying real relationships with others: 'I have always had a hidden wish, a frustrated desire, to run an hotel,' he revealed. The hotelkeeper, of course, greets his guests with the ever present meaningless smile like Heath's smile in his less sombre moods. The smile is charming, pleasant, but correct and distant; it would be addressed to his guests but all who come would soon go, ships that pass in the night. Not for Heath the dream of home, wife and children, only the impersonal hotel over which he presides and where undemanding transitory acquaintanceships, but not relationships, are formed. The narcissism of all politicians, like actors, is notorious, but even by Westminster's yardstick Heath's inability, as celibate bachelor, to choose someone other than himself as his loved one was the fatal flaw presaging his defeat by Margaret Thatcher.

Given his formidable intelligence, it is not surprising that his capacity to transmute his narcissism is more subtle than the increasingly vulgar displays of today's demi-monde Tory backbenchers: but nevertheless the blemish is chronic. As Chief Whip in yesterday's Macmillan government, his authoritarian detachment functioned well in a Tory party which was then more disciplined than now, but when the crisis of the miners' strike arose during his government he was alone, without deep personal resource.

Two years before that crisis arose I wrote of Heath:[1]

It is in times of crisis that the celibate bachelor becomes particularly vulnerable. Adult man, single or married, faced with difficulties that appear almost overwhelming, can still secretly feel a need to cry out for help from his mama: but his self esteem demands that he does not yield to such regressive tendencies and he must find an escape route to avoid recognising his feelings of helplessness and dependence. At such a time a man increases his narcissistic

defences: he can dangerously over-react to situations and individuals which remind him of his conflicts. To relieve himself of
his anxieties the bachelor, unable to sustain and enrich his inner
life by deep personal relationships, blatantly attempts to shore up
his self esteem . . . More genuinely-felt self esteem is rooted in a
confident sexuality, in the body giving and receiving love. Those
who feel themselves sexually inadequate often convert their disappointment into an aggressive competition . . . in the world of
power.

Heath needed private assurance and personal corroboration to
contain the miners' strike: that charisma was not part of his make up
and he inevitably turned to the country for a public confirmation of
his view, unnecessarily called an election for February 1974, and
received the rebuff from which he has never recovered.

When his humiliation was reinforced by the more decisive election
in October 1974 – which left the way open for years of Labour
government – the morale of the Conservative MPs, who had always
yearned for a virile, commanding father figure and had been long
uneasy with their celibate leader, totally collapsed. Too many MPs
suffer from manic-depressive swings of mood; they measure their
personal worth according to Gallup. When general elections take
place, anxiety envelops the Palace of Westminster. Most examina-
tions, if failed, can soon be taken again, but the election result is final.
Failure to the average MP means the destruction of his identity and
his world. So often a hollow man, he becomes increasingly and
utterly dependent upon his role; nothing exists behind the mask of
his persona. His rejection by the electorate is not coolly appraised as
disapproval of his political party: it is interpreted as personal rejection.
The election is not simply experienced as such; it is not conceptualised
as an event in itself, as something unrelated to his real inner life, as
essentially extrinsic to his self-evaluation. Failure means oblivion:
today a somebody, tomorrow nothing. To lose means the dissolution
of his world: all the various constellations of his relationships, all the
projects and plans which he has assigned himself will melt away. The
implications of failing to surmount the hurdle are so awful, so
intrusive, that for months before an election they cannot be put aside.
And at no time in my thirty years in the Commons was the shadow
of an election cast longer than during 1974.

When I returned to the House after the 1974 election, I found the
Tory MPs who had survived almost totally disorientated. Only a
few months before, their goals to personal office were defined: now
the achievement of such milestones was indefinitely postponed and

they felt, thanks to Heath's blunder, their roads would tremble with uncertainty. They knew the failed leader had to be overthrown but bungling speeches by Keith Joseph and uneasy involvement in the City by Edward du Cann led to the two most able contenders to the succession withdrawing from the leadership contest. The Tory MPs felt abandoned not only by the electorate but by those who may have rallied them and saved them from disarray. Thus rejected, they lost the cohesion of a triumphant horde and each man in his separate world, alone in his melancholia, was confronted with the pointlessness of his life. They were fearful and in panic and it was in panic that they made the choice to turn to Thatcher.

No one should underestimate the terror of personal dissolution felt by a failing politician whose self is stuck together only by the constant frenetic corroboration of public activity and consequent acclaim. His nightmare is to lose his seat and be compelled to discover an authentic private identity outside Parliament. His hollowness ensures that for him such a mature choice is unattainable. In a time felt to be overwhelmingly threatening, groups – certainly no less than individuals – make, in psychological terms, regressive choices. The Tory MPs' choice of Thatcher was made at a time when they were overwhelmed by feelings of helplessness; it was made to gratify an unconscious infantile need and did not spring from a conscious, mature assessment. It was in a despairing mood that they submitted to the lady and paved the way for the first woman prime minister in western Europe.

There were exquisite ironies in such a selection, for the traditional ethos of the Conservative Party is father orientated, even as the Labour Party is essentially mother orientated. The Labour Party's self image is that of the welfare party, maternally concerned, the provider, the bountiful, caring one. Indeed, the history of the Labour Party tells us repeatedly how all hell is let loose if its leader evokes memories of a tyrannical father: the rebellious temperament which brought so many of the Labour MPs into politics is then at once provoked. The Party is more at ease when it has leaders who are, or give the appearance of being, chairmen rather than leaders. This was Attlee's strength and Gaitskell's weakness in his relations with the Party: Wilson's colourlessness may explain in part the absence of rebellion against him during his premiership. It was the reconciling strength too of avuncular Jim Callaghan. Good uncles were preferred to commanding fathers. And on the rare occasion that inspirational leaders have captured Labour's imagination, their identification with their mothers is imperfectly concealed. When, as a youngster, long before I entered Parliament, I would proudly act as chairman to Nye

Bevan, I would find emerging out of the huge bulk of his frame a falsetto woman's voice rising ever more passionately the more he insisted upon his care for the sick: and hand on hip, with feminine stance, Jim Griffiths, the architect of our national insurance schemes, would be found at the despatch box insisting upon his legislation to support those maimed or unemployed.

When Jim Callaghan left, the subsequent contest for the leadership, even although electorally it was to prove deeply wounding, followed a familiar historical pattern. Two men were in the contest: Denis Healey and Michael Foot. The intellectually assertive, aggressive contender proved unacceptable; the Labour Party yielded to its emotional needs and chose the most loveable and honest man, the privately gentle Michael Foot, rather than the frightening toughie. Some, like Peter Jenkins,[2] associate editor of the *Independent*, even years after, still rail against Michael Foot and those of us in the Parliamentary party who supported him. Jenkins is an acute observer but he understands the Labour Party only with his considerable brain and not by instinct. In 1980 the hard left had temporarily seized the party machine: if the Parliamentary party had chosen Healey – perceived as he was by almost uncontrollably rebellious members as a bullying father figure – Benn would have been able to mobilise successfully his politically adolescent cohorts against the Parliamentary party, and the whole Labour movement would have been irrevocably split. There have been seven[3] serious breakaways or socialist rivals to Labour since its formation. I have lived through most of them and always the Labour Party has survived; but in 1980 the whole Labour movement was on the very edge of a precipice. We were fortunate to have Michael Foot who, among his many other qualities, has what some psychoanalysts have noted can be a special charm of some leaders: the capacity to tease out from his followers a response to his delicate need for love and protection.[4] That charm and the trust in him were to prove invaluable. Jenkins is right to regard the choice as irrational, and to think that it contributed to Labour losing the 1983 election. But it saved the Labour Party from destruction, the needed time to recapture the Party from the hard left was obtained, and Labour has been given another chance. The feminine, provident, maternal element which Labour requires in its leaders was available in Michael Foot – it was indeed a happy chance.

Early in 1975 when the Tory Party had its own turmoil, their choice of new leadership was even more irrational, certainly emotionally more regressive and decidedly more involuntary; political parties, like most men and women, often lack sufficient self awareness to be in control of their own destinies. In more usual circumstances the failed leader, Heath, would have been expeditiously succeeded by another man regarded as a stronger character – a woman would have been rejected out of hand by an essentially misogynist party – and their yearnings for a powerful father figure assuaged. For while Labour's mother's boys created the welfare state, the Conservative Party has never had time for such sentimental architects. It is a party basically paternalistic, if not authoritarian in mood. It believes in an élite; is comfortable in a structured fag system reminiscent of the private schools that many of its members have attended; and is ready, even in these less deferential times, to accept a Whip's rule, something which would be intolerable to a party more democratic and more sceptical of leadership principles. It has always seen itself as a man's party, impatient and suspicious of those who cannot stand on their own two feet. Self-reliance is the Tory Party's watchword and those of us who are unilateral disarmers are regarded as namby-pambys, too frightened to support needed military expenditure. But the paradox of ˣ such a party choosing a woman can be explained. In 1975 the freshly thrashed Tory MPs did not throng into the Westminster Committee Rooms to make their choice: the choice had been made for them in their nurseries.

2

Phallic Woman

BEFORE adult man discovers the vagina as a place of shelter for the penis, before he enters into the heritage of the womb,[1] he has to traverse a myriad obstacles. Often he misleads himself, becomes a fool to the signposts directing him only to a mythological place where terror, but no real solace, prevails. Then he may meet Medusa, upon whose head the snakes writhe: he has come to a land under the sovereignty of the phallic mother, where, if he is to become a protected citizen, he must renounce his manhood and become as a child.

And when political man on his public journey cannot advance further on his road and is suffering the narcissistic injury of the voters' rejection, then the loss of an election evokes all the prototypes of his earliest losses: the loss at birth of his mother's womb, the loss of her breast, withdrawn by his mother, the regular loss of his faeces under encouragement or threat. All these losses are but premonitions of what is to be the loss which he fears most, the loss of his penis. It is that fear of castration which the little boy must overcome to reach manhood. On that route he falters, some fatally, never to reach heterosexuality, but for most the faltering is but a hiatus, albeit one that can only be overcome by disavowal of all the possibilities of the consummation of incestuous wishes which would, as punishment, provoke the penis loss. The corroboration buried in the Greek myths, which caused Freud to name the conflict burdened wishes of the child wanting to possess his mother and slay his father as the Oedipus complex, also tells of the existence of the fantasy of the phallic mother: Medusa is but one of the phallic women to be found in the Greek mythology. Each year I drive up from my Italian home to the nearby Etruscan city of Volterra and there, in the wondrous museum, I see how three centuries before Christ, on the base of the funereal urns mounted by the sculpted figure of the cruel, enigmatic mother, the Medusa myth is depicted with terrifying vigour and immediacy.

The myth endures: it has been illustrated repeatedly in the art of the primitives, as in the allegories of Renaissance painters such as Mantegna and Giovanni Bellini, and now, with the arrival of Margaret Thatcher as leader of the Tories, it possesses a striking contemporaneity. In Britain it lingers on in the general coinage and has been reaffirmed in the issue of a new gold coin. Our own armed Britannia, with her phallic nature stressed both by an erect lighthouse in the background and her upright trident, protects us from dangers. Around Westminster the statuary of the protecting, phallic women abound. As the division bell called me from my office, I passed the female bronze group on Westminster Bridge dominated by a fierce Boadicea standing in a chariot with castrating scythe blades springing from the hubs of the wheels; and as I drove home passing under Admiralty Arch, above me was the amply-built female cradling a machine-gun in her lap representing Gunnery, perhaps the most unambiguous phallic woman in London. Only a little less explicit, when my profession has taken me to the Law Courts I am greeted by the feminine figure, veiled and draped, of Courage, conceived with a pre-Freudian lack of self consciousness in the form of a rearing snake's decapitator.[2]

Our home by the side of the Thames is on the site of the house where the poet David Mallet co-operated in writing 'Rule Britannia'. The loaded refrain continues down the centuries, perpetuating the theme of the helpless infant and the yearning for maternal protection. Abandoned by the electorate, the Tories were desolate and they turned away from manliness to obtain the protection of the woman whom they believed would be their Britannia; a goddess who was later to have her phallic nature made explicit by accepting as her title the Russian soubriquet of the Iron Lady.

Endowing the mother with a penis and renouncing the desired consummation, proffering submission in return for protection, creates a pause giving an infant time to breathe before taking the next courageous leap forward that will bring him nearer to manhood. But it is a faulty stratagem when used unconsciously in adult life, for the fantasy is an illusion and can be sustained only by denying or blotting out painful realities. In political terms, the incapacity of the Tory MPs to emancipate themselves from the thraldom has left the nation for a longer period than ever before in this century at the mercy of a prime minister unchecked by the operation of a genuine Cabinet and collective decision-making. The sight of the terrible Medusa made a man stiff with terror and froze him, and thus has Thatcher terrorised the Tories in the House. The extraordinary and total domination by Thatcher – up to the time of the defiance of Michael Heseltine – of the male, down-market Tory Cabinet, chasteningly illustrates how decision-making, guiding the destinies of a nation, can be determined by the interplay, at an unconscious level, between the residual infantile needs of a group of men and a commanding woman who refuses, through disability, to accept her full femininity.

There were particular cultural vulnerabilities which caused the Tory MPs to revert to so infantile a stage, and indeed to remain so fixated – for the over-determined stress they place on the manly virtues encapsulated within the public-school ethic reveals how precariously they hold on to their machismo. In 1975, they were experiencing their defeats as a threat of political emasculation and to ward off that threat, they selected Thatcher in a desperate feint to keep their intactness.

They laboured under the handicap of being brought up within the constraints of the English upper-middle-class families from which, at that time, most of them sprung. They had been tutored to respect the stereotype of the stiff-upper-lip, to be controlled Englishmen by mothers and nannies who were governed by a culture which disapproved of indulgence to children; they were not reared by disciples of Spock. Under such harsh regimes they passed through the cycle of infantile sexual life which Freud has told us is man's inheritance.

All our sexual lives are diphasic – occurring in two phases – and the rebuffs we receive in the first five years of our lives can leave far greater scars than those we romanticise in our second phase. All my political experience compels me to acknowledge that events which occurred in my colleagues' very early childhood and, of course, my own, play a much larger part in our collective decision-making than any other single factor. It is true that we are a disparate and diverse crew, but there is nevertheless no impress stamped more generally and clearly upon contemporary politicians than the spurning they endured when within what Freud has described as their phallic phase.

Among the principal findings of psychoanalysis is that sexual life starts with clear manifestations soon after birth and that it comprises the function of obtaining pleasure from zones in the body, a function subsequently, although sometimes imperfectly, brought into the service of reproduction. The first organ to make its appearance as an erotogenic zone and to make libidinal demands upon the mind is the mouth. Then we attain the sadistic anal stage when satisfaction is sought in aggression and excretory functions; and the third phase is the phallic one when a boy, from the age of about two or three, feels pleasurable sensations in his penis and learns to procure these by manual stimulation. This is the time, Freud has argued, that he becomes 'the mother's lover'. 'He desires to possess her physically in ways which he has divined from his observations and intuitive surmises of sexual life and tries to seduce her by showing her the male organ of which he is the proud owner.' It is the rebuff so many politicians receive at that time that ever reverberates around the House of Commons; it should never be forgotten that amongst politicians in the House there is a surfeit of rejected lovers.

The mother well understands that the infant's sexual excitement refers to her, and she begins the prohibitions which contain the explicit or implicit threat of castration – soon to be underlined by the spectacle of the woman's lack of a penis. The threat and the spectacle constitute, Freud insists, the greatest trauma in a man's life. To save himself, the child must make the renunciation which outlaws his sexuality, dissolves his Oedipus complex and permits him to live more serenely through a latent phase. Then, at puberty, the boy reaches his fourth phase – the genital phase – when the earlier oral, anal and phallic phases are subordinated to the primacy of the genitals.

But this process is not always carried out perfectly, and for some, the frustration of the phallic and exhibitionist activities at the height of their development at two or three years of age, by the very person towards whom the activity is directed, shapes their whole future character. The brusque mother or nurse who often from the beginning has given little encouragement to the healthy narcissism of the baby and has commanded rather than cajoled, praised and encouraged the boy to eject his excreta, is the mother who will show the maximum disapproval when he later shows his capacity for an erect phallus to her. The hurt to his pride is then immense and, never coming to terms with the rebuff he received at the phallic phase, the faulty child becomes as an adult what Reich has described as a phallic-narcissistic character, a character by no means resting on the genital organisation which, ideally, the pubertal boy reaches.

Reich,[3] enumerating the traits which belong to the phallo-narcissist, recites the characteristics of so many politicians. 'The typical phallic-narcissist character is self confident, often arrogant, vigorous and often impressive . . . ' The mother may have refused his erect penis but he will not accept her depreciating verdict; it is his special pride and it is not surprising that psychoanalysts find that such beings are characterised by a proud self-concentration on their own genitals. Typically, we are told, an analysis reveals the identification of the total ego with the phallus.

Undoubtedly the community has its gains from the persistent exhibitionism of those politicians who displace their phallic erective potency into their displays of political wares: the stamina, the compulsiveness which they show as they draw attention to themselves, ever inviting approval, means the community is treated to a constant stream of ideas, projects and programmes. Diffident, less clamorous and perhaps more mature men would not find such conduct endurable: but for the phallic narcissist – as Lord Beaverbrook once remarked, speaking of a whole range of politicians – 'The only bad publicity is no publicity.' The more they are in the news, the more they bloom. Inevitably, however, the genesis of their dynamism is not wholly concealed; the narcissism obtrudes in their insensitivity or in the spurious tones of their expressed concern for others and it is often revealed in the shallowness of the proffered ideational content.

The doctrinaire Tory with his stress on the virtues of individualism and personal enterprise, and his suspicion of any philosophy leavened by collectivism and social responsibility, possesses a political ideology which in no way mortifies his emotional predilection. It feeds and confirms his own phallic pride, and is indeed to some extent its product. With the political philosophy, the total ego and phallus so congruent there was no resource available to the Tory MP amidst the wreckage of his hopes. He was loaded with neurotic guilt, he felt his defeat was punishment, and wanted to atone for his phallic hubris. When he scrambled out of the shambles emotionally he retreated, not advanced. Clinical experience has shown that when those like the typical phallic-narcissistic type, who have failed in dissolving their Oedipus complex in a more conventional manner, are faced with such a crisis, they can endure what Freud called a degradation of libido, and a regression of the libidinal organisation to an earlier stage then takes place. In his unconscious, the Tory MP did not have to travel far to slip back to the security of the nanny. The historical accident was that a phallic woman was present and available to minister to him. Margaret Thatcher's temperament was the faultless template fitting precisely into his needs. He had found his dream woman.

3

Margaret at the Breast

MARGARET Thatcher, the lady who is not for turning, makes no concessions. In her bizarre entry to *Who's Who* – which she herself composes – she brutally repudiates her mother by suppressing her very existence. In it, she simply describes herself as the daughter of *Alfred*. She does not concede she was born of woman; she fantasises herself as an autochthonous Adam. 'Well of course,' she has said, 'I just owe everything to my father . . . ' No acknowledgment of indebtedness is ever made to her mother. On one rare occasion when close questioning about her mother forced her to give some reply, Thatcher's response was most revealing: in the same sentence that she protested her love, she also denied she had any relationship with the mother. 'I loved my mother dearly but after I was fifteen we had nothing more to say to each other.'[1] And realising that such an extraordinary response called for some addition she proffered to the puzzled listener this explanation: 'It was not her fault. She was always weighed down by the home. Always being in the home.' Since the home was most certainly not poverty stricken and consisted of some rooms above a shop, where two daughters and an active grandmother lived, the notion that household duties and chores weighed down the mother does not bear the slightest scrutiny. A contemporary at school and university, with understandable diffidence but more accurate recall, has said, ' . . . so I used to feel, just occasionally, that she rather despised her mother and adored her father.'[2] The contemptible mother is blotted out; even as Athena – goddess of war – sprang fully armed from the head of Zeus, so Thatcher claims a parthenogenic birth.

The ablation of a parent, the denial of a biological past and an insistence upon being self-made with no umbilical link to a mother's womb is a phenomenon not unknown to psychoanalysis. Such denials of one's ontology have been elegantly delineated and their private consequences explored.[3] The social consequences are more brazenly seen in the counterculture underground where the repudiation of the parent is expressed by an insistence upon a-historicity and a blotting out of any debt to the past. Ideally, it is claimed, identity can only be gained by a depopulation of the psyche by a total extrusion of the parental figures who have been internalised.[4]

In Thatcher's case, she has attempted to expel only one parent; the mother, Beatrice, has been sent into exile. But the affectation of psychological discontinuity is, of course, an illusion and is achieved only by massive self deception and an inauthentic philosophy. Thatcher's selective caesura in her personal biography is part of the same condition that precipitated her 'radical' assault upon the past – upon the historic Tory Party. Under Thatcher, the traditions of pragmatism and the domination of the Party by the aristocracy have been swept aside; she wants no lineage. The past is disparaged: when meeting a student of history she discouragingly informs him that his course is a luxury.[5] She emerges from no womb, even the womb of time. Visiting Paris for the first time as prime minister, Mrs Thatcher flabbergasted a senior foreign minister, Alain Peyrefite, by announcing she was the first post-war Conservative prime minister. Peyrefite seemed to recall names like Churchill, Eden, Macmillan, Home and Heath, but was sharply told they allowed socialism to be extended in Britain, whereas she was going to reverse it.[6] Since she acknowledges no legacy she favours the self-made man. Her Cabinet mirrors her own fantasised parthenogenesis. The Cabinet, moreover, must consist only of men. No hint of a mother image is permitted into Downing Street, only men in her father's image.

Heinz Kohut, the psychoanalyst whose emendations to classical Freudian theory have caused so much turbulence in the American psychoanalytical world, marshalled compelling clinical material showing that those whose psychic structure bears disproportionately the impress of an idealised father image, do so to compensate for their lack of a sufficiently empathetic mother. The baby needs an approving mirror for her healthy exhibitionism, and denied this by an unresponsive and negative mother, she turns as compensation to the father, trying first to idealise and then to integrate into her own self the father's abilities, skills and values. We must not, however, be blinded by Thatcher's constant public recall of Alderman Roberts's virtues.

The injury resulting from the mother's denial to the central self remains, Kohut insists, even when such compensatory techniques enable the individual to function. It is my belief that the deep wound the shadowy mother inflicted upon Margaret Thatcher's narcissism has never healed. All the decades I have sat opposite her confirm to me how overwhelmingly her primal narcissistic rage invades every issue to which she addresses herself. She is happy – indeed she seems only to exist – when she is furious: only then does she regain the self esteem she was not granted in her cradle.

Margaret was Beatrice's second child, born five years after her sister Muriel. When a second daughter is born to a woman without a son, it is often experienced as a disappointment and this may have contributed to the mother's lack of a positive relationship with her child, but more firmly established is the consequence of Margaret Thatcher's living-in maternal grandmother, Phoebe Stephenson, who evidently ruled the crowded household even if downstairs Alderman Roberts ruled his shop. She was, Thatcher has told us, 'Very, very Victorian and very, very strict.'[7] Margaret Thatcher's mother could not give her the warm responses which she in turn had never received.

The narcissistic deprivation Thatcher endured and her consequent ceaseless fury has reverberated around our domestic politics and has been dangerously injected into her conduct of Britain's foreign affairs. Too often the babe, denied the reassurance that her mother belongs to her, and the needed omnipotent control over the mother, becomes chronically and traumatically frustrated. Then chronic narcissistic rages with all their deleterious consequences will be established and will herald their later ideational companion – the conviction that the environment is essentially inimical. A paranoid impress is etched into the adult's individual perception of the outside world. When determining patronage within her own party, Thatcher asks, 'Is he one of us?' If enemies are not in existence, they will be created. No area of consensus politics can be permitted – the split between her side and the other must be total. Those accused of accommodation like Francis Pym, Norman St John Stevas and James Prior, are ruthlessly expelled from her Cabinet. And the politics of Neil Kinnock must be declared as alien and deported back to Eastern Europe.

Her determination to expel some of the most able Conservatives from her Cabinet illuminates some of the most pathogenic elements in her nature. It provides no little corroboration of the splitting process which many psychoanalysts in Britain who are followers of Melanie Klein claim takes place during the oral phase of the baby in its first three or four months, and which they describe as the paranoid-schizoid position. At that time the baby is unaware of persons, his relationship being to parts of persons, initially to the breast, and that breast is split into two parts, the ideal breast and the persecutory one. The fantasy of the good breast is confirmed by gratifying experiences of love and feeding by the real external mother, while the fantasy of persecution similarly merges with real experiences of deprivation and pain. Gratification therefore not only fulfils the need for comfort, love and nourishment but is also required to keep terrifying persecution at bay; Thatcher's divisive politics, in her Cabinet as in the country, suggests how meagre was the gratification she received from Beatrice Roberts, the affect-less mother dominated by the martinet grandmother.

The baby's necessary move forward to recognise and acknowledge the mother as a whole person was consequently never achieved and always in Thatcher's relationships that early polarity remains. While some ambivalence in all human relationships is natural and unavoidable, Thatcher will not tolerate it; persons, philosophies and institutions are all perceived as either friend or foe. Under no circumstances can she tolerate consensus. Casting herself as a prophet, she once told a rally, 'The Old Testament prophets did not say "Brothers I want consensus". They said "This is my faith and vision". This is what I passionately believe.' The lineaments of Thatcher's considerable failure to advance to a more integrated, albeit ambivalent, phase are embossed upon her personality structure.

During each election I have fought against Thatcher I have always been aware that my real opponents were Beatrice Roberts and the grandmother who, for the first ten years of Margaret Thatcher's life, enveloped the household. These women, of so little public importance in their lifetimes, rule us from their graves. Their denials and their imposed frustrations have left our premier with no affection for any legislative action that may recall the qualities with which mothers less atypical than Beatrice Roberts are so bountifully endowed: to nurse and nourish, to care and tolerate, improve and preserve. The welfare state, the National Health Service, are but mother surrogates, necessary evils which only electoral considerations inhibit her from totally destroying. When she publicly considers what her aptitudes are, Thatcher declares herself as eminently suitable as a prime minister and significantly stresses her lack of qualifications to be a nurse.[8] The cycle of emotional deprivation inexorably and inevitably reveals itself in all her assessments of the institutional fabric of our society, and pervades her stance on every political issue.

Sometimes her early wound presents itself in adulthood in the most exotic form. Such an occasion was when, as Education Minister, she made what even her most sympathetic biographers describe, perhaps hyperbolically, as the most wrong-headed political judgment ever made by a modern cabinet minister; it nearly drove her out of politics and made her for a long time one of our most hated public figures.[9] The *Sun* newspaper, stumbling into accuracy, called her the most unpopular woman in Britain.

Significantly the issue related to milk; the deprivation she felt at the breast was one which she in revenge and in return was now driven to impose upon the children in our primary schools. They were not to have what she always lacked. Punitively and irrationally she decided to end the £8 million a year free milk programme for primary school children. The public subliminally sensed she was acting out the role of a depriving mother, as indeed she was, and reacted with fury. 'Thatcher, Milk Snatcher' rang out at almost every one of her public meetings and, in the Commons, my less decorous colleagues cat-called every time she rose with shouts of 'Ditch the Bitch'. She was never to recover personal popularity until she became the warrior queen of the Falklands war.

Her oral anxieties, placing her sometimes into almost impossible political situations, always betray her. Because love and its symbolic equivalent, nourishment, were not warmly given at the breast, the early fear that the breast will not be available can be reawakened, and manifests itself as a fear of starvation. During the industrial troubles of the early 1970s, food shortages could have arisen if people had panicked by purchasing excessively, yet despite being Secretary of State for Education and consequently responsible for setting an example, Thatcher was discovered to be a hoarder. Her unconvincing defence was 'With my husband facing retirement, I see the prices rising so one does lay in a quiet store of food and household things that one thinks one will need.' Her unconvincing defence was properly derided; her husband is a millionaire, and he still has not retired more than ten years later. Her compulsive response to the threat of food shortage had no real rationale: it sprung from her primal fears of her unresponsive mother.

That unresponsive mother was not only the precipitate for our premier's political peccadillos: structurally embedded in Thatcher's personality are blemishes that have determined, often dangerously, her whole political style. Political journalists have often stressed how she thrives on confrontation and crisis, and languishes in her own estimation and those of the electorate when a calm interlude occurs in public affairs. The more sophisticated Tory political columnists revel in the success of her turbulence and only mourn that her confrontations are so indiscriminate,[10] but here the style is the woman and she lacks the freedom to focus her aggression. She is driven always to attack and the force driving her is unmitigating. She will attack loyal civil servants in trade unions at GCHQ at Cheltenham in the same fashion as she attacks Galtieri in Buenos Aires.

Insightful paediatricians have illuminated the source of such compulsiveness for us.[11] They have shown the consequences that arise in adult behaviour when the woman, as a baby, lacks the good care which allows a fusion of her aggression and eroticism. The motility that exists in the inter-uterine life as the babe kicks in the womb, and which exists when an infant of a few weeks thrashes away with its arms, is the precursor to the aggression which has to be purposively and meaningfully directed at specific targets if the child is to become a well-rounded person. For some, the environmental chance which enables the baby to ensure an integration of a personality is denied. They become not the healthy adults whose behaviour is purposive and whose aggression is meaningfully focused: they are the sick whose aggression is expressed like the babe who, without direction, kicks in the womb or thrashes away with his arms and upon whom we project the notion that he means to hit when, in fact, we have no right to make such an assumption. They are, in short, the men and women who have not lived their earliest times constantly discovering and rediscovering the environment by using their motility, as they snuggle and struggle within their mother's arms; they have not enjoyed that primal erotic experience within which they can fuse their aggression and love. For them, contact with the environment has not been an experience of the individual: lacking loving care, they lacked a series of individual experiences helping them on their way to integration, and suffered only an environment which was felt as an impingement.

The tragedy of men and women who have suffered such an early fate is that, as adults, they must constantly expose themselves to opposition that is vigorous, if not dangerous. Only in aggressive reactions to impingement can they feel real; and if the opposition is not in existence it must be provoked. They are deemed to have a personality which has developed falsely as a series of reactions to impingements and their only hope of possessing a total sense of feeling real is when they are in a situation which arouses opposition. In my Party we are only too familiar with them, for the character types of the hard Left display all these classical syndromes, but Thatcher illustrates no less clearly the hazards to the public weal when, like now, constant political turbulence is needed to ward off fears of personal dissolution.

Each year she is compelled to mount new provocations: for 1989 she has clearly selected the NHS and the dockers as her targets. She cannot desist, for there is no stillness in the woman: always she must be on the attack. Her traits caricature those found in so many politicians who seek to contain what is probably a heavy genetic endowment of aggression. The true base for the effective binding and modification of aggressive impulses is found in the essentially non-verbal communication received by the baby as it is held in love and safety in the mother's arms: and that baby can be strengthened by a mother's calm voice and by reassuring lullabies. I believe Thatcher lacked such an early blessing and that, therefore, to restrain herself from slipping into more primitive forms of aggression than is her wont, she uses words, even more than most politicians, to mollify her anxiety. For, with the end of early childhood, mitigation and control of the aggressive drive is effected by verbalisation; from then on, words are expected to take the place of muscular action. Dirty words must take the place of dirty actions such as a protesting defaecation; verbal abuse must take the place of physical attack. Not for nothing has the dictum stressed that the man who first hurled a word of abuse against his enemy instead of a spear was the founder of civilisation.

Unconsciously Thatcher fears she will yield, regress and display violence in a frighteningly savage form; verbalisation is the uncertain dam which resists and blocks the ebb tide of aggression that may otherwise engulf her. Talk and argument act as her defence and as her Cabinet and television interrogators know to their dismay, this is incessant. As David Howell, a minister in her government for four years, has put it: 'I think the general atmosphere in the government of which I was a member was everything should start as an argument, continue as an argument and end as an argument.' The phlegm of an Attlee is worlds away from Thatcher. However, verbal argument is not enough and a seepage of her unsatisfied aggression is only too often visible. Thus, vicariously, she has tried to be the hangman, and has urged and voted for the return of capital punishment, a punishment which gives her the opportunity of committing the same outrage as the murderer under cover of an act of expiation. The purity of her intentions, however, is frequently asserted by prefacing her violent view on capital punishment, as in a whole range of issues, with the seemingly quaint expostulation: 'Goodness me'. By such a reversal she seeks to mask the 'badness in me' which unconsciously she feels and fears.

It is not only Thatcher's intemperate prolixity which tells us of the long shadows cast by the grandmother; they are seen too in her vocabulary. She deploys evocations of the cultural ambience of the grandmother, doubtless echoed by Thatcher's lay-preacher father. The moral exhortations, as some observers have perspicaciously noticed, are culled from a wide range of pirated primary religious culture, Methodist hymns, the Bible and Bunyan's *Pilgrim's Progress*, and even when she is not making overt use of the language of the Bible, it emerges in the most unlikely places to shape the rhythm of her speech. It is indisputable that the impalpability of these references creates a powerful implicit sub-text which buoys up the banalities of her vision and gives to the unwary the conviction they are being offered a mysterious evocation of the universal truth.[12] There is, she preaches, no alternative to her way which, wrapped in the cadences of the Lord, almost blasphemously assimilates the development of capitalism to the exigencies of an absolute religious creed. In 1988, speaking to the Church of Scotland she presented her religious credo in its most shameless form: it offered moral absolution to the rich and a moral injunction only on the poor.

All the evangelising is conducted frenetically, incessantly. She unabashedly declares herself a workaholic as if the addiction to work has none of the pejorative overtones of an addiction to alcohol, but all the compulsive bustling and interfering has in public affairs a shadowy side as well as a positive value and reflects the fragility of her basic self: work is the glue keeping her together. In 1988 in a *Sunday Times* interview,[13] 'Why I can never, never let up', she proffered the improbable explanation that she cannot let go because she has not yet found a worthy successor: a more probable explanation is that it is she, not the country, who is in danger of falling to bits if she desists from hyperactivity, for she never received from the unresponsive mother the needed corroboration of her vigour and healthy narcissism. I believe she did not see herself as the gleam in her mother's eye for there was no gleam. The baby, deprived of the needed stimulating responses, lacking the assurance of joyful responses to her aliveness, can be depleted of self esteem and be left with a residual disposition towards depressing emptiness in adult life: the philanderer, the promiscuous homosexual and the drug addict are all desperately seeking, by the over-stimulation of manic excitement, to gain the stimulation initially denied them, for without their excitements they feel they will fall to pieces, and the workaholic, if sometimes less obviously driven and less anti-social, is no less afflicted with the syndrome.[14]

Her conduct in the House reflects her inner depressiveness. When an eloquent rapier thrust or some droll gaffe is made in the Commons, the whole House laughs but Thatcher rarely joins in the fun. The mothering smile was never bestowed upon her, and although she can jeer, the spontaneous laugh is not part of her equipment. The frown not the genuine smile is her emblem. The sophisticated raillery of St John Stevas could not be tolerated, self mockery could not be endured, and he had to be expunged from the Cabinet. Even her admired Reagan has been miffed by her total incapacity to appreciate his jokes.[15]

The straining after intactness reveals itself in the compulsive, humourless, remorseless action. Reflection cannot be permitted to cause delay. The time-span capacity[16] – the length of time for which an individual is able to tolerate the effects of exercising discretion on her own account – vary considerably. Emotional make-up even more than intelligence enters into the factor of being able to tolerate uncertainty. One's capacity for tolerating for increasingly long periods the uncertainty which arises when one considers a variety of options prior to making a final decision depends upon the duration and quality of early gratifying or frustrating experiences. Melanie Klein has taught us that the baby's experience of the period between breast feeding can have long term repercussions. When the mother is absent and is felt to be absent and the baby is not confident that the good breast will soon return, her later development reflects this with an intense anxiety if there is delay of any sort.[17] The well-founded complaint that although decisiveness may be seen in Thatcher's immediate reactions, under her control the government has no long term strategy, lends weight to the postulate that her policy making suffers from her lack of an early facilitating environment. The need for government policies to encourage scientific research and development – a prerequisite if Britain is not doomed to continued economic decline – has been ignored under Thatcher. Research, by its very nature, demands postponement of final conclusions and involves suspension of precipitate decisions: this is almost intolerable for Thatcher since she finds it impossible to await a result. She suffers so much suspense when England plays football that unless she finds out the result beforehand, she will not watch even a video replay.[18]

Her decision-making processes were illuminated by Sir William Pile who was her Permanent Secretary at the Department of Education when she was a minister. He has explained the odd way in which she came to make a decision. In a BBC broadcast he said:[19]

She is the only person I know I don't think I have ever heard say 'I wonder whether'. Most of us at moments of uncertainty or faced with a lot of conflicting circumstances and confusion of objectives will say, 'Well, what's it all about? What should we do? Any ideas? Should I do nothing? Should I do this? I wonder whether . . . ?'. 'I wonder whether' was not a phrase I ever heard on her tongue so I think her self-sufficiency amounted to always having ready the answer in herself, springing from her character. Equally, for that reason she never seriously delegated anything. I asked her on several occasions, 'You know this is quite a trivial matter, one of us can do that for you, if we get it wrong you can kick us in the bottom'. She said, 'No, I'll do it for myself'. She worked to all hours of the day and night, she always emptied her box with blue pencils and marks on. Every single bit of paper was attended to the next day.

Thatcher is a woman who dare not stop: in stillness she would collapse inwards. Her aggressive hypomanic activity is her defence against depression.

On one celebrated occasion after the 1979 election she cited St Francis, but the dulcet tune was off-key, and her listeners knew it. She never repeated that melody and soon she returned to her familiar raucous notes and her abrasive librettos. As the going got rough for her in the spring of 1988 Hugo Young, ever alert to the deceits of politicians, reported that her image makers had embarked upon an attempt to make her the soothing mother of the nation; she was to emulate Mitterand who has so effectively become France's father figure.[20] But Thatcher would never be able to play that role successfully for the slightest frustration in or out of her Party and she cannot refrain from using her bitter and effective tongue.

The biting language is compensatory satisfaction for her ungenerous suckling and, probably, her early weening. Two sub-phases have been identified during our early nursing: an earlier 'suckling' level and the later 'biting-sadistic' level, and those whose sucking impulses have been left ungratified seek compensatory satisfaction at the biting level to overcome their disappointment and deprivation. The displacement of her biting phase to her biting protesting language becomes almost embarrassingly self evident as under the pressure of interrogation twice a week in the Commons she unconsciously reveals the pathos of her earliest felt deprivation. To direct attention to the source of these bitter ripostes is not reductionism. To be steeped in Freud does not compel us to see only the child in the woman; the woman developed out of the child can also be observed.[21] And for eight long years, each Tuesday and Thursday in the Parliamentary calendar, as the chastened beholder, I wondered at the bitter potion she had received at her mother's breast, so potent that it sustains a limitless ambition never to be assuaged.

★

Peter Jenkins has made a valiant effort to trace the origin of Thatcher's ambition.[22] Thatcher, he writes accurately, 'was driven on and upwards not by the spur of poverty but by ambition and a spirit of acquisitiveness', and then warns, 'To take her at her own word "as a conviction politician", to see her as an ideologue engaged upon some lifelong crusade, would be to miss entirely the force of her ambition. It is of the small-town variety and there is none more ardent.' Jenkins tells us of the *petit bourgeois* world of Grantham and how its cultural and, in particular, its religious values would sanction and incite achievement; he explains that as the son of a small shopkeeper born in a little community in East Anglia, where values and prejudices were not dissimilar from those enveloping Margaret Thatcher, he has a special insight. 'I know Margaret Thatcher', he confidently asserts.

It is always a bold claim, despite the benefit of a cultural empathy, to claim one knows another person – even one's wife. Jenkins's explanation of Thatcher's ambition is intriguing but too slight to bear the weight of the phenomenon he is identifying, the ambition which drove her to the premiership. The culture into which one is born can certainly inflame ambition but it is unlikely to implant the limitless ambition of the kind possessed by Thatcher who, so obsessed with the drive for priority over all, heralded-in 1988 by postponing an important pre-arranged visit to Kenya to attend a self-congratulatory celebration, having beaten Asquith to become the longest continuous serving premier this century. Ambition to triumph over the dead as well as the living politician is an ambition which cannot be regarded as just a natural consequence of being a pupil of Grantham Girls' School: it has a morbidity as well as a strength of a different thrust. We need to turn to deeper sources of the characteristic.

Vexatiously, Freud gave his derivation of the character trait of ambition almost in throwaway lines rather than in a developed hypothesis. He attributed its source to urethral eroticism: the pleasure accompanying the function of urinating. Some understanding that such an unlikely source may promote dreams of boundless ambition is available to all of us with recollections of our boyhood, for we will have played games, alone or with others, when enjoyment of our urethral eroticism accompanied fantasies of omnipotence as we threw into the air our triumphant jets of urine. Freud, however, seems to have wrested his conclusion from his treatment of women patients, noting the intense, 'burning' ambition of women who had earlier suffered from enuresis; but it is in his unravelling of myths and legends that we find him in a whirl of intellectual excitements associating pissing with fire, and suggesting that behind the tale of the boundless ambition of Prometheus, who dared to steal fire from the gods, lay the story of a singular evolutionary advance of mankind: the advance was not, Freud claims, the making of fire but the quenching of fire, and interpreted the hollow stick, a fennel stalk, in which Prometheus concealed the stolen fire, as a symbol of a hollow penis tube which in real life harbours water and not fire.[23]

Pointing out how he had discovered in dreams that a reversal of procedures takes place, of inverting relationships, of the turning into opposites, of water into fire, Freud suggests that a firm link exists between urethral eroticism and ambition, illustrating the assertion with the legend of the most ambitious of all men, Alexander the would-be world conqueror, who was born during the same night on which a certain Herostratus set fire to the celebrated Temple of Artemis at Ephesus out of a sheer desire for fame.[24] These are heady speculations but in myths and legends allusions to a fire–water link and ambition and search for fame, certainly abound. More mundanely and less speculatively, I have, while spending thirty years of my working life with the most ambitious group of men possible to be placed under one roof, not failed to notice how frequently, when standing in the stalls of Westminster's lavatories, Members confide to each other, often by way of defensive jokes, their hopes and wilder aspirations. Propriety prevented me from having similar access to Westminster's Ladies' Rooms and I cannot tell of clinical material among women MPs that may confirm Freud's theory. Happily for this scrutiny of Margaret Thatcher this deprivation may not be a severe handicap, for even Freud's most loyal disciples, Karl Abraham and Edward Glover, as early as 1927, complained that his explanation did not penetrate to the deepest sources of the character-trait of ambition, conceding only that urethral eroticism reinforced the trait that came from earlier sources.[25]

We find earlier sources being suggested to us by both Heinz Kohut and Melanie Klein. Kohut tells us of the consequence of the unempathic mother brusquely negating the baby's need for corroboration of her healthy assertiveness and exhibitionism, and how a desperate and often pathological assertiveness then sets in in order to gain the recognition never voluntarily accorded by the mother: the baby cannot accept passively a world of unmirrored ambitions, and the self of the child – injured by the lack of the responsiveness of the cold mother – becomes dominated by unassimilated hostility. The enhancement of self esteem never originally freely and warmly given may, in the adult, as Kohut richly illustrates in his case histories, lead to a way of life of sadistic domination forcing continuous acknowledgments of superiority.[26] In some, a fruitless attempt to strengthen the rejected and enfeebled self is made by fantasies of sadistically enforced acclaim, in others it is effected by way of sick 'games' like tying up a sexual partner. But it is outside the private domain that the most havoc can be wrought; when ambition has such sickly roots it remains for ever inordinate and, if found in a prime minister, can, to satisfy its continuous and compulsive needs, lead to a demand that each and every ukase must without question be obeyed by Cabinet, civil service, press and nation.

Melanie Klein, like Kohut, found that the precipitate of boundless ambition is in less-than-adequate early mothering, but she explores the vicissitudes of ambitious yearnings by drawing attention to the source of envy. Envy above all else spurs on a craving for priority; for power and prestige.[27] Her view is consistent with Chaucer's who, in 'The Parson's Tale', tells us, 'It is certain that envy is the worst sin that is; for all other sins are sins only against one virtue, whereas envy is against all virtue and against all goodness.' Chaucer, placing it first of the seven deadly sins, knew how destructive and all pervading it can be, and knew that it should not be regarded as a mere peccadillo; it is endemic in the fiercely and increasingly competitive Commons where, to refute guilt, ambition to reach the top is claimed to be a virtue not a sin. Frustration and unhappy circumstances rouse some envy in everyone throughout life but the strength of the emotion and the way in which the individual copes with it varies considerably, and that variation depends on the mother's initial responses. In Klein's view, envy operates from birth, materially affects an infant's early experiences and, if not tempered at the breast, leaves permanent character defects.

Hanna Segal has written, 'Envy stirs as soon as the infant becomes aware of the breast as a source of life and good experience; the real gratification which he experiences at the breast reinforced by idealisation, so powerful in early infancy, makes him feel that the breast is the source of all comfort, physical and mental, an inexhaustible reservoir of food and warmth, love, understanding and wisdom. The blissful experience of satisfaction which this wondrous object can give will increase his love and his desire to possess, preserve and protect it, but the same experience stirs in him also the wish to be himself the source of such perfection; he experiences painful feelings of envy which carry with them the desire to spoil the qualities of the object which can give him such painful feelings.' Because the enjoyment of the baby at the breast is often marred and overshadowed by feelings of envy, which may give rise to terrifying destructive wishes, Melanie Klein – drawing on her clinical experiences – was led to the belief that the baby may react by fantasising that he had given birth to the mother and was the original possessor of the envied breast. So it was not the baby who wishes to rob the mother of the goodness of her breast but the mother who had already robbed the babe. From the baby's insistence that it was she, not the mother, who came first, Klein traces the determination of the adult man and woman to have priority and primacy of place. Her explanation was a development of the concept which had been presented by the paediatrician Donald Winnicott of the 'illusory breast' which suggested that at the beginning, the baby can believe she has created the world around her.[28]

Whether such unconscious fantasies of priority strongly persist in the adult, or whether they are mortified and substantially overcome, depends upon how hostile or facilitating the early environmental experiences were felt to be. In a happy development the gratification experienced at the breast stimulates admiration, love and gratitude at the same time as envy, and although these feelings enter into conflict with envy, gratitude can overcome and modify that envy. 'The ideal breast, introjected with love, gratification and gratitude', Hanna Segal has written, 'becomes part of the ego, the ego is more full of goodness itself. And thus, in a benevolent circle, envy lessens as gratification increases, the diminution of envy allows more gratification which in turn furthers the lessening of envy.'[29] But if the baby does not feel love and admiration is being boundlessly bestowed, there is no gratitude available to overcome envy and then 'overweening' and 'consuming' ambition – the adjectives betraying the early oral associations – becomes a permanent character trait. The curmudgeonly, affectless mother, shadowy and colourless as she may appear to the outside world, can, by negative reactions, bequeath such envy to the child that, when the infant grows up, all significant figures who come within her constellation must be usurped.

Sadly, perhaps, given the obstacles, some such intensive, envious spur is today a prerequisite for the achievement of the premiership. Those with a greater capacity and desire for pleasure don't compete; more rounded and balanced men have quit Thatcher's Cabinet rather than be subject to the continued assertion of dominance which springs from her ceaseless need for absolute priority, for they have other pleasures. Freud describes the infant's bliss on being suckled as the prototype of sexual gratification, and Klein believes that if the baby's excessive envy of the breast impairs this oral gratification, the resultant hatred and anxiety is carried forward to adulthood and paves the way for severe difficulties in genital attitudes. In fact, Klein goes further and argues that these early experiences at the breast constitute 'not only the basis of sexual gratification but of all later happiness and make possible the feelings of unity with another person; such unity means being fully understood, which is essential for every love relationship or friendship. At best, such an understanding needs no words to express it, which demonstrates its derivation from the earliest closeness to the mother in the pre-verbal stage.'[30]

No such understanding – none of the reticent communication

available in true friendship – can be found in Thatcher's Cabinet room, as so many of her talked-down former colleagues have attested. At Downing Street there can be no echoes from the bliss at the breast which is the blessed lot of some, for it was a bliss from which Thatcher was excluded. At fifteen, Thatcher has told us she had nothing to say to her mother. How could it be otherwise? For fifteen years before, the same woman could not speak, could not communicate to the baby at her breast. Poor little Maggie was so affected by the resultant envy that she would never know happiness, but only the sadistic triumphs of tawdry political and military victories.

4

On the Pot

THE description of adult character in terms of childhood experience is one of the basic principles of classical psychoanalytical
characterology and, indeed, the ontogenetic approach to human
personality has been claimed to be the essence of the theory and
method of psychoanalysis.[1] From the time that the influence of the
libido and the stages of its development were first divined there has,
however, been an insistence that there is no 'pure culture' to be found
in the character make-up of the adult.

Decades ago the traits of the orally ungratified type were listed as
arrogance, aggression, impatience, a tendency to collect and hoard
food, competitiveness and a quarrelsome disposition,[2] traits hardly
absent from Thatcher's personality. But what has undoubtedly been
more important in the shaping of Thatcherite policies is that her
orality has prompted a predispositional fixation which ushers in other
traits from later stages of libidinal development, and in particular of
her anal phase. When there is marked oral dissatisfaction, clinical
experience has taught that an admixture of traits subsequently occurs;
since those whose sucking impulses have been left ungratified desperately aim at satisfaction at the anal level. It is a goal they are unlikely
to attain, for a mother who is peremptory when the child wants
satisfaction at the breast is the same severe unempathic mother who
denies her child the pride in her own first creation, her faeces. The
child who is prematurely and strictly toilet-trained will all its life
unconsciously deploy stratagems to cope with the parental impera-
tives which far too brusquely compelled her to relinquish the phase
when the anus and defaecation are the major sources of sensuous
pleasure and form the centre of the infant's self awareness. A price
has to be paid by an infant if she is doomed to have a mother whose
own self is poorly consolidated and who, therefore, reacts by focusing
exclusive attention to the faeces and the anal region rather than to the
total, proudly assertive, anal-phase self of her child. With insufficient
compensation available to the child to make up for the parsimony

of the grudging breast, those traits which belong to the clinical phenomena of the anal character are built up on the ruins of an oral eroticism whose development has miscarried.

One of the most obvious traits of those who have been so cur-mudgeonly treated is an obsessive concern with order and cleanliness. From Thatcher's own account of her childhood we know that her Victorian grandmother imposed tidiness and scrupulous cleanliness upon the overcrowded household and so we can legitimately infer how negative the reactions to the infant must have been as she passed through the assertive anal phase. If excessive prohibitions were imposed upon the hapless little Margaret, the outlawing of any coprophilic impulses – of the pleasures of a proud infant looking at and touching her creations – would have left their mark on Thatcher's adult disposition. Explicitly echoing her grandmother, Thatcher, with never a hair out of place, has told us that in her league table of values cleanliness is next to godliness. Such an extravagant promotion of an attribute suggests the continued need for a defence against a nostalgia that she feels may pull her back to her unspent coprophilia. The hypertrophy – the magnification of the opposing tendency – is the reaction formation which forms a bulwark against the unacceptable impulses, too abruptly forbidden, which still endure.

This is sometimes revealed in a droll capriciousness. When Thatcher returned from a visit to Israel, an important statement was expected from her on the Middle East. Instead, as a priority, disturbed on the way from the airport by the sight of litter in London, she contrasted its unseemliness with gleaming Tel Aviv. To the vexation of the refuse collectors, who well knew that centrally imposed, local government cuts were limiting their services, she forthwith appointed a millionaire (who had made his fortune out of the commercial exploitation of pop music for the young), to lead an anti-litter campaign, and rationalised her gesture as a contribution to resolving youth employment. Some years later, forever preoccupied with uncleanliness, she was to be seen engaged in picking up carefully arranged, clean litter in St James's Park. By 1989 her overdetermined reaction-formations to filth led to her caricaturing herself: and the Prime Minister of Britain was to be seen in Downing Street enthusi-astically removing pigeons' droppings with a new high-powered jet spray water gun.

If the squeamish, compulsive and regular relinquishment of faeces was imposed on Margaret when an infant, then there could result more dire policy consequences than is shown in such whimsical campaigns. The dissonance between mother and child, destroying the elementary rhythm which can come from a mothering mother, means the resentful child is never reconciled to her loss. As an adult she will often passionately seek out the equivalences of the prized shit to which she has attached magical values. All the esteem which she felt in her creations and which she was so cruelly compelled to suppress, is transferred to that most ancient equivalent – to gold, to money. Gold, according to ancient oriental mythology, is the excrement of hell. And in dreams, as in folklore, Freud has told us gold is seen in the most unambiguous and magic way to be a symbol of faeces.[3]

Few of us could claim that we can totally regulate our relationship to money according to the demands of reality. In all of us an interest in money can in part be traced to the early excretory pleasures of defaecation, but those early libidinal influences can be so overwhelming for some that their relationship to money is leeched away from rationality. Thatcher's deprivation of her defaecatory pleasures made her an easy lay for Milton Friedman – her overvaluation of money led her to be an enthusiastic disciple of that monetarist guru – but although her monetarism may have given her supporters vicarious, sensuous delights, its infantile origin has meant, by its very irrationality, that it has destroyed much of Britain's manufacturing industry.

The passion behind her advocacy of monetarist doctrines elevates an economic hypothesis to a creed. In the late Lord Kaldor's words, it was adopted 'with almost the same solemnity as the Emperor Constantine when he embraced Christianity'. The doctrine was based on the retention and manipulation of the money supply measured by a mystical M3 (said to be the totality of cash and bank deposits). The anality of the theory, with its displacement of the visceral control of excretion to an economic hypothesis should have acted as a warning of its mythical nature. But the zealots possessed by such dogma have no doubts: they believe in the omnipotence of their thoughts. Such delusions of omnipotence, reflecting the baby's feelings as a Creator when she produces her faeces, are behind the Biblical myth telling us how man was created out of a clod of earth, of clay, the equivalent of excrement, when God breathed upon it; and when Thatcher breathed on her dirt, the magic of monetarism was commanded to emerge. In the real world there was no response to her ukase: by 1986, with two million lost jobs and tens of billions of lost output, the thaumaturgy was abandoned, and the Chancellor, at a Mansion House dinner, pronounced the end of the frenzied crusade. Still, however, though my colleagues take their seats every day in a Chamber where we are continuously passing motions, they would fiercely resist any interpretation of the nomenclature which would hint at the origins of our institutions and proceedings or of the mumbo-jumbo of monetarism.

The compulsiveness of Thatcher's attraction to money and her consequent incapacity to regulate rationally her relationship to it means she can stumble into political indiscretions that would otherwise have been avoided. Sometimes she has ignored the need for a prime minister to distance herself from action which gives an opportunity to the unkind to misinterpret as an abuse of her power and patronage. Her claim that, while on an official visit to Oman, she was batting for Britain when she urged a contract for the building of a university should be given to a British company was regarded as an unimpressive riposte by some of those who noted a payment of commission to Mark Thatcher by the company gaining the contract. 'We did pay him – and we used him because he is the Prime Minister's son', the company executive was quoted as saying by the *Observer*.[4] But the obvious lesson of this unhappy incident went unlearned. In 1987, yet again in the Commons, demands for a statement from the Prime Minister were being made following reports in the *Guardian* that Mark Thatcher had been engaged as a lobbyist by an American company bidding for the £1.6 billion Department of Health and Social Security contract. Moreover, when Tiny Rowland of Lonrho was thwarted in his attempt to take over Harrods he maintained, in vituperative letters to MPs, that the government, at the highest level, had behaved improperly in not investigating his claim that the Egyptian bidders failed to disclose that they were backed by the Sultan of Brunei. The *Observer*, owned by Lonrho, in reporting on the takeover struggles, added the ugly smear that the Sultan had 'presented her (Mrs Thatcher) with a gold bracelet studded with diamonds and rubies'.[5] If the *Observer*'s report is true, it was clearly indiscreet of Thatcher to have accepted the gift however untainted it may well have been.

There have been other occasions when her discretion has been questioned. She failed to stop her husband using Downing Street as a venue to oversee his financial interests. On Downing Street notepaper, Denis Thatcher was discovered to have peremptorily requested the Secretary of State for Wales to expedite the planning appeal of a company in which he had a financial interest. *The Times* commented, 'Ministers and MPs are rightly expected to make their business commitments public, and in some cases to lay them aside. Their husbands and wives are under no such obligation . . . Nevertheless the power they may have behind the scenes can be considerable and all the more formidable in that its extent is impossible to assess from outside . . . If ambiguous situations are to be avoided, a little more

care is needed than Mr Thatcher has shown on this occasion.'6
The warning comments went unheeded. Some years later in the
Commons, I drew attention to Denis Thatcher's continuing financial
involvement in a building company in dispute with an arm of the
Welsh Office and I deplored the inevitable conflicts of interest that
were arising in the litigation between Denis Thatcher and his friend
Nicholas Edwards, the Secretary of State. For the Thatchers the
odour of money overpowers all political caution.

Thatcher most certainly does not regard love of money as the root
of all evil. As her language so often reveals, she regards money as a
kind of materialisation of divine grace. Avarice, greed and profit
seeking is the motivation which is waiting to be rekindled in Britain.
Man is not to be viewed in his full humanity but as economic man,
and politics is related to a branch of economics. Too often the
vulgarity of her version of the psychodynamics of mankind, a version,
I believe, to be determined by her own emotional arrests at her anal
phase, invades Labour's vocabulary: the debate rages and becomes
virtually confined to a dispute over which party's economic programme will bring greater wealth to the desired materialist Britain of
the future. Debates about more profound human needs are considered
peripheral to the central argument as to which party will shower
more consumer goods on the electorate.

The nation's belief that there are other priorities must be expur-
gated; the tax cuts of 1988 are sacralised and we are invited to join in
worship at the counting house. As Jeremy Seabrook has written of
Thatcher's profane enterprise: 'The process of buying and selling has
long since ceased to be a simple inter-reaction between money and
goods but has become a parody of Holy Communion: an exultation
of the spirit, blessed by the advertising industry as a mysterious
marriage of desire with purchase.'7 Thatcher communicates with her
supporters by calling on them to pray at the Temple of Mammon,
and in the election of 1987 and the budget of 1988, she gave the
worshippers absolution at that Temple once again.

She has taught that 'caring' is a word to be whispered; henceforth
greed and avarice will not warrant guilt. On the contrary, these are
the impulses which will bring us to her 'moral' society. As she
presented it in 1971: 'Economics are the method: the object is to
change the heart and soul.' There is, of course, an irony, but no
paradox, that the initial economic methodology she claimed would
achieve her millennium was the promotion of thrift; the matching of
effort to appetite; the priority of duty over the allure of entitlement.
But like many a Mrs Grundy over-determinedly outlawing sex, in
the end she could not resist the attractions that she appears to

condemn. Surely she is recapturing the denied initial excretory pleasures not only by her political philosophy of declared retentiveness – of thrift – but also by the splurge. By so evoking the earliest delights forbidden to her, the years of Thatcher have brought an incontinent release of credit; she has brought about the casino society. It is the familiar story of the consequences of ideological leadership; *qui fait l'ange fait la bête.*

The florid ambiguities in Thatcher's economic policies reflect the pathetic battles which she once fought with the martinets determined to train her on the pot. The central position occupied by the training of our excretory functions during our early years may be modified but can never be excluded from the rest of our lives. The shit created by us, which in turn has created sensations for us, is a plastic source of fantasy and the very first object in which our relationship to others is concretised: to expel or to hold back, to give or not to give, to submit or to disobey, the seemingly trivial contest of wills forges a link, a meaningful nexus, between those involved. As Elvio Fachinelli, the Italian psychoanalyst, has emphasised, 'Within the nexus, a significant relationship of mutual tension and desire is gradually developed between the child and its mother.[8] Moved by love for her and by the fear of losing her, by the pleasure of gratifying its desire or the pleasure of being compensated for not doing so, the child slowly renounces total control over its new-found power and agrees to produce the golden eggs only when and where she demands. But in order to re-exert some authority over her in turn, to win her recognition and some revenge for all the wrongs inflicted on it, it learns at the same time to postpone, to disappoint her, to make her wait . . . ' Yet with sensitivity and love, a happy armistice can be achieved. The baby gives his great gift, the precursor of all gifts, and the mother's former prohibitions are now felt as wondrous approvals.

I believe no such peace treaty was ever signed between Thatcher and her mother and grandmother. The rumblings of the war continue; unconsciously she still strives to regain her denied earliest sphincter thrills by condemning the prohibitions which thwarted her. The restraints and regulations in the public sphere which she would now end are but displacements of the private prohibitions which once so profoundly irked her, and her coprophilia is but flimsily covered when she gives freedom to those who dabble deep into money. She is lured to preach a new antinomianism; under her grace many established regulatory and ethical codes are no longer binding. Even as the antinomians of old preached sin that grace may abound,[9] so she had preached freedom for licence: but if the ancient heretics used their licence to indulge the flesh, now the freedom granted is to be used to indulge the lusts for money.

Her evangelical fervour seduced millions into becoming first-time shareholders. Thatcher succeeded in initiating the electorate into a new form of gambling: her personal need to end the earliest constraints which she had endured, outlawing the joys of shitting and coprophilia, drove her to open the doors of the Stock Exchange and end its keep-out ambience and exclusivity; the whole nation was invited to wallow in magic money-making in the great casino. The Labour Party's cautious disapproval in the 1987 election was received by the voters with the same degree of enthusiasm as was Moses by the children of Israel when they danced around the golden calf.

As Labour's vote was ebbing away, I recalled my interventions in the House during the debates on the 1960 Betting and Gaming Act. Then, with an approval regarded as quaint, I had cited to my bemused Labour colleagues the words of Labour's one-time foreign secretary, Arthur Henderson. Speaking to trade union audiences he always insisted that 'Gambling is a greater foe to Labour than all the forces of capitalism.'[10] And so, forty years on, it proved to be. In 1987 perhaps a million of Labour's former voters, entranced by the speculative possibilities open to them by their new shareholdings, changed their political allegiances; but when they and others walked away from the Labour Party they walked backwards. Even as excellence in political leadership can move a nation into mature judgments, so a leadership afflicted with the emotionally regressive syndromes can reduce a nation to infantilism.

The aetiology of the urge to gamble lies in joyless masturbation and early, still-unresolved bisexuality: but Freud's elegant essay in 1928 on Dostoevsky,[11] which illuminates the dynamics of compulsive gambling, was literature unknown to my Labour colleagues who were exasperated and bewildered to find on the doorsteps a surly resentment that Labour should threaten to interfere with gambles on the privatised shares. Silly polls with sillier questions do not tell us of the unconscious motivations of an electorate deciding to vote; in 1987 more important than party manifestos was the cloacal atmosphere in which it was fought. In my view, Thatcher's frustrated coprophilia and her consequent unwitting reawakening of the electorate's early masturbatory habits played a considerable part in determining the result. It was not surprising that although Labour won the debate, Thatcher won the election.

Like many of us within the South Wales working-class culture of the depression years of the Thirties, in my late teens I attended for a season the local greyhound track, which was as much part of my entrance into manhood as had been my barmitzvah at thirteen. Although I claimed to have won more than I lost, my interest flagged after a year and on Saturday nights I switched to girls. That interest was more sustained and it was not until the post-war years that my attention again turned to gambling; but this time I was a solicitor, not a punter.

Then, for some years before I went into the House, I became increasingly professionally involved with one of Britain's largest bookmakers and football-pool promoters, by an accident of geography and his ageing. He was a great collector; he wanted to collect me too. But by insisting upon my independent status and refusing his offers to put me on his payroll, his appetite was whetted and I found him increasingly seeking me out for legal guidance. The greatest pleasure of this austere, childless multi-millionaire was litigation, preferably incestuous, involving his family. It was his leisure activity and filled many of my working hours. My close contact with him gave me a vantage point from which to observe and understand the shoddy and vast gambling industry of Britain, and indeed, its ramifications in Africa. Newmarket Heath on a fine early summer morning is certainly a delight, but the smell of the grass, the sound of larks singing, the rhythmic drumming of hooves on the turf, the touch of a satin pelt and the liberating sight of horses galloping through breast-high mists, is but the surface aspect of the sport of kings. The wretched saga of the acquisitive Lester Piggott is the reality behind the aristocratic pretensions of the oligarchic, self-perpetuating Jockey Club and the Ascot fashion parades.

My acquired knowledge of the gambling industry meant that I came into the House with no less a censorious attitude towards gambling than that held by the most severe non-conformist chapels in my constituency. I revealed my prejudices for the first, but not the last, time during the debates on the Betting and Gaming Bill in 1959 when, to replace street-runners, the opening of betting shops was given the go ahead by the government. I was first called to speak, immediately after a Member who anticipated Thatcherite doctrines by many years. He had concluded his speech by praising the Bill as 'a blow for individual liberty and commonsense which will show that we are an adult democracy and can afford to treat our people as such in future.' Before turning to the details of the Bill I prissily retorted:

My interpretation of the consequences of this Bill, including the moral consequences, are very different from those of the Hon. Member. Listening to the Home Secretary giving the amount spent each year upon gambling, it was chastening to think that in our society so many people find so little excitement in life and so little zest that they can gain a thrill only by this type of activity. I say to the Hon. Member that I think a more mature democracy would be seeking means to stimulate the imagination of people so that they dream other dreams than that of winning on a horse race.

Although some of us professionally engage sometimes in the farcical proceedings under the existing betting and gaming laws, and even though we want an effort to be made to provide a rationale to the betting and gaming laws, I can only agree to this scheme if the effort will not lead to further stimulation of gambling and will not make it still easier for gambling promoters to make still vaster fortunes out of the cupidity and credulousness of the most feckless sections of the community.[12]

I spoke strongly because I was aware of the evasions, cheatings and the exploitation of the credulous embedded within the gambling industry; but it was not simply the distress and disruption it brought into family life of working people that I regretted. More objectionable was the manner in which the glamorisation of racing facilitated and legitimised the demeaning of men and women who, by accepting the invitation to dream their dreams of gain, lost their adulthood. The considerable clinical material to which I had gained access in my professional work validated so many of the hypotheses within the psychoanalytical literature on gambling.

That literature had been stimulated by some revealing and startling asides within Freud's essay 'Dostoevsky and Parricide'. Freud found the causality of Dostoevsky's compulsive gambling habits in a particular variation of the Oedipal complex. It was a variation which probably plays a part in all our lives but was one which, because of Dostoevsky's particular infantile experiences, had a shattering impact on his adult life. Freud emphasised how when the child is in his Oedipal phase – in intense rivalry with his father, and resenting the father's possession of the mother – he not only has parricidal wishes against his rival but simultaneously has a desire to be the father's love-object. This bisexuality prompting the boy's wish to become both his mother's lover and to be taken by the father displacing the wife, can, in adverse external circumstances, bring about intolerable dilemmas which can reach into adulthood.

46

The boy fears that his wish to slay the father may bring him the retaliation of castration. At the same time he fears submission as a feminine love-object will bring about the same result. The ideal resolution of these dilemmas may never be possible, but for most of us, from fear of castration, in the interests of preserving our masculinity, we give up the wish to possess our mother and slay the father, and confine both impulses – hatred of the father and being in love with the father – to the unconscious. There, albeit imperfectly, they remain repressed, but still prompt in all of us a feeling of guilt and a need for expiation. Freud finds, however, that in those whose bisexual disposition has caused them especially to fear the consequences of their feminine attitudes, a pathogenic intensification of their feelings of guilt arises. In adulthood, such boys are prone to attempt to relieve their guilt by placing themselves at the mercy of fate and demanding that *it* provides a means of resolving their impossible dilemmas.

For, in the Freudian view, gambling is in essence a provocation of fate, forcing it to make its decisions for or against the individual. With every cast of the dice, with every turn of the card, with every spin of the wheel, the questions being asked over and over again reflect the earliest Oedipal dilemmas. Am I omnipotent, able by my secret wishes to kill off my father, and have I, if he is in fact dead, killed him? And simultaneously – since formal logic is not part of the unconscious – am I the beloved of my father? He loves me, he loves me not. If the gambler wins, he receives the affirmative answers to all his questions. He is the killer and the beloved. But in either case he must pay the price of emasculation, a totally unacceptable and terrifying conclusion. So to remain intact, the compulsive gambler never desists; he is determined to lose in order to survive. Only by losing does he gain relief from his guilt as killer and lover, for then he obtains the punishment he deserves for his parricidal and incestuous wishes.

During the years that I observed my bookmaker-client supplying these masochistic needs to thousands of customers, it was clear that although the punters, to maintain their psychic equilibrium, were determined to lose their money, the thrills they had en route were sustaining them. Those joyless thrills were paralleled by Freud to masturbation. Indeed, Dostoevsky himself described the tremulous excitement which losing afforded him and pointed out that the punishment of total loss at the end of a losing run led to orgasm.[13] Thus the psychic masochist pursues his lonely path, producing pleasure out of displeasure.[14] It is a solitary journey; onanism thus displaced turns its back on human relationships. There is no more lonely and sad a place than the silent, crowded gambling room of a fashionable, luxuriously appointed London casino. To enter one of them is to enter a lavish mausoleum.

The compulsive gambler vividly uncovers for us the determinedly infantile experiences producing his psychopathology; but the compulsive gambler's drive is only a caricature of the motivational forces operating on the less avid player. Writing of these forces, Freud observed: 'Infantile reactions from the Oedipus complex such as these may disappear if reality gives them no nourishment.' Contrariwise, the appetite grows if they are well fed. During the passage of the Betting and Gaming Act 1960, my efforts were directed to make the betting shops as austere as possible. I wanted them to lack the accoutrements, amenities and advertising displays that would lure customers into continuous betting, and I sought to nudge them away into unattractive side streets. The oracular nature of gambling makes it as impossible to ban as prostitution. But rightly, we do not encourage the siting of luxurious brothels in our high streets, even though, in some respects, fornication may sometimes be more of a maturational experience for the practitioner than gambling.

I soon found, in those very early days of my Parliamentary life, that such musings were not to the taste of many in the Commons; my arrogant belief that I had a special knowledge of the gambling industry and could pontificate without challenge was soon shattered. I discovered in the debates that my experience may have been considerable but unlike so many of my opponents, it was essentially vicarious. I was to learn that there are many politicians who are compulsive risk-takers and who persistently gamble with fate, sometimes within the political arena, sometimes by way of a concealed but scandalous private life, sometimes by direct wagering, and sometimes by using all three routes to find their date with destiny. Of course, few have the political talents of a Charles James Fox who, in the eighteenth century, lost £140,000 in three years, and, although an expert whist player who invariably won at the game, always preferred to play hazard, a game of pure chance, complaining that whist afforded him no excitement. In the House of Commons there were, and still are, not a few who continue the tradition of Charles James Fox's days when gambling was the principal activity of the political clubs.

A generation ago, I found that it was not only wealthy Tory MPs who were the gamblers: many Labour politicians, with far lower financial resources, made bets continuously. The police at Westminster acted as the illegal runners; they collected the money and slips, passed them on to the bookmakers and brought back the winnings and results. A network of unlawful gambling was part of the daily secret life of Westminster.

Yet, at least the gambling was furtive, and the public stance taken by enough of us ensured that the Betting and Gaming Act of 1960 contained many of the needed restrictions upon betting shops. How profoundly Thatcher – propelled, I believe, by her unconscious need to raise the prohibitions against her infantile coprophilia – had changed the ethos was chasteningly illustrated in 1986 when, to the satisfaction of the national bookmakers supporting the Tory party, all the restrictions were, by way of a Statutory Instrument, swept away. The betting shops are now on their way to becoming attractive social centres with all amenities including television beamed in, not just from the BBC and Channel 4, but also from a bookmaker-owned special satellite service covering all the horse and greyhound racing meetings throughout the day. The working-class punters are spurred on by the accompanying exciting commentaries into an orgy of gambling. The class battle has been won; gambling in luxurious casinos is no longer the prerogative of the rich, and boys coming from the working class like Norman Tebbit can, without any adverse comment, move effortlessly from the chairmanship of the Conservative Party to the directorship of a company controlling one of the largest bookmaking chains in the country.

This is a far cry from the time when Harold Wilson bitterly attacked what he saw as an ugly encouragement of gambling; the introduction of premium bonds by Harold Macmillan. But Macmillan understood a great deal about the strengths and weaknesses of working people and was careful to ensure the lottery was to be a gamble on only the interest and not on the capital invested. Thatcher would not tolerate such constraints. A change in the betting-shop laws impinging upon a significant part of Britain's billion pound gambling industry may be regarded as a peripheral issue: but it exotically illustrates her need to free Britain from what she has encouraged her followers to describe as the Nanny State, forever giving them the lead to mock the restraining mother.

The drive to make everyone a capitalist, to privatise the publicly owned industries and to entice millions to become shareholders is to assert the right of everyone to play with their own shit-money, to refuse to sit on the pot, and to stand defiantly on their own two feet.

A morally authoritative leader can persuade the populace, despite instinctual tugs, to turn away from the golden calf and pursue difficult but more mature ethical ideals, but Thatcher is no Moses and, submitting to her own emotional handicap, she played the timbrels and worked the electorate into a Bacchanalian frenzy. The trance could not, of course, be sustained. As always, reality asserted itself and the god was proved false. Black Monday came and the party, if not over, suddenly went sour.

All the erudition of the columnists and financial commentators has necessarily proved to be inadequate to explain the 1987 market tumble. But then, to analyse it without acknowledging the determinants of anality and masturbatory gambling is to follow the example of the Victorian novelists who wrote so fluently of marriage without mentioning sex. John Maynard Keynes well understood the sickness of the search for money beyond any reasonable need when he wrote, 'The love of money as a possession – as distinguished from a love of money as a means to the enjoyment of the realities of life – should be recognised for what it is, a somewhat disgusting morbidity, one of those semi-criminal, semi-pathological propensities which one hands over with a shudder to the specialist in mental disease.'[15] Such a specialist was Ferenczi, the early innovatory follower of Freud, who had already written in his essay, *The Ontogenesis of the Interest in Money*, ' . . . whatever form may be assumed by money the enjoyment at possessing it has its deepest and amplest source in coprophilia. Every sociologist and national economist who examines the facts without prejudice has to reckon with this irrational element. Social problems can be solved only by discovering the real psychology of human beings; speculations about economic conditions alone will never reach the goal.'

The international character of that 1987 market crash tells us that greed and gambling are endemic to mankind, but Thatcher's claim that the responsibility for the financial collapse fell wholly on the feckless United States and the economic chauvinism of Germany and Japan was unconvincing. That alibi could only be substantiated by wiping out from public memory the oscillations of her economic policies; from retentiveness to splurge – reflections of the swings of mood that sprang from her defiance of any external control of her private peristalsis. By the autumn of 1988, then backing her gambling Chancellor, her insistence that 'freedom' from credit control must be maintained made mortgage-holders flinch; and the world's bankers queued up to lend to Britain's willing suckers at usurious rates of interest, and so compensate themselves for some of the business they no longer dared to offer the Third World.[16]

Neil Kinnock, as the economic difficulties increase, has sensed the essential irrationality behind Thatcher's false alibis, and, mocking at her efforts to rewrite history, has stressed how magic and myth have taken over. 'Rewriting history', he has declared, 'does not merely involve ignoring the facts. It also requires the creation of the myth that consistent policy was consistently applied. The truth is that once there was monetarism, monetary targeting and a Medium-Term Financial Strategy built around the magical monetary measure of

£M3. Now all that is forgotten and borrowing and indebtedness can rocket where they will.'

Nowhere has there been greater rocketing than on the Stock Exchange. For years Thatcher has inflamed the bull market with her give-away privatisation. Lacking insight, unable to find a way to emancipate herself from the oppressiveness of her early upbringing, she encouraged millions to believe that to hold a share certificate was to possess a winning lottery ticket. Everyone was to play the market, able to play without prohibition or restraint with their own magical, creative shit. This was the politics of infantile fantasy; and when the Conservative MP for Anglesey abandoned reality and recklessly fiddled his application for privatised shares, he was but a paradigm of millions who were enveloped in that fantasy. He was not an evil young man and, when serving on a committee under my chairman-ship, given a firm hand, he could be a constructive contributor; he went to his nemesis because he was one of Thatcher's children. His political upbringing in Thatcher's permissive society led him to his particular delinquency, but there were millions of investors who had also assigned themselves parts in the grand charade of 'popular capitalism' and for them, too, the make believe had to end and, chastened by their losses, some faced the painful reality which Thatcher had denied.

The ethos Thatcher has established is not dissolved by one or two reverses: the parasitic financial services industry remains determined to drain adulthood from the investor. Exploiting the enthusiasms of *The Times* and the privatised British Telecom, the service industry is now able to keep the investor permanently emotionally arrested. Now the investor can remain literally hooked to his addiction for every moment of his day. Sponsored by *The Times*, Stockwatch is the gang the boys can join, and with their secret, 'unique' passwords, in their cars, homes and from public kiosks they will be encouraged to play the markets. Continuous betting spreads out from the betting shops to the new shareholders lured by Thatcher on to the Stock Exchange.

When their further losses come they will be more than financial. They, like so many infected by the Thatcherite fever, will have belittled themselves in their pursuit for gain. Karl Marx long ago demonstrated that money, by acting as the intermediary of exchange between people, can usurp the mediating activity of human social action; and so when man endows money with the role of intermediary between himself and others he himself is an exile, a dehumanised being. Man alone, Marx insisted, should be the intermediary between men and by giving this function to money he makes himself a slave.[17]

Then the intermediary becomes the real god, since the intermediary has the real power over which he mediates.

Marx's truth speaks in a language never taught to Thatcher; her earliest upbringing deprives her of the emotional maturity to understand or heed the warning, and so she goes blindly on, creating a society governed by fetish, where love of money supersedes love of man. And all the speculators, large or small, winners or losers, in the end suffer the same dissatisfactions, as all fetishists must. For the characteristic of money is that, in the words of Isaiah, 'It satisfies not', or, as one of the new millionaires, Mick Jagger, put it in his song: 'I can't get no satisfaction.'

★

Thatcher's one other major ally in creating the fetishistic society is the advertising industry, which rivals the gambling industry both in its size and in its capacity to debauch. Political parties are now in danger of becoming subsidiaries of the industry. After the Saatchi & Saatchi success of the 1983 election Thatcher was dismayed when in 1987 Labour procured an advertising team clearly superior to that of the Tory party. But my party needs to take care. The advertising industry is as unnatural an ally of Labour as it is a natural ally of Thatcher; for it is manned and directed by the mercenaries of contemporary capitalism.

Their task is to develop techniques which stimulate an insatiable appetite for objects which have been falsely sexualised. The desirable objects are all claimed to be absolutely necessary, they promise eternal gratification and pleasure and yet leave the purchasers unsatisfied, immediately yearning for more. Reimut Reiche described it as 'an attitude of striving toward ever greater satisfaction which dooms the individual to a state identical in its essentials to that of the sexual pervert who is for ever stuck at a preparatory stage of the sex act, and remains perpetually frustrated.'[18] Marx and Engels underestimated the capacity of the capitalist system to safeguard its processes of production and reproduction.[19] They believed that a destructive polarisation would occur and, as riches grew and fewer people would be allowed to enjoy them, making a revolution by a dispossessed class would be a pushover. But with the aid of the hired ad-men, sophisticated techniques have been developed to exploit the instinctual urges of the masses and turn them into frenetic consumers whose unceasing demands will ensure that production goes on.

The advertisers begin by luring children. Since, because of parents' apprehension, most children no longer go out to play in the streets and in the immediate neighbourhood,[20] and since the television, not the hearth, is now the centre of the living-room, the admen have a captive audience; the appetite of the child is inflamed by beaming in an unremitting display of the latest mechanical and electronic toys. The advertisers make their own disruptive contribution to the thieves of childhood, the television programmes illustrating every diversity and extremity of adult behaviour and pruriently lingering over every catastrophe and activity. The advertisers are in the vanguard of those destroying the natural-social sequence of growth of our children through which the natural world and society have, in the past, been very gradually experienced, and during which, in the child's own home, collective sentiments have been gradually established as a ground for personal character and for the regulation of behaviour within social institutions.[21]

The object-pushers next proceed by hooking the vulnerable adolescent; every television screen, film and hoarding promotes the addiction through sexual excitation and titillation. The cigarette, the bath soap, the branded drinks, the motor cars, the perfumes, the package tours, all are eroticised by overt salacity or innuendo. No symbol, however sacred, is exempt. Cardinal Hume was moved to protest when the May 1988 issue of the *Tatler* – the glossy house magazine of the fluff of the metropolis – used ruby and sapphire crucifixes and rosaries as erotic accessories to advertise patent stiletto shoes and purple satin slips with black lace. And against a background redolent of Catholic deity a young man and woman, wearing less and less and in increasingly contorted poses, were used to promote the sales of black hold-up stockings. A domestic shrine with Madonnas, candles and flowers was the backcloth for the primitive hill-tribe bracelets, gold crucifixes and silver-hooped earrings offered for sale.

The *Tatler*'s advertisement was more explicit than most, but the advertising industry uses the same technique, if more subliminally, on a huge scale. The commercial artist is required to clothe the offered product in symbols often oral, anal or phallic, in the hope that the response coming from the viewer's aroused erotogenic zone will take the form of a sale. But if the overstimulated viewer lingers too long over his purchase, he may become corrupted. In the end, he may find he is stunted; the component instincts ensconced in his more primitive erotogenic zones may not have been adequately subordinated under the primacy of the genitals in the service of reproduction. Even if he is able to copulate, he is unable to make love. He fucks, but lacks concern and is unable in intercourse – beyond the pleasure – to take responsibility for the result. He can acquire objects but cannot relate to a subject. He lacks a truly genital character; he possesses only what some of the German new-left writers – blaming the manipulative nature of late capitalism – describe as the genital facade.

The mask is worn by more and more yuppie parents. They are seduced by commercial advertising into the illusion that only by taking on larger homes and mortgages can happiness be achieved; the houses are stuffed with consumer goods and empty of love. Two out of three of the mothers of young children now go out to work, but how many of them do so for acquisitive reasons rather than personal satisfaction? The mother in the one-parent family has usually no option but to work to keep herself above the poverty line, but, for most, the compelling economic necessity is not present. With only a derisory provision of state nursery school made available, the mothers and their children have become the victims of the beguiling ad-men. The children find their parents, as real parents, are missing. Too often there are no legitimate targets available to the children against whom they can rebel; no authority because it cannot be pinned down to any particular person. The child never learns how to resist: her family unit is a sham and a totally unsatisfactory training ground. The love–hate relationships, the identification with parents, all of which must be worked through if adulthood is to be achieved, become arrested. Now we have so many growing up with bodies of adults and the feelings of pubescents. We cannot expect an adult concern for children in such people and, in political terms, a serious concern for the next generation.

The Thatcher family, if not a paradigm of the ills of today's family, reflects uncomfortably so many of its weaknesses. For Margaret Thatcher, the intimate and deeply moving experience of childbirth itself is relegated in importance to a contemporary external event; one significantly related to a competitive game where there are unblurred and final scores with exact measurements and firm allo- cation of rewards.[22] Did Margaret Thatcher recall the experience of the birth of her twins? 'I had the children the day we won back the Ashes – do I remember!' she responded. The emotional shallowness of her response to her children is again revealed by her emphasis on the chores which are necessary to maintain cleanliness. 'When children are very tiny it is very exacting because they need a lot of feeding and there is a lot of washing . . . '[23] Not surprisingly, Thatcher was back at full-time work when the children were one year old, though she explained this by pointing out ingenuously that she was only twenty minutes away, 'if I was needed'. Her children's reaction to her being absent for a fortnight astonished her and her help had to explain to her the importance of talking to the children.

A mother who knew the family well when the children were small has said, 'When Margaret first got elected, the papers were full of headlines like, "New woman MP calls for the return of the lash", yet she never raised a finger to the twins. Instead, she used that low hypnotic voice of hers at times when I would have belted my kids. I vividly remember her saying, "Now Mark, you mustn't poke that sharp stick into your sister's eye, otherwise she won't grow up into a pretty little girl". I'd have walloped him, and hard.'[24] But the permissive mother, wrapped up in external pursuits, is not in touch with her child and does not recognise the child's need to have limits set on its propensity to act rashly. An empathetic in-tune parent will not permit a child's play to become dangerous to himself or another. The child may protest vigorously against the restriction but will also soon recognise that the restriction is appropriate. When the child grows up without the certainty of being protected by parental restrictions, and senses that the parents' kindly permissiveness is really an excessive involvement with their own concerns, then the permissiveness is experienced as indifference and the child feels unloved and uncared for. The child will then begin to push, to risk, to provoke all in the unconscious hope that it will be stopped by the concerned adult who thus demonstrates that he or she cares. The 'spoiled child' is really the child crying out for someone to care.

The escapades of ad-man Mark Thatcher have achieved notoriety and have often been catalogued. His 'antics',[25] as his twin sister has described them, have included mendaciously claiming professional qualifications he lacked; recklessly engaging in sponsored motor-car racing and desert journeys; signing himself up with a Japanese clothing firm to model mock-suede jackets; and tenuously involving himself in a company engaged in an arms deal with Argentinians during the year of the Falklands.[26] He has caused so many embarrassments to his mother that it would be difficult to explain them except as the syndromes of a spoilt child. His move to the USA was a relief to senior-ranking cabinet ministers who feared he could pose a serious threat to his mother; but biographers sympathetic to Margaret Thatcher tell us, 'She won't hear a word against Mark.'[27] There are public consequences of this failure to release her fury against him. To be spurned by unruly and provocative behaviour disconcerts the permissive parent who does not acknowledge the hollowness of the nice kindly treatment she convinces herself she has bestowed. Inhibited by her own narcissism from feeling or releasing her anger upon her own child, insisting that no child of hers could possibly be bad, her rage is displaced upon others. The public relevance of this private familial disorder – which justifies the scrutiny – is the consequent use of the badly behaved children of other families as scapegoats. Thatcher is strong on law and order for others: punishment is always her prescribed remedy for anti-social conduct. During the 1987 Conservative Party Conference, she applauded all the delegates who demanded more severe penalties and carefully distanced herself from her Home Secretary who sought to ward off some of the worst excesses coming from the floor.

She eschews an exploration of the aetiology of violent crime. At the 1988 Conservative Women's Conference she would brook no suggestion that a fourteen-year-old delinquent may be a victim of his upbringing. The deprivations of the inner cities, and the homes where parents attempt to buy off their children with goods rather than give love, are all acquitted of responsibility. She declared:

> The most likely British criminal is a fourteen- or fifteen-year-old boy. You do that child no favour if you suggest that he is not responsible for his actions. He won't change and improve his life if he doesn't accept responsibility for it. Those who commit crime must be held personally responsible for what they do. If they learn that lesson, then there is hope for them and for us. If they don't learn that lesson we must hold them to account. In dealing with crime we have to make life as tough as possible for the criminal.

This untempered anger against any expression of criminality is the rage of Caliban seeing his reflection in the mirror.

The Prime Minister's family is perceived by many to contain at least some of the disorders which contemporary capitalism imposes on the family: the harassed but ambitious working wife; the beaten, retreating husband who drinks too much; the tearaway son, they are unhappily familiar stereotypes in the determinedly free-enterprise society that Thatcher urges upon us. As for Carol Thatcher, it is to be hoped that the grim concatenation of shaping-events which I believe link Phoebe Stephenson, Beatrice Roberts and Margaret Thatcher, does not extend to her, and that the chain is broken: and since Carol Thatcher, for the most part, has creditably chosen to maintain a low profile, it would be a prurient intrusion, and not one prompted by the public interest, to attempt a scrutiny of her private life. As I have written elsewhere, children of MPs already have sufficient burdens without intrusive monitoring of their conduct.[28]

The incapacity of Thatcher to acknowledge her own domestic failures, and the consequent displacement and projection on to the public scene of the inner tensions of the Thatcher family unit, lead us to be subject to harsh public chidings condemning failures, personal or institutional. And, as Thatcher delivers her condemnations telling us of other failures – never her own – we are aware that her chidings are possessed of a special quality, the quality described by Ernest Jones, Freud's biographer, as 'oughtness'. 'It is astounding', he wrote, 'how many tasks and performances can symbolise in the unconscious the act of defaecation, and thus have the mental attitude towards them influenced by the anal erotic character traits when these are present.' When Thatcher was on the pot, it is my belief she was peremptorily required by her mother and grandmother to do her duty; so she brings to her performance 'a special sense of duty or oughtness . . . especially moral tasks . . . The person has an over-whelming sense of "mustness" which brooks of no argument and renders him quite incapable of taking any sort of detached or objective view of the matter; there is only one side to the question, and it is not open to any discussion at all.'[29] She must, unhindered, proselytise.

Therefore, she is forever preaching. Whenever Thatcher goes out campaigning – and she rarely stops – she is not on an ego trip but a super-ego trip, preaching the need for a return to the old values before the Fall. She regards Victorian England as Paradise, an era when the primal wisdom had its natural reward in Britain's respect and unrivalled position in the world. There is no recall for her of the oakum pickers in the workhouses; of the child prostitutes; of the cholera and stillborn children; of the domestic slaves; of the humbug and nauseating hypocrisy which was part of Victorian England.

The super-ego of a man or woman blessed with an understanding mother which enables a successful negotiation of the anal phase and, later, of the Oedipus complex is of a different quality to those who lack such a benediction. For such a super-ego will have internalised not only a parent's prohibiting admonitions and punitive threats but also the providential and protective elements of a caring, loving parent. But a super-ego which is possessed only by a parent's strict-ness and severity, its primitive character, can – when it drives a public figure of high intelligence and mistress of dialectical skills – have lamentable public results.

For the super-ego is more than a conscience which prohibits us from doing disapproved acts – it also includes the concept of the ego-ideal by which the ego measures itself, which it emulates and whose demand for ever greater perfection it strives to fulfil. Political super-ego-tripping begins whenever political action is taken on the assumption that whatever satisfied the demand of the super-ego would be the most effective in obtaining realistic goals: if it makes the tripper feel good, then, delusion though it may be, the super-ego-tripper claims virtue for the proclaimed policy.[30]

A demanding super-ego insisting upon obeisance and constant

placatory gestures, can compel the grant of priority over reality to its *diktat*. Such a jealous and ruthless super-ego can have been formed by a prohibitory mother who is brusque and prematurely insists upon early toilet training. Thatcher's political philosophy, as most Victorian creeds, is replete with what Ernest Jones once described as sphincter morality.

It follows that, so driven, she insists no one can do the tasks the super-ego sets other than herself; she finds it impossible to delegate, the trait her permanent secretary so pertinently remarked upon. Delegation means lack of personal control. Denied by the command-ing mother the right to control her own motions, she is unable, in adulthood, to allow the possibility of further frustration. Power must be centralised. The British educational system, lacking uniformity and essentially under local control, must be challenged and Keith Joseph and Kenneth Baker must become her agents and must im-plement what she as a junior minister was unable to do when she held the education ministry. The local authorities and the miners must be brought to heel and the trade unions castrated. The BBC's independence must be challenged. The Conservative Party itself must be centrally organised and the influence of the local associations diminished.[31]

In the autumn of 1987 her ministers were extensively leaking to the press their concern that she was overworking – their concern was humbug. With Thatcher running the slimmest cabinet machine since the war, holding fewer cabinet meetings than any other post-war prime minister, the opportunities for ministers to participate in collective decision-making, or to formulate policies in cabinet com-mittees, free of her dominating presence, have dramatically diminished.[32] The ministers' anxieties were not for her health but for their exclusion since she was now determined to chair and control all the cabinet committees engaged in the task of implementing the election manifesto.

This boundless need to control also acts as a threat to the indepen-dence of our judiciary. We are acutely aware of the battles Reagan had to extend his power by appointing congenial if not pliant lawyers to the Supreme Court; we are less alerted to the creeping blight of Conservative lawyers appointed during Thatcher's régime to the judgeships of the High Court. With, as a result of administrative changes, only about sixty High Court judges now in existence, their influence becomes more concentrated and potentially more dangerous. The power of patronage by the Lord Chancellor is enor-mous; it is in theory absolute and in practice has only been limited hitherto by the intercession of his confidants who sit as judges in

the Lords or the Court of Appeal. Thatcher, upon whose patronage
the office of the Lord Chancellor is dependent, is, however, not
even content with such vicarious influence. Now, in 1989, having
appointed a Lord Chancellor whose political experience is limited to
being an unsuccessful Conservative candidate, she incites and sup-
ports the new appointee in his bid to establish a framework which
the judges protest will allow executive control of our whole system
of justice. The discarded Lord Chancellor, Lord Hailsham, has declared that the legal profession is being treated like a corner shop in
Grantham.

Such protestations from Hailsham, however, come late in the day:
he cannot exempt himself from his obeisance whilst Lord Chancellor
to Thatcher. As recently as 1988 he was proclaiming, 'You have got
to put her in the same category as Bloody Mary and Elizabeth I',
confirming his submissiveness, ambivalence and his fear of her. His
own inertia and prejudices, and, above all, his failure to stand up to
Thatcherite policies of a Treasury refusing to provide needed public
funding, cast a shadow over all my efforts to reform our family law;
a major preoccupation of mine in the last years of my Commons life.
The 1969 Act I had sponsored, which transformed our divorce laws,
attempted to cope with the prejudices then prevailing but necessarily
contained a built-in obsolescence. The societal changes since then
demanded new laws and courts which could buttress marriages and
give greater protection to children of divorcing parents. Although I
built up enough pressure to wrest some minor legislation out of
Hailsham,[33] over whole areas of law relating to conciliation, proceedings in matrimonial disputes and custody of children, all I levered
out of the government was the appointment of procrastinating committees dominated by the Treasury, designed to postpone a resolution
of the problem.

The Family Courts Campaign, which I helped to form and activate,
brought a pledge in the Conservative manifesto of 1987 to introduce
family courts, a promise which, with the approval of Hailsham and
senior judges was reneged on immediately after the election. And
now that the delaying committees reluctantly appointed by Hailsham
are at last reporting, canvassing as they do the need for the establishment of a national conciliatory service,[34] it means little advance in
the implementation of their brave schemes can be anticipated. A
politically naive Lord Chancellor with a department depleted in
numbers and quality is unlikely to regain the needed independence
to fight Thatcher at cabinet level for the legislative time and the funds
so urgently needed. Lord Mackay may seek to deny, as he has,[35] that
all that may result in the field of family law is the obtaining of

planning permission to enlarge his department's pigeon-holes, but that unhappily is the likelihood. Past Lord Chancellors and many High Court judges, now that Thatcher's passion for control is encroaching on them, may rage: but, for the most part, they have in the past acquiesced. The woman who was a less than successful junior barrister and who was bruised, not inspired, by her encounters at the Bar in her short professional life, will bestow no special favours on them as she asserts her elective dictatorship.

The recent track record of the judges certainly does not inspire confidence that they can be effective guardians of our unwritten constitution which depends upon a delicate balance between the executive and the judiciary. Yet the need for a confident assertively independent judiciary has never been greater: for we have a prime minister who, I believe, is unconsciously, ceaselessly attempting to gain the control in her adult life which was denied to her on the pot. It is a dangerous drive. All my political experience has taught me that if liberty, diversity and tolerance are to be maintained, power must be distributed: the compulsive need of Thatcher to control by centralising power is one of the most dangerous aspects of her psychopathology.

5

Oedipal Rivalries

IN 1984 Thatcher claimed she had found the secret of life. 'You see', she emphasised, 'really to me the whole secret of life is to stop looking at things in the terms of men politicians, women politicians, men in power, women in power. You come to a certain time when you look at the personalities available . . . and you forget whether they are men or women.'[1] If Freud's emphases are valid, the time when Thatcher decided to blot out the difference between man and woman would not however be in her adulthood but when, as all little girls, she suffered the trauma of the discovery that she had not and never would have a penis. If that fact is never acknowledged, if unconsciously the differentiation is denied, then indeed we have the phallic woman to whom subliminally the Tory MPs of 1979 submitted. The phallic woman is the woman who has not passed through rites of passage which bring her to a resolution of her Oedipal problems and to fuller emotional maturity.

Freud has delineated the route a woman can take to reach that destination. He believed that to attain a creative femininity, a woman had to sustain the travail of Via Dolorosa; at one of the stations of her cross, he asserted, she was destined to endure the trauma of realisation. Ideally, to help her assuage her pain, her libido – as Freud puts it – 'slips into a new position along the lines of the equation penis-child'. Her wish for a penis is replaced by the wish for a child, and then she is on her way to womanhood. But for some girls, full renunciation of the penis-wish is incomplete. Cursed with penis envy, there follows a failure to deal with masculine sexuality and to make sufficient room for her femininity. Her identification with the father and desire to possess a penis overwhelms her and, so compulsive is her yearning, she will not yield priority or give up her wish. And Thatcher has of course never renounced her fixation upon her father: all her actions reveal it. Essentially, Freud, despite criticism from some female psychoanalysts, held fast to his phallo-centric theory that the girl passes through a masculine phase based on the clitoral

61

zone and a consequent feeling of being a castrated creature. Then this phase has to be abandoned and the 'superior' male organ has to be acknowledged.[2]

To reduce the dynamic of the Thatcher phenomenon simply to penis envy, to a symptom of unresolved Oedipal problems, would, with justification, prompt the charge of reductionism which is so often levelled against the more vulgar interpretations sometimes proffered by those who plunder classical psychoanalysis. The gale force which drives Thatcher along has certainly a more complex aetiology: there is no inevitability that all of us must be shipwrecked; that we must fail to steer our way through the tumultuous currents of our Oedipal experiences. It is the response of parents that determine whether, despite ourselves, we reach safer harbours.

Some response, malign or benevolent, has to come from the parents when faced with the sexual and aggressive strivings enveloping the child during its brief Oedipal phase: it is the echo of the parents that determines the consequence. If there are excessive or negative responses, the child is the casualty. If the father's response to his daughter's sexual striving is too intense or too defensive – and even if it is tacit and comparatively silent it nevertheless can be all pervasive – then it is deleterious to the child's developing psychic apparatus. No one can doubt, both on the known facts and on the constant recitations of adulation by Thatcher of her father, the intensity of the relationship between Alderman Roberts and Margaret. It can be certain too that a mother who so insensitively bequeathed such a permanent impress of the anal phase upon her daughter would, when the child entered into the inevitable Oedipal rivalry with her, have displayed the self-same insensitivity with similar malignant consequences. And everything points to the father being a man suffering a narcissistic imbalance with an affectless wife unable to give him the admiring, approving responses he desperately needed. Roberts was a moderately successful lower-middle-class shopkeeper, who fought to maintain respectability for his family in the over-crowded rooms above his shop. Lacking formal education and social status, with his ambitions unassuaged by the often muted responses he commanded in his chapel and on his local council, he wanted more: his admiring daughter supplied his need, and he in turn gave her his undivided attention.

That ensured the older daughter Muriel was brushed aside. Sibling rivalry is not to be underestimated as a determinant in character formation, and since Muriel was a presence in the Roberts' household until Margaret was thirteen, the notorious and often remarked pushiness of Margaret as a child, found, no doubt, a spur from her place within the family constellation. The second child can resent the advantages and privileges which it so often finds the older child already possesses and, unless parents respond with tact, the younger child can determinedly refuse to yield priority to the older sibling, and will insist upon a triumphant usurpation.[3] Muriel in later life has obeyed Margaret's injunction not to give any interviews but, on a rare occasion, when she wrote a few sentences about Grantham, the account she presented seemed more a protestation against Margaret's depreciation of their mother than an objective recall.[4] Muriel's eulogy of her mother suggests a determined idealisation and is in striking contrast to Margaret's devaluation of Beatrice: they do not appear to be speaking of the same woman. Muriel in making her tribute claiming Beatrice was an avid reader even attempts to endow her retrospectively with a considerable intellectual capacity, a suggestion which repudiates Margaret's, and indeed everyone else's perception. The explanation for the conflict of assessments of the mother by the two sisters would be that an alliance of sorts was built between the mother and Muriel, as the one was excluded and the other displaced by Margaret's takeover of the father.

The symbiotic conjunction between Margaret and Alfred was not, however, total – the merge was highly selective – but each fed the other with the corroborative grandiosity they wanted. Achievement and vocational educational goals were stressed to the impoverishment of other values; concern and care were to be expressed but they were carefully rationed like the groceries in the shop. It was a *folie à deux*, and its essential morbidity was to have the consequence that, in adulthood, the daughter was locked into the prejudiced and simplistic assessments of the provincial small-shopkeeper. It is not surprising that the more sophisticated grandees of the Tory Party, and those wishing to be grandees, recoiled from what they perceived as the essential vulgarity of the woman, an assessment known to have been explicitly expressed by Harold Macmillan. The Tory MPs of the old school have often spoken to me of 'that common woman'. Their self image is that of belonging to those who provided the carriage trade, and Thatcher, of course, the father imago encapsulated within her, was someone whom they at the most may occasionally patronise at the shop. One Tory MP indiscreetly, but accurately, said that Britain was being governed by the Wraith of Alderman Roberts, a sort of ghost of recessions past, and that he had handed on to his daughter a set of beliefs, values and social attitudes which she was now employing to guide the affairs of our nation. He added that since Alderman Roberts told her that you cannot spend more than you take at the till, she chops away at public spending for all the world as if it were an unnecessary new hat; and since Alderman Roberts told her to work hard, she wished to cut unemployment pay.[5] Such comments and such depreciation she found intolerable; possessed of the paternally bestowed narcissistic grandiosity and an incapacity to tolerate self doubt – for even a scintilla of a self query could puncture the absurd inflation of self which carried her along – she swept the grandees out of the Cabinet. The 1945 election was supposed to have marked the end of the old Conservatism, yet the Tory cabinets which ran from 1951 contained no fewer than eleven hereditary peers of the realm. Such anachronisms were to be ended: when they were not replaced by the son of a pawnbroker's shop assistant like Norman Tebbit, they were for the most part to be replaced by men of the same ilk and the same class as her father. Napoleon's dictum has been fulfilled, rather than Marx's vision: the ruling class are now the petty bourgeoisie.

The contribution of the intensive Oedipal rivalries between Margaret and Beatrice to the provincial Poujadism informing Thatcherite domestic policy cannot be dismissed: no less, as Thatcher's reveries reveal, can the same pervasive influence be ignored in any serious study of British policies in relation to the Commonwealth, the USA and Europe. Before she became prime minister, Thatcher was asked which other person she would have liked to have been.[6] Her choice was unexpectedly exotic: 'Anna of Anna and the King of Siam'.

The political scientist Graham Little has seen the significance of Thatcher's fantasy, for Anna in the story is given a role which is not quite wife and not quite mother but as intimate as both. 'Politics', writes Little, 'and personal life come together in this fantasy of being consort to a King and at the same time a kind of Queen Victoria, bringing British civilisation to a backward people . . . Mrs Thatcher's choice of Anna as a model is a useful condensation of her adult politics which combine femininity and a mission to civilise what she regards as an unruly world. It points as well to the roots of her politics, to the relationship the young Margaret might have believed she had with her father.'[7]

Thatcher's continued yearning to be the consort by the side of her idealised father seen, as so many little girls see the father, as a king, has inevitably brought her into conflict with the real Queen. With the collusion of her father, Thatcher ruthlessly swept aside her older sister and usurped her mother. If the constraints were not present she would undoubtedly have been driven to encroach upon the Queen's sovereignty, for the prime ministership leaves her dissatisfied. She would like to usurp the Queen's role, and become, at least, President, a secret wish that in a moment of speculative candour she once imparted to her most senior official.[8] Her efforts to challenge the role of the Queen as head of the Church and Commonwealth has apparently led the Sovereign to have as little affection for Thatcher as Queen Victoria had for Gladstone. In December 1988, without any consultation with the Sovereign, Thatcher, determined to prevent the Queen from visiting Moscow, instructed her pliant press officers to leak the story that any invitation would be refused.[9] The Queen had other views, and a contest was only avoided by Gorbachev not immediately extending the expected invitation. When the invitation came in April 1989 the Queen's wishes prevailed, but not before Thatcher had gained priority by obtaining an invitation to visit Russia before the Queen: only then did the turbulence Thatcher's veto had caused subside.

In July 1986 the *Sunday Times* claimed that it had been given a briefing by 'sources close to the Queen'.[10] The paper 'had received an unprecedented disclosure of the monarch's political views.' 'The Queen', it was stated, 'considers the Prime Minister's approach often to be uncaring, confrontational, and socially divisive.' It seems unlikely that the Queen would in fact have conveyed her views in such a manner, and so explicitly: but the *Sunday Times* story was not wholly without substance, and understandably gained credence for it was not the first or only time that conflicts between the two have been reported.

Thatcher was infuriated by the Queen's approval of the St Paul's Cathedral Falklands' Service where prayers were offered for all: both the British *and* the Argentinian combatants who had died. As a reprisal the Thatcherites, with the aid of the squalid Cambridge New Right, attempted a – happily unsuccessful – putsch to depose the Dean of St Paul's (though as soon as the good Dean did retire, Thatcher appointed a member of the Carlton Club to replace him). Since the Falklands' Service, Thatcher has continuously incited her anchorites to attack the Archbishop of Canterbury: five years after the event, the Dean of Winchester, the former Speaker's Chaplain in the Commons, bluntly declared that the campaign conducted by the Thatcherite press against the Archbishop had its roots in his refusal, with the Queen's approval, to grant Thatcher the triumphalist service she desired.

There are moments, more droll than pernicious, when she fancies herself as monarch. Her travels to the Middle East, to India, to Malaysia and to Indonesia were described by the conservative *Spectator* as her Royal Tour, except that in her euphoria, her gushing tributes to foreign dictatorships were in marked contrast to the Queen's careful courtesies on such occasions. Encouraged by the

South Asian government's extravagant use of honorifics she had her husband playing his part to the full: 'The illusion is completed by Denis, inching respectfully two paces behind. Somehow the process has affected him too. He has developed the ducal habit of clasping his hands behind his back.'[11] Not surprisingly, by 1988, the *Observer*'s political correspondent was reporting, 'Britain has increasingly had the feel of a nation ruled by two queens. Both refer to themselves in the first person plural. Both speak of "my" government. Both put in gracious appearances at ceremonial occasions, and visit those injured in national disasters.'[12] When in March 1989 she became a grandmother, the fantasy took over completely. She announced she had created a dynasty. 'We have become a grandmother' she told the bemused public.

Such pretensions are but asides: the profound difference between the role the Queen plays within the Commonwealth and the one Thatcher would affect are of a different order. The Queen has all her life dedicated herself to the Commonwealth. She treats it as a family and never ceases to stress the value of its multi-racial character in a world so rent by racial conflict. The Labour Prime Minister of New Zealand, David Lange, has, without sycophancy, described her as the glue holding the Commonwealth together. The head of the family of the Commonwealth carries the image of the caring mother, a designation which becomes the Queen, but which cannot be comfortably donned by Thatcher. The nurturing Queen has developed a public role of her own for which the Commonwealth is a natural stage. Thatcher's attempts to edge her way on to that stage and become the leading lady are more than disruptive.

As a Jew, I am well aware that any comments or actions which can be interpreted as racial prejudice are never forgotten and rarely forgiven by those against whom they are directed. Through the valuable Parliamentary Commonwealth Association, which brings together Parliamentarians from many countries, I have frequently found myself engaged with black or coloured legislators and I have been reminded by them on so many occasions of Thatcher's Powell-like statement in 1978 when, they believe, she voiced sympathy with racist sentiment in Britain. She had then spoken in sympathy with British people who feared they would be 'swamped' by the influx of black people; the comments were too explicit of the endemic prejudices of the petty bourgeoisie for comfort and now, with the South African sanctions issue to the fore, that speech has been frequently recalled.

As prime minister, her relations with the Commonwealth leaders began badly when she made a gaffe of sanctions in Canberra in 1979.

It was thanks to the skills of the Australian Premier, Malcolm Fraser, that the damage was contained, but in 1981 there were further signs of tension. In a radio interview, Thatcher put into doubt the visit of the Queen to the Lusaka Commonwealth meeting – where the Zimbabwe–Rhodesia sanctions issues were to be discussed – by claiming the right to advise the Queen whether it was safe for her to attend. Thatcher was speedily told to mind her own business and that the Queen was free to take advice from the appropriate Commonwealth leaders of whom the Prime Minister was only one. Tory MPs at the time were keen to keep the Queen's influence and sympathy with the African Commonwealth in the background. The Palace had other intentions and, in the event, the Queen went and played a conciliatory role which has to this day earned the admiration of President Kaunda. Thatcher's lack of sympathy with the responses to the insulting apartheid made by non-white leaders in the Commonwealth has continued to bring new threats to its unity. More recently, Thatcher, finding that her opponents were calling for sanctions against South Africa on moral grounds, extravagantly suggested they were on the side of Satan: not all may accept that sanctions would be God's punishment but it was totally unbalanced to present them as the devil's work. The Tory editor of the *Sunday Telegraph*, Peregrine Worsthorne, saw the dangers of her stance and expressed them in an article entitled 'Worse Perils than Collapse of Commonwealth'.[13] He saw that Thatcher was risking a direct confrontation with the Queen by threatening the destruction of the Commonwealth. Worsthorne wrote, 'Unfortunately it is the Queen's Commonwealth that Mrs Thatcher would be destroying . . . Politically speaking, that is the only serious problem for Mrs Thatcher. The fact that the Church of England, the BBC, the Opposition, the establishment, even some business people, oppose her on South Africa might not matter, since the same groups opposed her to begin with over the Falklands operation. But for a Conservative Prime Minister to have the monarch in the ranks of the critics – that obviously does matter quite desperately; even to the point, if the worst came to the worst, of becoming a resigning matter.'

In the event, Sir Geoffrey Howe was called upon to intervene and cool the situation; but it was not the first time Mrs Thatcher discovered that the Queen could not be pushed aside like Beatrice Roberts. When the USA invaded Grenada, Thatcher called a cabinet meeting to take decisions on the issue without first consulting the Head of the Commonwealth. Even as the Cabinet sat, the Queen sent for her and would not accept the excuse of the continuing cabinet meeting as a justification for delay. Thatcher was peremptorily required to attend and when she hurriedly arrived it was widely reported that the Queen did not give her the customary permission to be seated during the audience. The tensions have continued, and when the Queen is given priority at Commonwealth conferences, Thatcher is guaranteed to behave badly. Her outrageous behaviour at the Vancouver Conference in 1987 led the Canadian Premier to protest that she was insulting her hosts. It was fortunate that the Queen had arranged to remain in Canada after the Conference and was able to dissipate the bitterness.

Always a hostage to her father, Thatcher's Oedipal problems intrude just as overtly in our dealings with the United States of America, and Europe. Her special relationship with Ronald Reagan was only too real; although the claimed special relationship between Britain and the United States of America becomes increasingly tenuous as Washington's concerns turn away from Europe to the Pacific Basin, to South America and to the consequences of deficit budgets. There is a growing recognition in the USA of Europe as a trading adversary and a growing belief that Britain's defence contribution to the alliance – as a help to the security of the United States – is almost an irrelevancy. The need for us to reappraise our role has long been obvious, but it is a reappraisal dangerously postponed by the staging of the fairy-tale romance between Thatcher and Reagan: their musical-comedy act distracted us from objective assessments. In June 1986,[14] I put to the House of Commons that:

> Constant apologies for our subjugation to American policies come from the Prime Minister and from the leader of the Social Democratic Party, who, in the past few weeks, has lectured us about the dangers of anti-Americanism. That constant refrain, which we heard again from the Foreign Secretary, is based on their belief that our defence security wholly depends upon America.
>
> If we act on such an assumption, we are on the road to Armageddon. The aeroplanes from American bases here could one day carry H-bombs inviting our obliteration. It is nonsense to believe that military necessity leaves us with no alternative but to condone Reagan's self-indulgent caprices. The Libyan intervention shows how important it is that we free ourselves from our thraldom to the United States.
>
> There are more than 300 million people in Western Europe with tremendous industrial resources and long military and diplomatic experience, who are potentially able to defend themselves militarily and diplomatically against some 200 million Russians who are contending at the same time with one billion Chinese on their

borders, with the rising dangers of Islamic fundamentalism in Eastern Russia and with all the disgruntled peoples of Eastern Europe. If we had a government who genuinely placed upon their agenda the Europeanisation of West European security, instead of attempting to sabotage it – as occurred with the Anglo-American attack on Libya – we might avoid the final disaster.

Those who accuse people who speak like me, British people, of anti-Americanism and those whose emotional attachment to the United States is similar to that of the Leader of the SDP or the Prime Minister – who complain that the British seem to have been seized with an anti-American mood – are mocking the realism which they lack. It is no use us pretending that Reagan's America is that of Roosevelt or of Kennedy. There is abroad in the United States a dangerous politicised fundamentalism, an unhappy form of Christianity, that is soaked in gnosticism, a belief that this world is so sunk in evil that rescue is necessary. Such gnostic beliefs lead to the conclusion there is a demiurge, or a limited evil power. That power is said to be the satanic representative of cosmic evil. It can then be speedily identified as the Russians and, therefore, must at all costs be overcome . . .

It is becoming increasingly clear to assist . . . ourselves we need a considerable lurch in our foreign and defence policies.

The view I put then was still unfashionable. However, in an important address at Brussels in the spring of 1987, Geoffrey Howe, with the backing of the Foreign Office, belatedly initiated a questioning of the attitudes and assumptions of our relationship with the USA, formed more than forty years before.[15] 'We need to be alert to trends in American thinking which might diminish our security, perhaps not today or tomorrow, but possibly in the long run.' That all his comments should be so painfully tentative is not surprising for they are dangerous thoughts: the possibilities he canvasses are brushed aside by Thatcher.

For her, the relationship between the United States and Britain is as securely anchored as was her personal relationship with Reagan; because they were loyal to each other she denied there were any conflicts of interest. He gave her support on the Irish issues and on the Falklands, and she supported him without qualification on star wars and Grenada; in his attempt to murder Gaddafi from British soil she was ready to give full approval. Any suggestion that the national interests of Britain and the United States are not necessarily congruent infuriates her: she attained as high a decibel rating in her public displays of anger as she is ever likely to reach when, during the Libyan adventure, I linked her relationship with Reagan to her refusal to be prudent about British interests. Hansard records:[16]

Mr Leo Abse (Torfaen): Is it not clear from all the statements the Prime Minister has made that her passionate political infatuation with Reagan is leading her to the misjudgments of a giddy girl? Why is she feeding the paranoia of Gaddafi? Why is she providing him with corroboration of his crazy conspiratorial theories? Why does she provide him with a theatre in which he can place his self-immolating terrorists and allow them, as they obviously now will, to come into this country? Is it not abundantly clear that the real immediate effect of her collusion is inevitably the importation of greater terrorist violence into Britain?

The Prime Minister: The United States stands by the NATO alliance, this country and Europe in defence of freedom. For that purpose it keeps hundreds of thousands of troops in Europe. In that capacity, American forces have been subject to terrorist attacks: and the complicity of Libya in those attacks is beyond doubt. Yet the Hon. Gentleman is asking me to refuse the United States, in the face of those attacks and planned terrorist attacks, any right of self-defence, to use its own planes and its own pilots to defend its own people. It would be ridiculous to refuse it.

She could refuse Reagan nothing, for he is indeed her ideal man, a man in her image of her father.

Their attachment to each other was profound, but over-determinedly asexual. The woman denying her mother is claiming the father is hers – that the mother never slept with her husband. Perforce the sustaining of such a myth places the incest taboo at risk: it is too dangerously close to its explosion. No man must be chosen, therefore, who is threateningly sexual. No doubt Denis Thatcher, apart from his money, brought the bonus of having had a previous wife and, given the original triangular Oedipal situation, entering into such a triad may have toned up her zest for the marriage. Essentially, the elderly husband must not be a symbol of virility, a claim that no one is likely to make for Denis Thatcher.

Thatcher often reveals her penchant for unthreatening men. The gentle Sir Fergus Montgomery, her long-term Parliamentary Private Secretary – to whom she remained intensely loyal when an unsubstantiated charge of shoplifting hung over his head – has always had a head full of idle stage talk. Like another of Thatcher's favourites, Cecil Parkinson, he has the good looks of yesterday's matinée idols who were part of the magic Thatcher still recalls, with excitement undimmed, of musical comedies of her youth like the trashy romantic American export musical comedy, 'The Desert Song'.[17] Poor Parkinson, one-time chairman of the Conservative Party and now reinstated as Secretary of State for Energy, is a charming, non-assertive vacillating man, publicly buffeted around by wife and mistress; he was protected by Thatcher to the utmost until and after his enforced resignation and she had him back in the Cabinet as soon as propriety permitted. Her other cabinet appointment was John Moore, a good-looking husk of a man who was soon to be seen as promoted beyond his capacity. And her political flirtation with David Owen, attempting the not too difficult task of seducing him into the Conservative Party, was sparked off by his good looks as much as by his notorious lack of firm political principle. She is too calculating to be wholly stage-struck but she cannot resist the indulgence of having attentive men around her, even as a wealthy nineteenth-century Italian woman, with her husband too preoccupied with worldly affairs, would have a *cicisbeo*, a 'walker' who was not her lover but an asexual playboy.

Reagan, the B-film hero, has acted out his political life in words and deeds eagerly included in this section of Thatcher's lexicon. Graham Little, in an arresting essay, has pointed out the asexuality of Reagan.[18] Reagan invokes the latency period of a man's life, the period which, psychoanalysis maintains, extends from the dissolution of infantile sexuality to the onset of puberty and constitutes a pause in the evolution of sexuality.[19] It is the period of emotional quiescence between the dramas and turmoils of childhood and adolescence, the period of play, not of sexual exploration and activity.[20] 'Reagan', Little writes, 'is a *Saturday Evening Post* version of youth, a freckle-faced boy, tousle haired, leaning on a picket fence, baseball mitt in hand. There is no image of young women. And the male version – conveyed in the President's jeans and horses, his sports talk, his innocently quizzical tilt of the head which makes dissension seem unfriendly, is pre-adolescent: before sex, before religious and moral doubts, before universalist ideals and politics.[21] The youthful American Reagan invokes is a latency youth . . . ' Reagan has listed his priorities and passions as 'Football, drama and politics'. Thatcher enjoyed his insouciance when he played, as she does, the contradictory role of hero of the consumer society, preaching an old-fashioned Protestant ethic; and she enjoyed all Reagan's hometown soliloquies and platitudes, all his oft-repeated declarations to cut down bureaucracy at home and gain more respect abroad. All his yearning for tax cuts, all the ideological clutter so encapsulated in Thatcher was so reminiscent of her father's stances: but she relished all this without fear, without the threat of sexuality which would always have had to be held in check in her relationship with her father.

That this was a fine romance with no kisses does not mean it lacked either intensity or reciprocity, for Reagan, displaying some of the same syndrome that originally determined the choice of Thatcher as leader by the Tory MPs, found that she supplied him with more than admiration: she also supplied his pronounced dependency-needs in a fashion he evidently found irresistible. His autobiography, and his recounting to others of his early years, reveals how he vacillated between feelings of dependence on others and longings for independence, and the part that these oscillating personal feelings have played in formulating his political ideas must not be underestimated.[22] Describing Reagan's upbringing in a family with a father whose alcoholism made him dependent upon his do-gooder wife for the management of all the family affairs, the historian Robert Dallek concluded, 'Reagan's childhood implanted in him powerful feelings about dependence and independence, loss of control, and self-possession. He finds great appeal in self reliance, and he strongly dislikes dependency, partly, current psychological understanding suggests, out of unrecognised fears that he is like his father. Indeed, what is striking in the President's life is his idealisation of freedom, autonomy and self mastery and his antipathy toward, or belief in the need to overcome, totalitarianism, external control, and dependence on forces outside one's self. He has played out these feelings in both his private and public lives.'[23]

His deep-seated fear of being as dependent as his father meant that the one-time beach lifeguard made the most extravagant and often disastrous political gestures by launching upon rescue missions aimed to help those who are most helpless. The rugged individualism he preached, the virtues of self help, were all proclaimed too noisily as he warded off his fear of yielding to his yearnings for dependency; for he is his father's son as well as his mother's boy. In Europe, we had good cause to be frightened as he made his emotionally-charged, Rambo-like excursions into Libya or South America. Irangate ensured that, at home, the mask of the strong leader was torn away and his dependence upon his staff starkly revealed. His was a 'hands-off leadership'; he preferred, as one commentator put it, to be cheerleader rather than coach. Reagan looked for strength in men he felt were more powerful than himself and structured his government at the White House to protect himself from the complex uncertainties of 'hands-on' leadership. In public, his wife, Nancy, fixed upon him her notorious 'gaze', loving, controlling, proprietorial: she was the strong woman whom Reagan called 'Mummy' and in the bewilderments of Irangate she was his powerful protector. Such a man as Reagan was a natural victim for a 'strong' leader like Thatcher; he did not have to be politically seduced, the chemistry operated for both of them and they fell into each other's arms.

It was a reckless liaison, a Bonnie and Clyde affair: each encouraged the other's adventurism. Real national interests and the interest of the international community were often treated in scatterbrained fashion. She encouraged his misshapen star wars schemes, supported his attempts to bring down the Nicaraguan government, reluctantly but passively accepted his Grenada intervention and colluded in the Libyan bombing; and he sealed his troth in the supply of Intelligence and support for her Falklands war. The curbs which the USA put on Eden's Suez spasms or the constraints that Attlee put on American military strategy in Korea were all lacking. These two leaders fuelled each other's fantasies. And the whole world suffered.

6

Burying Beatrice

I BELIEVE no single phenomenon has contributed more to Thatcher's domination of the electorate than her incapacity to mourn the death of her mother. Few would dispute that her electoral triumphs rest on her Falklands victory and her success in persuading the electorate of the imperative need of her nuclear defence policies, yet in a British political climate so often bereft of insight, to insist upon a firm link between Thatcher's notorious belligerency and the hostility she felt towards her mother is to invite incredulity. Without an understanding, however, of the malign result of the failure to endure a bereavement by mourning, there can be little appreciation either of the aetiology of war or the psychotic anxieties which prompt a nation to opt for a nuclear policy which is totally lacking in credibility and is able to be acted upon only at the price of total annihilation.

The immediate aftermath of the Aberfan tip tragedy of 1967 demonstrated most poignantly what happens when the mourning-through process is blocked. When I was about to be interviewed in a television studio in Cardiff on some trivial issue, a large group of Aberfan parents whose children had been buried alive poured into the building demanding – although I was not their constituency MP – to see me. I, of course, listened to them, inevitably with shame, as, in their awesome agony, they poured out wild complaints and demands; but it was well beyond my capacity to contain their terrible grief. I could but condone their accusations of responsibility for the disaster, and not by insulting logic attempt to spell out the irrationality of their extravagant demands. Although some weeks had passed since the disaster, they still could not begin to accept the deaths of their little ones; and to maintain their denial of the terrible reality, they had launched a paranoid onslaught upon all around them.

The miners and their wives who had come to me had, in more usual circumstances, well-tried conventions to ease the pain of bereavement. When a miner was killed in an accident, the pit stopped, the workforce accompanied the dead man home and the village would attend the funeral. When I was young, even in the towns and cities of Wales a death would bring down the blinds in the whole street and a community would share the grief. Death now is unhappily more private and too often almost clandestine. But even within the traditions of the Welsh mining community no artifices were available to cope with the terrible slaughter of almost all their children: and, lacking precedent, the parents turned to the paranoid alternative which for so long after the disaster was to bedevil the organisation of relief funding and work and to become enmeshed in all the physical and psychological reparative efforts. No defined mourning ceremonies were, in the unique circumstances, available to them, nothing to assist them to weather the immediate and intense impact of death, enabling them to undertake the process of mature internal mourning at their own time and pace.[1]

The abruptness and the scale of the tragedy could not be absorbed by the parents within conventional funeral ceremonies. On the death of anyone near us we feel profound guilt, for ambivalence to our loved ones is a necessity; we can only be indifferent to those we do not love. The depression that bears down upon us when we lose a parent, a spouse, or a child, comes from our guilt, for unconsciously each man kills the thing he loves many times over and, when death comes, unconsciously we are possessed with the belief that our malevolent thoughts have caused the fatality. Our mourning ceremonies are attempts to exorcise the anxiety which falls upon us. Our fears that as a father or as a son or daughter we are killers are exteriorised in the Greek myths of Oedipus killing his father, or of Cronus the devourer of his children, and in our unconscious those myths retain their force and validity. Unless we can expel our irrational sense of responsibility for a near one's death, we can be possessed by fears of retaliation by demonic forces; the spirits of our departed ones. We have devised social mechanisms to defend ourselves against such depressive anxiety, mechanisms which, although inadequate to contain the agony of Aberfan, could, until recent times, operate more or less successfully.

The psychoanalyst, Elliott Jaques, has succinctly spelt out one of these mechanisms.[2]

The bereaved are joined by others in a common display of grief and public reiterations of the good qualities of the deceased. There is a common sharing of guilt through comparison of the short-comings of the survivors with the good qualities of the deceased. Bad objects and impulses are got rid of by unconscious projection into the corpse, disguised by the decoration of the corpse and safely put out of the way through projective identification with the dead during the burial ceremony; such mechanisms are unconsciously aimed at the avoidance of persecution by demonic figures. At the same time good objects and impulses are also projected into the dead person. Public and socially sanctioned idealisation of the deceased then reinforces the sense that the good object has after all not been destroyed, for 'his good works' are held to live on in the memory of the community as well as the surviving family, a memory which is reified in the tombstone. These mechanisms are unconsciously aimed at the avoidance of haunting by guilt-provoking ghosts. Hence, through mourning ceremonies, the community and the bereaved are provided with the opportunity of unconsciously co-operating in splitting the destroyed part of the loved object from the loved part, of burying the bad destroyed objects and impulses and of protecting the good loved part as an eternal memory.

In more primitive societies where little capacity for internal mourning seems to exist, other social mechanisms are deployed as a defence against the psychotic anxiety a death can provoke. Ornate ceremonies are devised to exculpate the mourners from their own guilt and project the responsibility for the death upon others. The apogee of such rituals – when a tribal leader has died – is war, which must be waged against those whose persecutory thoughts had caused the death. Franco Fornari, one-time President of the Italian Psychoanalytical Society, in a profound work[3] using as a springboard the writings of a French sociologist, Gaston Bouthoul,[4] and that of ethnologists, has hypothesised that the group of psychic manoeuvres that take place when a leader dies and war is waged against a neighbouring tribe is a paranoid elaboration of mourning. While the propitiatory rites and sacrifices are made to the ancestor gods for having wished and therefore caused the death of the ancestor, these still do not assuage the feelings of guilt nor sufficiently reduce the fear of retaliatory action by the ancestor gods. Only by accepting a paranoid stance – projecting blame on the neighbouring tribe, and slaying them as sacrifices – can the ancestor god be appeased and the followers of the leader demonstrate they were not disloyal to him.

We certainly cannot afford to be too condescending when ethnologists explain to us such roots of the wars of primitive people, nor be dogmatic in asserting that hints that such precipitates play a part in contemporary wars are meta-historical and meta-political. The phenomenon of mourning and its paranoid elaboration following the assassination at Sarajevo were certainly not extraneous to the outbreak of World War I; and, although it is often forgotten, Hitler when mobilising the Germans felt it necessary to claim to the British Ambassador Neville Henderson that he was justified in attacking Poland immediately because Poles had castrated and killed a number of Germans. Perhaps, in justification of our own bellicosity, we are being over-sophisticated when we search only for economic, religious or ideological causes of wars or conflict and ignore more archaic compulsions. Although the pogroms which have been endured by Jews in the Christian world throughout the ages have usually been explained away on economic grounds, they can only be fully understood as a paranoid elaboration of mourning. The accusation was continuously made, as it was made against me when I was the only Jewish child in my infant school, that the Jews were sons of Judas and were the descendants of Christ's murderers. 'You killed Christ,' was a taunt with which, in my childhood, I was to become well accustomed. Fornari has explained such accusations:[5]

> The fact that the Jews have always lived as a minority in Christian countries has constituted a most favourable condition for the paranoid elaboration of mourning. For the Christian, the entire world of guilt is based on the fact 'sins are the cause of Christ's death'. Every Christian, therefore, at the moment he feels guilty is apt to say that his loved object has died, that it has died through his fault, through his failure to observe the precepts of his Church. Depressive anxieties of this sort are rather hard to endure, and anti-semitism offers Christians a way to avoid mourning and the sense of guilt for the death-loss of the love object by projecting on to the Jews the cause of the death and betrayal of Christ.

In Britain the avoidance of mourning is now bringing both the disruptive dangers of paranoid projection and a denial of therapeutic relief to the bereaved. It is not only the secular who are depriving themselves of the possibilities of diminishing their depressive anxieties: the established Church itself colludes in the conspiracy to deny death. Recently in the *Observer*[6] a perceptive country vicar wrote of his dismay when he attended the funeral of an old friend, another priest, where the 'Alternative' Service Book was used. Complaining that the words could no longer bear the weight of the funeral and resenting the superfluities of the language which broke up what little pace and drama existed, he wrote:

> I was not sanctified but angry. I was deprived by those obsequies of the opportunity actually to grieve, to mourn the death of

my friend. For, pervading the service was a relentless forced cheerfulness. They even wore white stoles instead of the customary purple or black. I am convinced that my late friend does now truly find the light perpetually shining upon him; but we must go through death before we reach heaven. To pretend there is no sadness and sorrow – to behave in fact as if there is no death – is to abuse the psychology of the funeral service which exists to bear our grief . . .

What appals me is the violence these ignorant and psychologically incompetent revisers have done to the rites of passage – to those services which we all require eventually.

The loss of faith which is reflected in such banal funeral services shows how a process of shallow secularisation is accelerating. Now all must be euphemistic and vague. The social mechanisms which have always served to contain our psychotic anxieties are crumbling: we are becoming enveloped in a miasma of free-floating depressive anxiety. We may try to escape it in widespread hypochondria and demand yet more pills from the Health Service; we can turn to the elixirs of the health clubs and farms; we can desperately seek to jog away from our pursuing furies: but it is of no avail, for no society can seek to refute the existence of death without being suffused by anxiety. It is a depressive anxiety akin to that experienced in the nightmare when we feel an internal interior Terrifier choking us to death.

So desperate a society is vulnerable to a false messiah. The sadistic impulses that have prompted the guilt and caused the resultant depression can be deflected outwards onto a commonly shared external enemy, an enemy who the false messiah, acting out his or her own problems, presents to the followers as an antagonist whom they can without guilt and with good cause, destroy. By such projection the paranoid anxieties in the whole community may be alleviated or at least transmuted into fear of known and identifiable enemies since all the sadism turned outwards returns not in the form of internal terrifying persecutors but of actual physical attacks which because it is experienced in reality, not fantasy, is manageable.

Thatcher is finely tuned to play the role of such a false messiah for if the depressive anxieties of contemporary Britain are acute, hers are chronic, and she survives them only by incessant discovery of enemies: she must find the enemies within and the enemies without. She is doomed to have no alternative and so, of course, insists that there is no alternative way of seeing. The compulsion to obliterate the unempathic mother who, in Melanie Klein's phrase, 'left a child with a breast taken in with hatred',[7] means necessarily that she has a singular need, by denial, to deal with her own guilt brought on by the accompanying death wishes against her frustrating mother.

Indeed, she has no capacity to accept guilt in any circumstances. She will never accept responsibility for any of her personal political blunders, a characteristic which a minister like Leon Brittan was to discover when he had to take the blame for the deceits over the Westland affair. In the twice-weekly question hour she turns around her interrogator's criticism by projecting blame upon the questioner, making him or his Party always responsible, however tortuously, for the fault the questioner is seeking to highlight. Political commentators have often pointed to her strange quirk of distancing herself from her own side. When complaining that the changes she would like to see are not being effected quickly enough, she blames *her* government for tardiness. Indeed, during the 1987 election campaign when, in her morning press conferences, she attracted hostile questions which blamed her for government errors, later in the day she would intrigue reporters by stepping out from her morning personage and, by referring to herself as 'Maggie' in the third person, dissociate herself still further from blame.[8] As her water privatisation schemes were falling apart, she turned upon her Environment Secretary, Nicholas Ridley, and publicly announced 'The subject of the privatisation of water has not been handled well or accurately.'[9] By May 1989 she was blaming Nigel Lawson for the growing inflation rate. Roy Jenkins was describing these deep-seated schizoid-paranoiac reactions when he commented on what he called her 'peculiar quality'. 'She manages to be a powerful leader of her government and detach herself from her government – to be in a sense leader of the government and leader of the opposition at one and the same time.'[10] And James Prior, who suffered so much from such schizoid conduct, has similarly bitterly commented on her 'remarkable habit' of 'often being the leader of the opposition when she wants to be'. She was, he has told us, a great distancer from policies which she was not certain would succeed: others, never her, must take the responsibility for any failure.[11] Reshuffles mean new scapegoats.

These paranoid techniques, pushing blame away from herself on to others, stem in no small measure from her desperate attempt to elude the internal Terrifier which retaliates against her for her death wishes. Thatcher's incapacity to endure the more normal, painful but salutary process of mourning the loss of her mother means that she is propelled along the alternative paranoid path. The experience of mourning then manifests itself not as sorrow for the death of a loved one but as the killing off of an enemy, a political opponent or a political doctrine.

This flawed protective technique, a tragic and costly system of refusing even to acknowledge to herself her secret, leaves her forever fiercely translating internal anxieties into external dangers.

Her perspicacious but not unsympathetic biographer, Penny Junor, has sensed that Thatcher has unusual reactions to death. She tells us that when Beatrice Roberts died of cancer 'She was very upset: this is always something which shocks her very deeply, irrespective of whether it is someone whom she knows or not. She becomes very quiet and pale looking, quite visibly shaken. But, as with every emotion, she very quickly masters herself, certainly at the back of her mind.'[12] Repressed emotions, however, are not extinguished emotions; if, in some form, our emotions are not to govern us, we have to face them, not vainly dismiss them. Thatcher, on Beatrice's death, reassured eight-year-old Carol 'Don't worry. Grandma will go to heaven.' As so often, reassurance to others can be an attempt to reassure ourselves, and here one suspects Thatcher was seeking to comfort herself that Beatrice was at last banished to another world.

Whenever confronted with death, she predictably acts as Penny Junor has described: she quickly puts it 'at the back of her mind', and then, like a member of a primitive tribe, she speedily seeks an enemy to attack. When in 1989 the Hillsborough disaster struck, she consequently showed an insensitivity which outraged her own backbenchers: incapable of tolerating the delay of the prolonged mourning so desperately needed by the stricken Liverpool community, she made a quick visit to the hospitals and then, to everyone's astonishment, before the dead were cold, insisted that, irrespective of the recommendations that may come out of the proposed inquiry, her scheme to control soccer hooligans by an identity card system was inviolate, and was to be put on the statute book. In the week following the tragedy she called cabinet meetings to impose that view upon her doubting cabinet colleagues, and even wooed Heseltine to gain his support for the scheme.[13] At the very time when the relatives of the victims were being supported, thanks to the Catholic Church's Requiem and to the community spirit within the idiosyncratic enclave of Britain which is Liverpool, Thatcher blundered in, blazing against hooliganism, stirring controversy when peace and solace were compellingly needed. Her riposte to death is manic denial and attack: her conduct at the time of Hillsborough revealed she was barred by her upbringing from genuinely joining the mourners.

She is, of course, not the only politician incapable of mourning: but some of them are often driven to take another route, no less mined, but one not open to Thatcher. They utterly deny the death of their loved one so that no guilt may fall upon them, and by turning passionately to the ideology of a political movement, their beloved continues to live embedded within their dogmatic political party. Fornari has explained: 'Thus while the paranoid elaboration of mourning seeks to defend against the destructive tendencies and feelings of guilt for the death of one's love object, by projecting them into the enemy, the elaboration of mourning through ideology makes use above all of the mechanism of denial, that is the loss of the love object is denied through a manic elaboration of mourning. The dogmatised ideology becomes an omnipresent object, a god on earth, in a manner. The mechanism of negation, as a typical manic defence, leads to specific distortions of reality . . . ' An unusually articulate and literary politician, Ignazio Silone, the great Italian novelist, socialist leader, and one-time communist, with his developing insight, saw this process operating within himself. When as a young serviceman I met him for the first time during the war in Rome, I was shocked to find one of my heroes so intemperate in his attacks upon the Italian Communist Party which, however ignobly its subsequent strategies may be judged, had a proud wartime record. It was not until later that I understood I had rudely intruded into Silone's private and still not worked-through grief. He was to write of quitting his loved Communist Party thus: 'My leaving the Communist Party was for me a very sad event, an occasion of grave mourning, the mourning for my youth and I come from a place where mourning is observed longer than anywhere else.'[14]

The avoidance of the paranoid elaboration of mourning by using ideology as an instrument of manic denial of the mother and the attendant guilt is not a course open to Thatcher. Her ideology itself is intrinsically a too thinly disguised, exteriorised onslaught upon her mother. The Welfare State – the mothering state – is her enemy. Cursed as she is with her psychic structure she sees a suckling State as a destroyer, a destroyer of morale and initiative, and she compulsively attacks the mother surrogate. Such an ideology, perforce, provokes yet more unconscious guilt: she is trapped and can only strive still more desperately to find new enemies and therefore must continuously provide Manichaean interpretations of events which are good or evil: there must be no compromise and if no real external enemy exists she must create one. Without enemies she cannot survive. The radicalism attributed to her – the constant affirmation that the momentum must at all costs be maintained – is often not founded on rational reappraisals of state institutions or traditional political structures. The appearance that she is in the driving seat is often an illusion: she is, in fact, a driven woman.

There would be no question of such a leader having the capacity to apply the brakes to avoid a collision course with the Argentine leadership. On the contrary, Galtieri as an enemy was a God-send to her; and the world watched with bewilderment and astonishment that a mature democracy, famed for its diplomacy, should be propelled by Thatcher into a war over some rocks in the South Atlantic whose sparse inhabitants could have been adequately protected by negotiation. The bravery of our forces and the incredible incompetence of the Argentine government saved her from disaster and has given her a triumphant dominance over Britain rarely yielded to any prime minister. But the outside world's disbelief that Britain would engage in such a costly war, and indeed one which to this day is bleeding Britain and severely distorting our whole defence strategies, was based on the common fallacy that the specific factors generating war must be economic, political, ideological, religious or racial.

In the Argentine conflict there was clearly no compelling reason for Britain to wage war. Labour's Ted Rowlands, who visited the Falklands on behalf of the Callaghan government in 1977, came to the conclusion that what was required was 'to keep British sovereignty over the islanders but give Argentina sovereignty over the territory'. It was 'the people, not the land itself' which seemed to him to constitute the crucial issue. This distinction could be met by a leaseback proposal in which sovereignty would be granted to Argentina while government control remained in the hands of Britain. When the Thatcher administration took over, Nicholas Ridley continued to pursue such a settlement. But Thatcher would have none of it. Before he went out to the Falklands in 1980 to consult the islanders, he was subject to a fearful mauling for his ideas by the Prime Minister.[15] She would not give him a clear mandate and insisted that the leaseback idea could only be presented as an option. The fate of Ridley's mission was then predictable. 'The younger and more cosmopolitan islanders tended to be sympathetic to some accommodation with Argentina; and the view was that between one third and one half of the 1800 population might have accepted some form of leaseback. Islanders of this persuasion argue that, had Ridley come down with a firm announcement that the islanders had now to rethink their future, that the British were seeking leaseback and would compensate any islander who wanted to leave, the mood might have been more constructive. But Ridley had been given no such mandate by the Cabinet.' A peace based upon a rational compromise could not be suffered by Thatcher; and she had no difficulty in persuading most of the nation that a pacific solution of the problem was intolerable.

There are deeper almost irresistible factors that can override traditional economic and political assessments. All too easily, conflicts connected with specific historical situations can reactivate the grave conflicts which all mankind experience in infancy in the form of fantasies in our affective relationships with our parents. War is an institution to which man has clung since time immemorial and that it is no longer ritualised, as often in the religions of more primitive tribes, must not permit us, in an act of self-deception, to disguise the tragic reality that, hitherto, man has always needed wars to ward off his psychotic anxieties – to preserve his sanity. Such an assertion, of course, infuriates the political ideologues who correctly see such an interpretation as a demand for ideological demobilisation, and a call for insights which subvert their doctrines. But the extortions of external reality which Thatcher needed to contain her internal anxieties, the elaborate paranoid projections which she compulsively and exotically enacted in the Argentine conflict, ruthlessly condoning the unnecessary sinking of the *Belgrano* rather than risk peace, unhappily found resounding echoes in the legislators and in the electorate: for all born of woman have had in their infancy some sadistic fantasies as Thatcher has had, although fortunately most have come to terms with them in less malignant fashion. She was the detonator but the charges lay buried, waiting to be exploded in a frustrated nation suffering from almost forty years of peace.

On 16 April 1982, more than a month before the Task Force landed at San Carlos, Thatcher's intentions were made clear in the leaked transcript of the conversation between Reagan and the US Secretary of State, General Haig: the United States President said, 'Maggie wants a skirmish.'[16] She broke off negotiations and, using her customary projective technique, blamed the Argentinians for the breakdown.

On the eve of the landing when she was making her self-justifying speech, I faced a hostile House when I intervened with the question: 'Since, at the end of the day, every rational man and woman knows that we cannot sustain indefinitely the sovereignty of those rocks 8000 miles away, why is the Prime Minister showing such extraordinary impatience? (interruption) Why will she not continue to seek to negotiate when the alternative is carnage and bloodshed which will have no good effect at all?' The Prime Minister replied, 'Because the Argentinians do not want a negotiated settlement. They want sovereignty of the islands and they are using protracted negotiations to procure that objective. I do not believe that they are genuine in their negotiations.'[17]

Her father would have been proud of her contempt for negotiation. In 1945, in his inaugural mayoral speech, he saw war as an inescapable therapy in this vale of tears.[18] 'Again and again in our human life we learn that without the shedding of blood there is no remission', he declaimed.

His daughter echoed his words and, on that night, the Commons – reflecting the now aroused anxieties and passions of the electorate – gave her overwhelming support: only thirty-three of us voted against the adventure. Amongst our small band were Tam Dalyell and Andrew Faulds, both shadow ministers, who were immediately dismissed from their posts. The rabble-rousers were soon at work: a populist Liberal MP broadcast a demand that as traitors we be put on trial for treason. In such seasons it is important never to bow to the storm. Having failed to obtain an apology I issued a writ for defamation from my law office and twenty-four of my colleagues asked to join me in the proceedings. That curbed some of the overt vituperation against us. In the event, some years later, after a long and circuitous process during which I was thankful that I had some knowledge of the law and the rules of Parliamentary privilege, an apology, legal costs and damages were wrested from the offender and the broadcasting company. (A curious, beneficial side-effect was that by collusion between myself, the Law Society and the legal correspondent of *The Times*, the occasion of the announcement of the settlement in court marked a little piece of legal history, for we obtained the right to address the court without employing barristers and so I became, to the chagrin of the monopolising Bar, the first solicitor ever to be granted audience in the High Court. But such relish was for the future; at the time the tide was running murderously against us.)

With such passions aroused I was fortunate to have had my political base in Wales. In Anthony Barnett's spirited polemic on the Falklands War[19] he correctly asserted:

Within the UK it seemed that backing for the war was stronger in England than in Scotland or Wales in intensity if not in numbers. English nationalism appears to take the form of great Britishness: The cross of St George does not have enough colour in it for the English, and they need a larger geographical entity than their own nation. This may be most obvious in England's attachment to Northern Ireland, but the attitude emerged sharply during the Falklands' War. For Thatcher especially, a *united* Kingdom means an expansionist assertion of nationalism, revealed by her claim that she had put the 'Great' back into Britain. This feeling is more prevalent in England, which has still to accept its small country status than in Wales . . .

By chance the Welsh Labour Party Conference was being held as the troop ships were assembling to take the task force on the journey and so I had the opportunity to challenge the conventional view and protect my political base. The *Guardian* reported my stand.[20]

One of the Labour rebels who voted against the Government on the Falklands issue, Mr Leo Abse the MP for Pontypool, yesterday explained to the Wales Labour Party conference in Swansea why he dissociated himself from 'the whole of this miserable episode'.

'It was a vote against Mrs Thatcher's handling of events and not a vote against Michael Foot, the Labour leader,' he said.

Mr Abse recalled his experiences in a troop ship during the last war and contrasted that fight with the Falklands campaign.

'There were hazards and miseries but we knew why we were sailing, we knew how it came about and what the objective was.'

He added: 'This whole folly has come about because Thatcher and her Government left those islands utterly defenceless. As a result of their folly we found that our boys, not Thatcher's boys, are being involved in a battle which we know can never mean bringing about the continued sovereignty of the Falkland Isles.'

Mr Abse emphasised: 'We cannot sustain indefinitely those islands 8,000 miles away. We know full well at the end of the day the United Nations has to make a resolution on the position of sovereignty – so those boys are asking for what they are dying?'

The islands' sovereignty had been given away and Britain had now estranged all of South America, bruised relations with her European allies and quarrelled with the Irish Republic.

The Prime Minister had satisfied the militaristic sections of her party – 'she has her triumph and we have our tragedy', he said.

The younger Welsh MPs, however, eloquently put the case of the Labour Party's leadership, that the battle to be fought was for liberty against dictatorship and that it was as necessary to fight Galtieri as we had fought Hitler in the anti-Nazi war, a war which, because of their youth, had been denied to them. In the Anglo-French colonial war against Egypt, there had been similar strident pleas, and there was a hiccup before the Labour Movement recovered its poise and fought against Eden's disastrous nostalgic attempt to relive his anti-appeasement youth at Suez. But although I was able to prevent the Welsh Labour Conference from condoning Thatcher's adventure – thanks to the aid I received from the Welsh miners – such a refusal

to be overwhelmed by the rhetoric of the Prime Minister was idiosyncratic in the May days of 1982.

*

It takes two to tango. The nation gave Thatcher's Falklands adventure
overwhelming support. At certain historical moments – and the
Falklands War was one of them – there is a fit between a leader and
the group. If Thatcher's posthumous duel with her mother led to
war, so did the nation's inability to accept the loss of their Empire.
The English have refused to attend or acknowledge the funeral of
their past, far-flung power. Thatcher's call during the Falklands crisis
and in the 1983 election to put the 'Great' into Great Britain was for
them irresistible. If there were lurking but substantial doubts that a
death had occurred, then Thatcher's war and clarion calls have provided them with the illusion of a resurrection.

I believe that we have used the magic of the monarchy to delude
ourselves that we could perpetuate the Empire in a purer form by
way of the Commonwealth; no longer as colonies held together by
force but as an association of free peoples with the lesser breeds of
the new tremendous heterogeneous Commonwealth looking to us –
with the Queen in London as head of the Commonwealth – for
leadership. This heady rubbish I was to hear for years in a House of
Commons which resisted entry into Europe. From both sides of the
House, led by Manny Shinwell and Derek Walker Smith, these
children of the Empire eloquently miseducated the nation instead of
shaking it out of its dreams of grandiosity.

That grandiosity had had, in fact, a diminished correspondence
with reality since the latter part of the nineteenth century. During
the last century Great Britain was the centre of a world-wide Empire,
ruler of the seas, the balance of power in Europe and actual, if
unofficial, protector of the isolation of the western hemisphere. That
power had been considerably undermined by the end of the century,
when Germany and the United States became the two industrial
giants. At the time the First World War broke out Britain was not
able to maintain the balance of power without having to enter the
arena herself. She could no longer confine herself to the exercise of
her sea power and to minor land operations in support of some
continental allies as she had done during the Napoleonic wars. Instead,
she had to throw a drafted major army into the bloody battle and
even then victory had to await the intervention of the United States.
The subsequent disarmament of Germany and the isolation of Russia
following upon the revolution, and the withdrawal of the United
States into temporary isolation, enabled England to deceive itself that

it was still a great power but by the Second World War pretensions had slipped.[21] Victory was won at a very heavy economic cost and for all but those who were wilfully blind, England was no longer a superpower.

Yet still, politicians, even of great experience, attempted to evade the consequences. I recall my surprise when soon after I entered the Commons, at a small private meeting of MPs, I listened to Attlee who had come down from the Lords to address us. His antagonism to continental Europe revealed his prejudices but he knew that Britain could not use the Commonwealth to maintain itself as a superpower. Therefore, he seriously canvassed the view that Britain should become the 49th State of the USA; quietly but arrogantly making clear that Britain's sophistication would enable it to take over the leadership of this new Federation. I had no taste for such fantasies and when the crunch came and the decision had to be taken by Parliament whether or not we entered Europe, I voted against the official party line of non-entry presented by Harold Wilson. In the Commons I gave my view on the issue bluntly because I was impatient with those refusing to face reality.[22]

The narcissism of all of us politicians, the manic dispositions of our parties, have conspired to mask the reduction in Britain's role.

The Dutch, like ourselves, had open seas and they had an Empire. But immediately we go to Brussels and the Commission we are struck by the European spirit there, particularly amongst the Dutch. How can they take such a different attitude from ours? One of the reasons is that the Dutch knew that their Empire had come to an end. They lost the war and then they knew they had to assume a new role in Europe.

But, under Attlee's administration we transformed our Empire into a Commonwealth. As a result we brought to our nation perhaps an excess of solace. A public obeisance to our changing position was adopted by all the political parties, but there was a stubborn retention of the inner fantasy that still the sun never set upon our Empire. The Prime Minister (Sir Alec Douglas Home) with his East of Suez policy, was matched by my Rt Hon. Friend the Leader of the Opposition (Harold Wilson), with his daydream that our frontier was on the Himalayas. So, together, we all failed to adjust to reality.

Now the moment of truth has come. Unfortunately, it is too painful to be endured – understandably by many outside the House, but, less pardonably, by too many in the House . . . Not a few have debauched themselves by self-administered opiates which gained them the delusions of the grandeur of a Britain with which, with rare conceit – and none of us lack that – they identified. Now we are having an ugly chauvinism which distorts all arguments. Every fact is selected to the effect that alone Britain is great and the Community is nothing. An eager public proffered such fantasies by men of great rhetorical skill, applaud these false soothsayers and turn savagely on the realists who would take away their sweet dreams.

Eleven years later, even after we had entered into Europe, still the recurring grandiose dreams helped Britain to sleep. Thatcher and the nation were, in the Falklands adventure, to act out one of the recurring dreams of Europe: the arrival at the Fortunate Isle, the magic island which has been so variously named, Meropis, Kronos, Atlantis, the Garden of the Hesperides, and appears on so many medieval maps.[23] There is indeed an irony that the windswept and forsaken islands of the Falklands were to be the lure, as potent in their attraction as the exotic Fortunate Isles themselves. But the rocks, to meet that need, had to be beautified and romanticised. Keenly aware that this metamorphosis took place, Anthony Barnett sought to explain Thatcher's successful evocation of a powerful social empathy with the distant islands in terms of the nostalgia for a dreamt-up rural arcadia which industrialised capitalism had prompted. He points to the centrality of rural ideals in British political life from the mid-nineteenth century to the present, well illustrated by Stanley Baldwin's adage, 'England is the country', and Jim Callaghan's pose as a farmer. It may well be that English life is permeated by the nostalgic vision of a tranquilly rustic mode of living, prompted by the massive depopulation of the actual countryside.[24] But there were deeper wells that were tapped on this occasion: the combination of the rural idyll and the island setting had a fatal appeal. When, to applause, Thatcher brought her speech to an end in the fateful Commons debate she put forward an absurd proposition which cannot bear scrutiny: 'The people of the Falklands like the people of the United Kingdom are an island race.' No matter that 'an island race' is a phantasmagoria, I knew her ringing declaration had meant myth had overthrown reality. Britain was on her way to regain Atlantis for her Empire.

★

Who can resist distant islands? An invitation to Desert Island Discs or the Greek Islands? Although I have long since learned from the Welsh psychoanalyst, Ernest Jones, that all aspects of the idea of an island paradise are intimately connected with womb fantasies – with our deepest feelings about birth, death and mother – still the holiday brochures of the magic islands beguile me: the innocence of the armchair dream survives the journey, rarely the arrival.

I would not deny that there must have been a strong undercurrent to the tug which has taken me to campaign against devolution in the Shetlands; to plead for copyright protection on behalf of British publishers with Taiwan ministers at banquets in the island's capital, Taipei; and to address large gatherings in the island of Mauritius under the chairmanship of the former prime minister – the famed 'Ram' (who, fusing my brother and myself, always introduced me as a poet-politician). I would not plead mere chance that I have found myself on the platform at packed meetings at the Mansion House in Ireland's capital, urging the creation of a divorce law in Eire; or that for some years I became, in effect, the MP for the Seychelles, after a visit in the days before the island had an airport and independence, insistently putting its problems before the Commons; and I doubt whether it was just coincidence that, in the midst of the Tamil troubles in Sri Lanka, I found myself in heavy discussions with President Jayawardene in Colombo. The rational explanations I could afford for my presence on all these and other islands would rightly be suspect: Prospero's magic, sometimes black, reigns over all of us and the siren calls coming from islands can dangerously bemuse us. Ernest Jones,[25] drawing on his exploration of its geography in his clinical work, instructs us that the Fortunate Isle is the paradisiacal intra-uterus land where all wishes are fulfilled, from whence new souls emerge and to which dead souls return to rediscover limitless happiness. We covet such imagined, wondrous isles: we will not release them from our dreams and though they may be chimerical, we will not easily yield to reality and see them as they are. On the Falklands as on the Northern Ireland issue, the politicians of all parties fiercely attack interlopers who dare to scoff at their hallucinations.

No intervention I ever made in the Commons brought upon me, as I had anticipated, more fierce vituperation than one I made in 1974, on the morning following the ruthless IRA bombing in Birmingham, when an outraged House was furiously expressing its indignation and its united determination to fight to the end to wipe out the IRA.[26]

Mr Abse: May I put an unpopular view? Do not these appalling events, as the notorious strike of the Protestant workers, emphasise that the well-intentioned vanity of successive governments in seeking to continue to cajole and coax the people of Northern Ireland into a settlement is an illusion that we shall have to face (Hon. Members: 'Shame'). Is it not high time – I am convinced this is the wish of the overwhelming majority of British people – that we save further blows falling upon innocent people, upon the Army, upon the police and upon our precarious economy by unequivocally announcing that we must have a phased withdrawal of the British presence so as to leave the people of Northern Ireland, as we shall have to do in the end, to determine their own tragic, self-inflicted destiny? (Hon. Members: 'Disgraceful')

The Secretary of State for the Home Department (Mr Roy Jenkins): My Hon. Friend is fully entitled to put forward an unpopular view. It often requires courage to do so. I think my Hon. Friend will recognise that it did not command the support of the House.

As the years wore on, and as we still remained bogged down in Ireland, my speeches on the issue did not raise the hackles of the House in the same manner, but they were always sulkily received. Five years later in 1979, I used the occasion of a visit by American congressmen to Eire to set out the absurdities of Britain staying on in Ireland.[27]

Mr Leo Abse (Pontypool): Recently, when in Dublin, Mr Tip O'Neill, the Speaker of the House of Representatives made what I regard as a wise and perceptive speech. That speech was intemperately criticised both by the present Prime Minister and, in my view, by Mrs Shirley Williams – both women apparently being seized by a bout of tetchy jingoism.

When in Dublin, Mr Tip O'Neill quoted James Joyce's yearning that Ireland should awaken from the nightmare of history. Britain, too, needs a jolt to awaken her. Britain, and, in my view, particularly the Labour movement, has to emancipate itself, as it has not yet done, from the dreamy delusions of Imperial grandeur. Self-deception by nations, as by individuals, brings disaster, as reality ultimately shatters all the deceits. The policy of successive governments in Northern Ireland bears the impress of our imperial pretensions.

Our Empire was not abruptly ended, as was Holland's, by a disastrous war that compelled the Dutch to pursue a new and constructive role becoming to its new station. The dissolution of our Empire into a Commonwealth provided us with a dangerous balm for our narcissistic wounds. For overlong – I detected some of that theme in the speech of the Minister this afternoon – we have affected the capacity to assume an Imperial role and dodge the compelling necessity to recognise our genuine rather than our inauthentic capacities.

Coming to terms with themselves helps nations as well as individuals to make mature decisions. The theme that I wish to put to the House is that it is time to acknowledge the brutal fact that Ulster is our last colony. In the interests, moral and economic, of our people as well as the people of Northern Ireland, Britain should once and for all complete its process of decolonisation.

Holding this view makes it clear that I do not concur with the opinion expressed by the Leader of the Opposition that the tragedy of Northern Ireland is not to become a party issue. Bipartisan policy, founded upon Sunningdale, genuine partnership and power sharing is one matter, but a bipartisan approach based upon the consequences of the blackmail of a group on a minority government – in other words, blackmail by Unionists – is another.

All the anguished protests made by the press and the politicians against Tip O'Neill's assertion that Northern Ireland had become a political football in this country and had not received its proper priority are too overdetermined to convince any objective observer from overseas . . .

The sooner that Labour sloughs off the slime of the political football ground upon which the murky game was played, the sooner will it gain its self-respect. It is important for Tip O'Neill and the five distinguished Congressmen who accompanied him on his Irish visit to know that his speech finds resonances in the House and that there are some in this country who hope that they will continue with their pressures. Certainly they have no less right to criticise our policies in Northern Ireland than we had to criticise American follies in Vietnam. We here, as did the Americans over Vietnam, have placed ourselves in danger because of continued stubborn entanglements that have debased our values. We have been arraigned before international tribunals accused of torture and have passed legislation that is an affront to all our libertarian traditions. We are now being presented by the present Prime Minister, as her response to the Northern Ireland position, with a few platitudes in the Queen's speech and her announced conviction that the rope must be brought back to deal with terrorism.

Thus we reduce ourselves to the same level of brutalisation as that of our opponents. This 'hangwoman' Prime Minister is strong on conviction and coarse on sensibility . . .

Of course we receive not only good advice from abroad; we also receive bad advice. Senator Conor Cruise O'Brien from Dublin, or from his editorial chair at the *Observer*, never ceases to inform us that Britain must remain enmeshed, since the alternative is a bloodbath in Ulster. In private life sage men learn not to respond to a hysteric; seeking to convert others to his or to her will by threatening suicide.

If the people of Ulster are hell-bent on turning the Province into a Lebanon, that is their grim choice. My experience, however, in meetings that I have had in the past both with the UDA and the Provos make me sceptical of Senator O'Brien's gloomy prognosis. But if he is right and I am wrong, certainly I am not prepared to tell my constituents in Wales that they must pay not only the moral price but the economic cost of buying off Ulster's unnecessary self-immolation . . .

By what right have the Senator O'Briens of this world, and, indeed, the right Hon. Member for Down, South (Mr Powell) to lecture us that we must continue with an open-ended commitment, military and economic, to this turbulent Province? In Wales we, too, have passionate differences, but we resolve them, as we have recently, by debate and referendum in a civilised manner.

Senator O'Brien would no doubt claim that Britain's historical responsibility means that nevertheless we must continue to pay. The years, however, go on. There are limits to what can be wrested out of Britain by way of reparative guilt, and that limit has been reached. It is better that the people of Ulster are bluntly told that. The generation of young British soldiers being cruelly slain in Ulster is not, by some immutable law, required to bear in perpetuity the cost of the follies of their great-grandfathers . . .

The Senator O'Briens of this world need to be told that if we took the course that they commended we would still be in India, Palestine and Cyprus. Of course there was bloodshed there when we withdrew, but of what avail would it have been, in terms of life and economic expenditure, if we had been insane enough to attempt to linger on? We would have become, as we have in Ulster, the scapegoats for every paranoic complaint, and we would then have provided the opportunity to all who prefer to whine rather than to resolve their own problems.

Our continued presence in Ulster provides a hundred spurious alibis to all the elements who are obstructing bridge-building in the Province. Britain does not owe Ulster a living. Our largesse, by way of hapless troops and economic subvention, is creating a sick dependency-relationship, corrupting in values both to donor and donee . . .

It is the duty of a Labour Opposition not to trail along colluding with the government on the continuance of direct rule, importing, as that inevitably does, tragic violence into this country and imposing an unnecessary and grievous economic burden on all our people. Ulster must realise that the Labour Movement will not continue to be manipulated for the benefit of Unionist MPs, and that the 'Brits' are not indefinitely to be suckers doling out money and receiving death and destruction in return.

The time is drawing near when we should bring down the curtain and Ulster should understand that. Unless the people of Ulster come together themselves, ere long the so far suppressed majority belief of the British people that the troops should return and the subventions end will become so overt and compelling that no collusion of the leadership in the established parties will be able to resist the legitimate pressures of our people.

It is to be hoped that, for the sake of the people of Northern Ireland, they will not be deceived into believing that the patience of the people of Britain is infinite. It is not, nor should it be. Some of us hope, indeed, that by the pressures that will be exerted it will soon be demonstrated that the patience has come to an end.

I had made that speech after visiting Ulster where I talked with the leaders of the Protestant para-military groups and with the leadership of the IRA. The ageing, fatigued IRA leaders, who have now been replaced by even more brutal younger men, were struggle-weary and their prison experiences had given them the self-same pallor I so often encountered when, as a lawyer, I defended the criminals of the South Wales docklands. To diminish the tension I stressed my Welshness to the IRA, and in the prolonged discussion in what was, in effect, a no-go area, I listened to their passionate denunciation of the English. Their language, which was not without eloquence, and, indeed, not without poetry, was of more interest than the stale content of their views.

As the hours wore on in the bare room above the down-at-heel pub, there was for me in the imagery enveloping their presentation a chastening corroboration of Ernest Jones's assertion that no other culture is so impregnated with the various beliefs and legends of an island paradise. The number of Erse names for it are legion: Thierna na Oge, the Country of Youth; Tir-Innambeo, the Land of the Living; Tirno-nog, the Land of Youth; Tir Tairgire, the Land of Promise; Tir N-aill, the Other Land; Mag Mar, the Great Plain; Mag Mell, the Agreeable Plain. This is where we find the fountain of life, the golden apples, children come from it and this is where, on death, we return. And if the Magic Isle has so many names, so has the land where the Catholic cult of the Virgin Mother reigns: the feminine names abound: Caitlin Ni Houlihan, Morrin Ni Cullinan, Roisin Dub (little black Rose), Shan van Vocht (old woman), Seau Bheau Bhoct

(Dark Rosaleen) and the names of three queens of Tuatha Di Dannan – Eire, Bauba and Fodhla; all these names evoke ideas of woman, mother, nurse and virgin.

It is no far step to infer the two themes are connected: surrealistically the Magic Island and Ireland are superimposed upon each other, glorified idealisations of an Irishman's birthplace. With the English still refusing to abandon their right to call their kingdom the British Isles, which includes Ireland, appalling events as in Enniskillen and Gibraltar will continue. Britannia – with a Union Jack embossed heavily upon her shield by the Ulster Unionists – has no place in the hierarchy of Irish mythological figures. The myths collide in the heavens and, on the ground, men possessed by their fables relentlessly slay each other.

So, too, Thatcher's fantasies of the congruence between the Island race of Britain and the Kelpers of the Falklands, and her vision of the Malvinas as the Arcadian Isles, a glorified idealisation of every Englishman's birthplace, bring disaster. Now when Thatcher gives guided tours at Chequers, she proudly directs her guests to a particular spot. 'This', she tells them, 'is the chair I sat in when I decided to sink the Belgrano.'[28] Let those who will rejoice, rejoice with her in the victory; but I weep for all the young dead, Argentinian and British. They were killed by politicians lured into Thatcher's dream.

★

Upon the arrival of the 1987 election Thatcher brought to the electorate her remaining credit as a triumphant warrior queen; ready to persist in debauching the skilled working class by offering absolution for their avarice and bestowing moral approval to their yearnings for embourgeoisement, she held one further trump card: her defence policy. Yet again it was to prove fatal to Labour.

When Enoch Powell, in response, while sinking into the political bogs of Northern Ireland, intervened into the national–defence debate to protest against Thatcher's defence policy, he described it as 'barmy'. I was then reminded of the recounting to me by the psychiatrist John Denham, who introduced into Britain the concepts of community care and crisis intervention in the field of mental health, of how in a mental hospital the patients, unlike the trade unionists in the large factories in my constituency of whom I was complaining, never yielded to the delusions of paranoid leadership. The patients, however sick, rumbled to the madness of their fellow inmate. Analogously, Powell powerfully demonstrated, in his customary eloquent style, the lack of credibility in Britain's dependence upon Trident missilery. On this rare occasion his premise, as well as his subsequent conclusions, were logical and valid. But it was of no avail. His intervention recalled to me the crowded, apprehensive CND meetings during the Cuban crisis when I shared platforms with Bertrand Russell. I was made aware how Russell, eschewing depth psychology, seemed to imagine that he only had to point out stupidity to overcome it. Politicians and the electorate, alas, are not made wise by being told they are stupid or barmy.

Powell and the Labour Party argued that the American-supplied missilery made it farcical to imagine our claimed deterrent was independent; that from this small and crowded island we would never send out atom bombs when the inevitable retaliatory response would mean our total annihilation – and the enemy would *know* this to be the case, but nevertheless, the majority of the electors voted for the 'barmy' view. During the election campaign when Thatcher was asked by Jonathan Dimbleby why, if Britain needed nuclear bombs for its security, all other sovereign states should not acquire them, she replied, 'This is no ordinary country.'

The nation basked in her absurd grandiosity – although there has probably never been an occasion when, if rationality prevailed, it should have been easier to dismiss as a paranoid delusion Thatcher's vision of a powerful Soviet army sweeping across Europe and occupying Britain, deterred only by our bomb. Even as the electoral campaign was being conducted, Gorbachev was making his disarmament proposals; the electoral contest had hardly begun before the pathetic weakness of Soviet defences was exposed by a German teenager flying his plane unobstructed to Red Square; and before polling day was reached the Pope was visiting Poland, greeting millions who visibly demonstrated the lack of genuine unity between the members of the Warsaw pact. Moreover, China – always feared by Russia – exploded by way of a test, a large atom bomb. Finally, the anniversary of Chernobyl had led to western journalists being allowed to visit the stricken atomic energy station and area for the first time and enabled them to report that atom bombs, wherever the Soviets dropped them in Europe, could blow back self-destructively, devastating Soviet territory.

All these events were muted by Thatcher's opponents. The Labour Party was fearful of making defence the main issue of the election, for it sought to avoid being singed as it had been in 1983. Yet again the way was open for Thatcher to find her enemy; now Moscow – where but a few months before she had been warmly welcomed – supplanted Buenos Aires, and her customary paranoid elaboration commenced as she alarmed the electorate with the prospects of Russian domination of Britain. She argued that without the bomb

Britain was helpless; and it is helplessness which both the individual and the group cannot tolerate.

The Chicago psychoanalyst, Ernest Wolf, has emphasised the significance of narcissistic rage – the rage evoked by a threat of helplessness – and, following Kohut, believes it is legitimate to speak of the group self of nations. He has written:[29]

Nations or nationality groups when they feel threatened by helplessness react with violence. War and terrorism are the result: the Arab-Israeli conflict is an example. On the one hand the Jews, after two thousand years of sometimes violent persecution and with the memory of the recent Holocaust could not possibly bear the feeling of helplessness that would come if they found themselves a minority in an Arab controlled state. They will fight to the death to prevent that. The Arabs, on the other hand, after several centuries of having to endure helplessly the advance of the West upon their once mighty Empire, suddenly find the feared enemy in their midst, apparently expanding without anyone being able to stop Israel's growing strength. It is an experience of unbearable helplessness also for the Arabs and the narcissistic rage seems inevitable. I think Kissinger recognised the dilemma and tried to manipulate the Yom Kippur war in such a way as to give the Arabs a feeling of some sort of victory, of being in control of their own fate again; and I think he succeeded to the extent of making it possible for Sadat, some years later, to make some sort of peace.

Clearly, such an hypothesis leads to the conclusion that the long peace between the United States of America and the Soviet Union, based on a so-called balance of terror, has succeeded so far not because of fear of the consequences of nuclear war but because neither side has felt helpless vis-à-vis the other. It is helplessness that is unbearable and would lead to violent action. The star wars programme which is designed to make the USA invulnerable but leave the USSR vulnerable is a recipe for disaster: for to incite one power to be so far advanced in its defence and aggressive capacity as to make the other helpless is indeed a guarantee for a pre-emptive strike.

The Labour Party needed to persuade the voters that Labour's conventional arms strategy would not leave them helpless and gave them as much real protection as could be obtained in this uncertain world; but competing with Thatcher's spurious alarums to the electors, my party failed. It was not that, in reality, they were obtaining greater security, it was because they *felt* they were. Denis Healey protested that Thatcher's policy was sabotaging the nascent disarmament proposals and Gorbachev bitterly commented on Thatcher's obsession with nuclear weapons. But Labour could not allay the fears Thatcher had aroused.

Thatcher's passionate attachment to the bomb, like her belief that its possession makes Britain great, is an exotic symptom of her psychopathology. To underline the obvious by pointing out the corroboration the energy-charged penis-shaped bomb affords the phallic woman, would still not explain why she is ever yearning for Britain's grandeur and why she particularly selects the bomb as the symbol of that greatness. Grandiosity, a feeling of omnipotence, narcissism unlimited, is the endowment of the self for all of us in our early years. The ultimate test is our capacity to transmute our grandiosity into self esteem and self confidence as we grow into adulthood. For that transmutation to take place, our first carers must not regard our earliest claims as arrogant and self-serving; as demands to be fiercely denied. Instead, they should acknowledge them joyfully and with empathy until the soothed baby – no longer compelled to test her power to command – weans herself away from the need for total narcissistic gratification, gains self confidence, and in the end will obtain her self gratification and esteem from her own activity and creativity. Thatcher's carers, her mother and grandmother, suffering from a marked strangulation of affect, clearly did not meet Margaret's needs; the transmutation from narcissism to self esteem was consequently faulted and the baby's archaic, unsatisfied hunger for grandiosity now manifests itself both in her election slogans of making or keeping Britain great and in her provocative, didactic lectures to Europe asserting that Great Britain's sovereignty will remain untrammelled, never subject to checks from foreigners on the Continent.

There are singular clinical manifestations which Kohut has traced back – in the analyses of his patients – to the type of narcissistic injury which Margaret suffered and which has resulted in her identification with a very 'great' Britain. Initially, the infant sees the mother and her parts as extensions of herself and hence, to use Kohutian nomenclature, as self-objects, and Kohut describes what happens when these self-objects fail to respond. 'When the child's self-assertive presence is not responded to by the mirroring self object his healthy exhibitionism – experientially a broad psychological configuration even when single body parts, or single mental functions are conspicuously involved as representatives of the total self – will be given up, and isolated sexualised exhibitionistic preoccupations concerning single symbols of greatness (the urinary stream, faeces, phallus) will take over . . . Ultimately, the clinical manifestations of an exhibitionistic . . . perversion may arise in consequence of the break up of those broad psychological configurations of healthy assertive-ness vis-à-vis the mirroring self object . . . '[30]

Kohut's observations were about patients who were seeking help to free themselves from their more overt exhibitionist perversions. But the distance between those unhappy perverts and the phallic woman who is under a compulsion to possess and exhibit the bomb-phallus to make her feel great is not immeasurable. Recalling that the amputee often feels the presence of a phantom limb, we could ask ourselves whether our PM is a phantom flasher? Even though *we* do not need the bomb, *she* does. We are dealing with a symptom of a narcissistic personality-disorder, not a rational defence policy.

7

Sounding Brass

'THOUGH I speak with the tongues of men and of angels, and have not charity, I am become as sounding brass . . . ' Freud thus quotes his fellow Jew[1] when he explains his conception of libido and, with unashamed romanticism, he tells us how Eros can hold all living things together. Nevertheless, Freud recognised that the destructive Thanatos may overcome Eros – his eternal adversary – leaving the community increasingly narcissistic and atomised, and bereft of binding libidinal ties. Far from providing the needed cohesion, a leader suffering from a narcissistic personality-disorder adds to our confusion. Thatcher speaks with no charity, is felt by large sections of our society to be uncaring, and, despite her Parliamentary majority, she leaves society divided.

Although her declared value system rests on a fake version of Victorian ideals, in one important respect she is a woman of our times. Most of the patients who seek help today from mental health professionals suffer from what have come to be called 'disorders of the self'. It is much less common nowadays to see a patient with one of the classical psycho-neuroses described by Freud. Instead, patients suffer from character disorders associated with feelings of emptiness, deadness, meaninglessness, diffuse ego boundaries, hypochondria, feelings of not being together or of lacking a cohesive sense of self. Often they are inflicted with depression, despair, hypersensitivity to slights, lack of zest and are suffering from insomnia. Not infrequently these persons attempt to shore up their crumbling self esteem through perverse delinquent behaviour or addiction to drugs, alcohol or a frenzied lifestyle, thus striving to keep empty depression at bay.

They are adults whose childhood lacked the needed stimulation and psychological nourishment, even though, without empathy on the part of their carers, they may have been well fed and well clothed; these are the adults who felt, as children, uncared for and unresponded to.

One of the explanations for the increasing morbidity of these self disorders is the shrinking importance of the stable family, the dissipation of the extended family, and the incapacity of the under-funded, hard-pressed, over-extended educational system to act as substitutes for the parents. To have a leadership that corroborates the original, uncaring attitude is to ensure a dangerous spread of the anomie in our vulnerable society; Thatcher shares some of the ills which afflict so many, and, having lacked sustenance, cannot give it. Her political actions betray a blankness, a void, which comes from a lack of comprehension of the imperative need of a leader to strengthen libidinal bonds within a society.

Not surprisingly she has consequently led her party into conflict with the bishops. The Church of England is no longer the Tory Party at prayer and its refusal to condone Thatcherism infuriates Hailsham and the Tory MPs, who are accustomed to the Church's acquiescence. In the end, the persistence of Christian belief rests upon the equal love bestowed on all Christians by Christ; the Church's survival depends upon its libidinal structure. Freud has described its operation:

> This equal love was expressly enunciated by Christ: 'Inasmuch as ye have done it unto one of the least of these, my brethren, ye have done it unto me.' He stands to the individual members of the group of believers in the relation of a kind elder brother; he is their substitute father. All the demands that are made on the individual are derived from this love of Christ's. A democratic strain runs through the Church for the very reason that before Christ everyone is equal, and that everyone has an equal share in his love. It is not without a deep reason that the similarity between the Christian community and a family is invoked, and that believers call them-selves brothers in Christ, that is brothers through the love which Christ has for them.

The tension between many of the bishops and Thatcher is inevi-table. Her whole philosophy constitutes a belittling of the importance of community: Alderman Roberts was the self-made man and she is the self-made woman, and that suffices; the community will benefit from the spin-off of the deeds of the independent man. The ethos she has promoted heralds in an increasingly narcissistic society in which libidinal ties are devalued and the needs to which the Church has been ministering for centuries are denied.

The ideals upon which the libidinal structure of the Church is based are confirmed by the concepts of contemporary self-psychology. One of the most prominent of the Kohutian psychoanalysts has put the position bluntly:[2]

One . . . aspect of the study of the self makes it unpalatable for many people. Here I am referring to the inevitable discovery, when studying the self, that the self cannot exist for long in a psychological vacuum. In fact, the very emergence and maintenance of the self as a psychological structure depends upon the continuing presence of an evoking-sustaining-responding matrix of self object experiences. This discovery heralds the end of another cherished illusion of Western man, namely the illusory goal of independence, self-sufficiency and free autonomy. Self psychology strikes deeply at a political value system in which the self-made man is hero. We now have a deeper appreciation of man's inescapable embeddedness in his environment. Man and his environment are inseparable and cannot be studied in isolation. The psychoanalytical study of the individual inevitably, via self psychology, becomes not the study of the person-in-vacuo but of the study of man in his surroundings, that is the study of the self and its self object as a subjective, experiential phenomenon.

No one is more determined to pursue what the psychoanalyst here describes as the 'illusory goal' than Thatcher. At the opening of Parliament in 1987, the Queen's Speech was, as the *Observer* editorial commented, 'a blueprint of what Thatcher confidently expects to be a new kind of society. We know now where she is driving: it is towards an ideal of individual self-sufficiency where the emphasis is on private endeavour and responsibility, at the same time not simply weaning the weak from the welfare dependency, but ripping the drip feeds from their arms.'[3]

She sees the trade unions in particular as an obstacle in her path, and indeed they are, although not for the reasons which she peddles as justification for the legislation which has been introduced to subvert them and divide their membership. For though metropolitan, over-sophisticated opinion often mocks the trade unions and cynical journalists regard the language in which their members address each other – as brothers and sisters – as risible and quaint, my life experience has taught me how stabilising, not disrupting, are the libidinal ties which can join men and women together in their union branches and lodges and when the Tory press presents lurid pictures of fratricidal struggles in the unions they forget that fratricidal struggles can only take place between brothers.

Before my RAF bounty enabled me to become a solicitor after the war, I worked through my teens on the factory floor, and the membership I acquired then of the Transport and General Workers' Union I proudly maintain. Indeed it was largely because of the help

I was later able to give the Welsh branches (fighting for damages for their industrial accidents), that reciprocally – through their voting strength on the local Management Committee of the Constituency Party – I was selected to become an MP. On the factory floor I had learned that the union branch could bind workers together and that the binding was not simply to fight employers for more pay and better conditions, but, albeit inarticulately, to give both courage and fun to workers who had to endure the dreary monotony of factory life. As in the RAF, comradeship could be real and supportive.

Nowhere was that role more clearly demonstrated than in the miners' lodges in South Wales and although, as the years went on, my mining constituency gradually lost all its pits, the communality which had radiated from those pits continued, although ever diminishing, to permeate the lives of my electorate. Initially, the miners' lodge was the centre not only of industrial life, but of all political and social life as well. Local health schemes began there and blossomed in the National Health Service as Nye Bevan applied to the nation the lessons he had learned in the Monmouthshire lodges. From the lodges came the miners' institutes, their clubs and their libraries. Through the lodge the miners acquired their own cinemas, their billiard halls and even a corporately owned brewery. The male voice choirs and the brass bands were all spin-offs from the lodge. The sublimated homo-erotic bindings, established in the hazardous work in the darkness of the pits, came above ground and made life on the surface a community, not a society.

None of this was understood by Thatcher when, in the 1985 dispute, she set out to smash the miners' union. Their loyalty to each other – a deeply embedded value within their culture – was exploited by a prolix, paranoiac leader to lead the miners to their doom, and Thatcher rejoiced. When I participated in delegations to Peter Walker, then the Energy Secretary, he would be flanked by the Secretary of State for Wales, Thatcher's satrap, who was ready to sabotage any efforts made by the well intentioned, ever-smouldering and unhappy Walker to save the miners from their own leader. No concessions were available; Thatcher, as ever, wanted total 'victory'. But smashing the miners meant more than the weakening of union powers: it meant smashing the cement that kept whole communities together.

All this was done at a time when there is an urgent need to arrest the increasing anomie in our society; for the transfer of miners into the factories means that alienation in the workplace increasingly threatens. One hundred and forty years ago Marx was already warning, 'Owing to the extensive use of machinery and to the division of labour, the work of the proletarians has lost all original character, and consequently, all charm for the workman. He becomes an appendage of the machine, and it is only the most simple, the most monotonous and the most easily acquired knack that is required from him.'[4] But Marx could not have anticipated the remarkable escalation in mechanisation and automation which has brought the triumph of the machine over man – of dead labour over living labour. When I took motor-component workers from my constituency to view new robots installed at British Leyland's factory at Longbridge, I sensed that their wonder at the robots was tempered by their concern at the role of the robot minders. Robotics was isolating those men from their fellows and, in effect alone with their robot, they told me they were lonely and missed the old fellowship of working in a group. Indeed, the foreman supervised his section of the factory on a bicycle, pedalling hundreds of yards from one worker to another. Our technology can thwart Eros's binding purpose, for in these large factories, men and women increasingly work alone, not libidinally bound to their fellow workers but chained to a machine. The threat of technology to social bonding is awesome. When Freud – following philosophers like Hobbes or sociologists like Durkheim – posed himself the question 'what holds society together?' his conclusion was distinctive. For him, Eros was not a glorified herd instinct binding large numbers of individuals together, nor did he accept the Aristotelian view that man is 'by nature' a social animal; he most certainly did not believe our society was the result of a social contract or an instinctive tendency of individuals. Still, his belief that society was held together by Eros, not necessity, was qualified. In order for Eros to function as the basis of social bonds, it has to be deflected from its compulsion for pleasure, relinquish its sexual aims and form the base of an identification of each individual with the whole society and with its ideals and leaders. If every collective ideal apart from a vulgar and anachronistic display of the Union Jack is mocked by the leader, and if social cohesion can only be maintained by finding threatening external enemies, then, indeed, given modern technology, the decline of religious belief, and the weakening of working-class solidarity, the centre of our society will not hold and it will fall apart.

We are already having to confront the consequences of what has been labelled the 'new narcissism'. The modern narcissist has been accurately delineated by Yiannis Gabriel thus: 'the characterological profile of the modern narcissist combines megalomania and hypochondria, an ethic of hedonism and an ethic of survival, a recognition of anxiety and a profound individualism, a fear of death and ageing and a careerist mentality, and above all consumerist orientation towards objects, peoples and images.'[5] These are the desperate who, without faith, idealism or moral values, turn to themselves as the objects of their desire. Unable to love, frightened to be loved, their lives are a frenetic and futile attempt to embellish their own egos so that their self esteem may be obtained by self admiration. The paradigm of the modern narcissist is to be found in the City jungle where the Big Bang blew away such remnants of the square mile's collective commercial ethics as remained. Its inhabitants left their universities uninterested in genuine scholarship and, debauched by Thatcherism, can measure themselves and evaluate their success only by salary and by the size of their tax-avoidance expenses.

There are others, and in far greater numbers, who are also lost in our increasingly loveless society; the unemployed young, particularly the young blacks in our inner cities, relapse into apathy. Apathy or a-pathos is a withdrawal of feeling and there is a dialectical relationship between apathy and violence. Violence is the ultimate destructive substitute which surges in to fill the vacuum when there is no relatedness. The anonymous cannot endure their apathy interminably; they wish to force us to acknowledge that they do exist, and inevitably and increasingly if these needs are not acknowledged, they will move into words and destructive behaviour which gives them the hope that they will shock both society and themselves into feeling again. The very reactions they provoke give them the renewed confidence to declare, 'We also are here.' Thatcher was not prompted by compassion when, immediately after the 1987 election, she announced that inner-city problems were, in a committee under her chairmanship, to receive priority. It was a reaction prompted by the Tories' fear of the electoral consequences if they continued to ignore the plight of the inner cities.

Moreover, her intervention presages the creation of some centrally controlled bureaucratic organisation designed to usurp – to a substantial degree – the functions of an elected local authority. Clearly alarmed that Thatcher's approach may head into serious trouble, Lord Scarman, endowed with an expertise originally founded on his inquiry into the Brixton riots, issued a warning: 'Can a viable partnership with local people flourish if one sidetracks their local representatives? I doubt it . . . '

Certainly, it must be conceded, models of such a bureaucratic organisation are available to Thatcher; the New Towns Development Corporations have with no little success now almost completed the task laid down by the New Towns legislation of the post-war Labour government. Such Corporations are governed by a Board all of whom are nominated by the Minister and none of whom, unlike local councillors, are elected: at their service they have a bureaucracy answerable only to these ministerial nominees, and not to the electorate. Having had experience of such a Corporation operating in my constituency (where a New Town was started and almost completed during my Parliamentary tenure), I am only too aware of the pitfalls. Within temporary bureaucracies there is always a danger that since commands, plans and directions emanate not from persons but from offices, the domination of the organisation is transfigured into an administration.[6] Repeatedly over the years I was compelled to use my political muscle to prevent clumsy chairmen of the organisation running rough-shod over my electorate and to ensure by pressing the Minister that he appointed to the Board of the Corporation local authority councillors who were so respected in the area that their selection would not be treated as treason by the local council or constituency party. On some occasions, when persuasion was not sufficient to modify provocative actions such as excessive rent rises, I was prompted to activate and lead demonstrations in order to ensure the bureaucracy knew that they were not the masters. But for the most part, my task was to act as an emollient; enabling the outside, alien organisation to be spared the overt expression of hostility that was always simmering beneath the surface.

Bureaucratic intervention into the institutions and social systems created within a well established, South Wales valley community endowed with a singularly politically mature local leadership is one matter: intervention into the combustible inner cities is another. When such an intervention is based on a preconceived rigid ideology of 'enterprise' and fails to appreciate the vital role that local community organisations play, then there is trouble ahead; for such organisations, particularly in the more anomic and disturbed inner cities, serve other functions than the expression and gratification of libidinal impulses in constructive social activities. They also act as a defence against profound individual anxieties and though they may often fail on the accountant's cost-effective terms, they are clung to as changes in social relationships threaten to disturb the existing social structures.

In his study of the culture of a large factory,[7] the psychoanalyst Elliott Jaques explored the nature of the psychic defences often afforded by group organisations against the paranoid and depressive anxieties of the individual; and in a later paper, 'Social Systems as a Defence against Persecutory and Depressive Anxieties', he illuminated experiences MPs know only too well – to their cost. In their constituencies they often find that an organisation – be it a union branch, a constituency party, or community or local district council

– can be dominated by a disturbed individual who is so afflicted with anxieties that he lights up his fellows, stirs up their anxieties and disrupts the whole group activity. In my own constituency political and council action was, over one period, dominated by one such unfortunate individual until, happily for himself and the community, he ended in the mental hospital, and, in the case of another, the community had sufficient insight to recognise he was a suitable case for treatment and isolated him. Such individuals abound and proliferate in the organisations of the inner cities.

The force of these psychotic anxieties should not be underestimated; nor should the therapeutic value of the local organisations which hold them in abeyance, organisations which, if overthrown or devalued by the bureaucracies, can fall victim to the most turbulent paranoiac individuals within the organisations. What has to be grasped is that it is one thing to bring about organisational changes; but if the required readjustments to the underlying fantasy are not made by the individual member of the organisations but are peremptorily ordered by some outside agency, then the individual's social defences against psychotic anxiety are dangerously weakened.

★

Like all fathers I have watched my children, as babies, going to sleep contentedly, making certain noises and movements with the mouth or sucking their fingers, and I can accept the Kleinian inference that the child believes that he is actually sucking or incorporating the breast and goes to sleep with the fantasy of having the milk-giving breast actually inside himself. And my recollections of being a young father so often disturbed at night by the screams of a hungry baby lead me to offer little resistance to the Kleinian view that the fierce child is actually attacking the frustrating breast in his fantasy, tearing and destroying it, and that he experiences the screams which rack his body and hurt him as the torn breast attacking him in his inside. He is not only experiencing a want but his own hunger pain, and his own screams may be felt as a persecutory attack on his inside.

Those early fantasies, the internalised persecutory anxieties and expressions caused by the guilt of being a ruthless attacker of the breast, pass, according to the Kleinian meta-psychology, through many vicissitudes as the child develops; but they are still present in the adult, and can be dangerously activated if provoked by a hostile environment. If the inner-city dweller is contained, reassured, by the affection and libidinal binding of a community-based group, he can find his guilts and depressions at least partially dissipated. His internal, persecutory feelings can, together with those of his colleagues in the community-based organisation, be projected out of himself on to some external enemy whom he can attack without the burden of excessive guilt. At best, that can be the drug pedlars in the district and, at worst, the police force, which may have failed to integrate itself within the local community and is felt to be the hostile outsider.

The local authorities or community-based organisations in those deprived areas with large black populations are inevitably precariously poised: they often lack the emotional balance and resource to cope with the all-pervading envy in their areas, an envy which expresses itself in horrifying large-scale vandalism. The problem of vandalism is not, of course, confined to such areas: I recall the distress in my valley when, after I had participated in a tree-planting ceremony to mark the planting of some groves in a large park, within a few days all the saplings were destroyed. We learnt from that experience that it was more important for the youngsters of the area to plant the trees than the local MP. Seemingly senseless spoliation, a comparatively rare phenomenon a generation ago, has lamentably become a commonplace phenomenon in urban life; yet it is futile to respond with fury rather than understanding. Melanie Klein[8] demonstrated that envy was one of the most primitive and fundamental emotions; and it is insights into the dynamics of envy that may help us to modify some of its wretched consequences.

Clearly the envy of the unemployed youngster – faced with the affluence held up to him on every TV commercial – is an envy which cannot be dismissed as being other than reality based. But such envy has precedent: it will have stirred soon after birth, as it does with all of us, when the infant becomes aware of the breast as a source of life and good experience. The clinical work of the Kleinian child analysts has led them to the view that the child feels the breast is the source of all comforts, physical and mental, an inexhaustible reservoir of food and warmth, love, understanding and wisdom, and the blissful experience of satisfaction which this wonderful object gives will increase his love and desire to possess, preserve and protect it. But the same experience also stirs in him the wish to be the *source* of such satisfaction; he experiences painful feelings of envy which carry with them the desire to spoil the qualities of an object which gives him such painful feelings.[9]

How, as adults, we cope with these infantile, envious feelings largely depends on the quality of our very early environmental experiences. The fortunate may be so blessed that gratitude overcomes, or at least modifies, envy. If the fantasy of the incorporation of the good breast repeatedly takes place, accompanied by feelings of love, gratitude and gratification, then it becomes integrated within our ego which itself is increasingly replenished with goodness. Envy lessens as gratification increases and then, in a benevolent circle, the diminution of envy allows more gratification which in turn furthers the lessening of envy.

Such a benign personal history is not everyone's lot: the breakdown of the family, the competitive claims of work, career and the home, means the strains of motherhood are felt, and the goodness of the breast is experienced as too meagre to overcome the deep-seated envy. With envy untamed, the youngster lashes out destructively, acting out the spoliation which in fantasy he had imagined against the breast and so bewildering the more conventional in our society who are unable to understand the source of the apparently senseless vandalism.

It is indeed the spoiling aspect of envy that – given care-less environmental conditions – the child analysts have found is so destructive to personal development. Envy aims at being as good as the object and when this is felt to be impossible, it aims at spoiling the goodness of the object, thereby removing the very source of the envious feelings. It is a two-part relationship in which the subject envies the object and it is the precursor to jealousy – the triangular relationship based on possession and the removal of a rival – and in the event that early envy has been inadequately mortified then, when fused later with jealousy, it can have terrifying consequences. What the child psychoanalysts describe in the babe, I have encountered in the naked and fierce expressions presented to me when I have sat in cells with murderers who I have been professionally defending.

The weaker the sense of the community, the more ramshackle the group institutions, the higher will be the incidence of violence and vandalism. 'What appears later on in society', Freud has written, 'in the shape of Gemeingiest esprit de corps "group spirit" etc does not belie its derivation from what was originally envy . . . Thus social feeling is based upon the reversal of what is first a hostile feeling into a positively toned tie in the nature of an identification.'[10]

These days, MPs need only scrutinise their fellow members to recognise that the weakening of allegiances to the group results in the growth of envy. During the thirty years I was in the House the ethos changed dramatically. Dedicated and determined amateurs have been replaced by professional politicians who bring with them a fierce individualism which is expressed in unbridled competitiveness. Those of us who are rooted in outside vocations, professions or industries, peter out; the pay, once derisory, now approaches that to be gained in commerce; and the expenses now available enable MPs to claim car allowances and to provide themselves with secretaries and research assistants, most of them genuine but, as is now notorious, some selected by younger Tory MPs for a command of statistics not to be found in government Blue Books.

Certainly it can be argued that the work load of MPs has substantially increased. The electorate are no longer submissive and activated by television and consumer interests, batten down upon their Member, while the never-ending interventions of all governments compel the MP to act not only as welfare officer but also as ombudsman as he wrestles with clumsy bureaucracies. Moreover, the growth of lobby and the partial disintegration of party, has meant the MP is incessantly buffeted by special interests. Consequently, the change to a House composed of full-time, career-orientated MPs may be inevitable; but it brings some unfortunate consequences. We have seen an unhealthy manipulation of the political machine as outside interests employ MPs as 'consultants' – though the chosen politician often has little knowledge of the issues outside the briefs provided for him by his pay-masters; and we have seen the power of the prime minister grow as the Tory MP – now that he is increasingly dependent on his salary and consultancy fees – forfeits his independence and submits to the caprices of Thatcher and the extravagances of his constituency associations. A fevered ambience has been created leaving the homogeneity of the political parties, of the regional groups, indeed of the House itself, sorely frayed. Now that becoming an MP is seen as an entry into an institution which has a career structure comparable to a large public company, the scramble to advance higher becomes increasingly unseemly and the presence of the green-eyed god becomes more evident daily.

This expression of envy is raw. It is not like the politics of envy masked in the hard-left ideology of class struggle and it lacks, too, the refinements of Gaitskell and his heirs who, not satisfied with the doctrine from each according to his ability, to each according to his needs, always stress that socialism is above all else about equality, a doctrine not always conspicuous in their lifestyles and one far removed from the realities of the factory floor where the battle has always been for a fair wage and just differentials. An odour of envy pervades many of the writings and speeches of the Gaitskell theoreticians and one suspects that in their early battles with their siblings for the love of their parents they feel they lost out: a guarantee of equality means no one else can be the favourite son. Certainly, similar early sibling rivalries fuel the envy which now, reflecting the outside competitive culture hallowed by Thatcher, is so visible in the House.

Within such a Parliament, the mote in their eyes unacknowledged, the majority of Tory MPs accept the Thatcherite policies which defiantly declare that individualism, not collectivism, is the answer to our inner-city problems. Soon after Thatcher declared, post-election, that she was now going to tackle these problems, her obedient Chief Secretary to the Treasury, John Major, made clear that the government's special understanding of psychology, not the spending of public money, was to be the panacea. No blank cheques, *The Times* headlined, were to be given for inner cities: 'Prosperity had returned to Britain because the Government was curing the British disease. But it had not used medicine, instead it had relied on the self-healing properties of individual and business initiatives. By working with the grain of human nature and not against it we have tapped a willingness to accept responsibility. We have enabled the British to cure their own disease. Individual effort and self-reliance have replaced paternalism.'[11]

Mocking at paternalism to a population so often deprived of the benefits of fatherhood, and refusing to help create or strengthen the family spirit expressed in collective and community organisations is an error only further compounded by inciting envy through the eulogising of rampant individualism. The targets of the Thatcherite argument are, of course, the democratically elected councils which, despite their many blemishes are, and are felt to be, the possession of the local community. Thatcher will not tolerate the yielding of a serious measure of control to them, for they are her father's enemies and she is the avenger. On only two occasions has Thatcher been seen in public in tears and one of them was when she recalled the deposing of her beloved father as an alderman by the manoeuvrings of his political enemies on the Grantham Council. Her revenge was taken by the abolition of the Greater London Council.

The trauma experienced by the young girl witnessing the fall of her father reverberates through all Thatcher's condemnations of local councils; but her determination to limit control of the inner cities local authorities has still earlier roots. The consequences of her early toilet training expressed in an irrational determination never to delegate control have already been canvassed; yet the aetiology of her compulsion to control needs further exploration for this manic defence provides an understanding not only of her responses to inner-city problems, but of the whole tone of her political conduct and declared political philosophy.

8

Les Trahisons des Clercs: Academic Perfidy

IN the Roberts' household the unfortunate Margaret was brought up in a severe, sober world; application not fun or fantasy was the firm rule. Order, not disarray or flightiness in imagination, governed. Duty prevailed, not unseemly laughter. 'To outsiders it seemed there was never much gaiety or laughter in the Roberts household' reports one well researched biography.[1] And Thatcher herself has, in an unguarded recall, confirmed her dire upbringing, 'When I was a child we did not often go out to have fun together. I suppose my parents first didn't have very much spare time – they believed it was wrong to spend very much on personal pleasure. Dancing was frowned upon by my parents – dancing was forbidden . . . My life revolved completely around the church . . . in a way I was cut off from my school friends . . . '[2]

Apart from the chapel, all interest was centred on money making in the shop which had to be protected from theft, and available to customers at all times. As a consequence one biographer concludes 'There was no real family life. Alfred Roberts made it a rule that either he or his wife would be on duty during opening hours, which meant that the family could never take a day off together, with the exception of Sundays and bank holidays, and very seldom were able to sit down to a meal together.'[3] And on the Sunday, 'There was no question of either girl being permitted to play with friends, or even to play snakes and ladders with each other. Their grandmother wouldn't even let the girls sew or knit on a Sunday. It was a day for God, reserved for religious thought and discussion.'

Even on a weekday poor Margaret was never free to indulge in childish frivolity. There was no garden behind the shop for her to play in, no bicycle to ride. The pathologically mean father, although increasingly prosperous as Margaret grew up, with his two shops doing good business, was too parsimonious to spend money on the house: the family remained with no running water, no bathroom and no indoor lavatory. Baths were taken once a week by carrying hot water from the tap. Holidays were few, a week perhaps in a Skegness boarding-house, but never taken as a complete family unit; mother or father had to be left behind to safeguard the shrine, the grocer's shop. And the profits of that shop had to be hoarded: only miserly expenditure was permitted at any celebration. That rule applied when Margaret's sister, by coincidence or determining family ethos, also married a millionaire. A family acquaintance has recorded that as a bridesmaid at the pre-wedding party, Margaret was required to hand round milk and plums since the Alderman held that coffee and biscuits were too expensive an extra.[4]

Whatever passions rumbled below the surface they were to be determinedly controlled. 'I try to be controlled,' she has said, 'I was brought up to be. My parents, who were the main influence in my life, and on my attitude to life, including politics, taught us – my sister and me – to *be* controlled.'[5] The parental prohibitions may produce the obedient child but a price has to be paid for such quenching of emotion. Repression brings distortion: the harsh, defined parameters within which the family must operate give an appearance of safety, but authentic inner security never comes by banishing passion. Our emotions cannot be exiled.

Unfortunately even some of our most sophisticated political scientists are misled by Thatcher's idealisation of her early life; they reconstruct it as an idyll. In 1987, Dennis Kavanagh, in a formidable work on Thatcherism,[6] was writing, 'From her secure family background come the values of self reliance, hard work, thrift, the family, and a belief in just desserts and not looking to the "nanny state".' Thatcher's 'values' do indeed emerge from her family background, but they spring from the negative aspects of the uninviting family life of Alfred and Beatrice Roberts. The more Thatcher's political beliefs are seen to be epiphenomena (the reflections of her inner insecurities), the more one is alerted to the dangers of their application to our national life. Today we are paying for the vigorous suppression of fantasy imposed upon little Margaret.

It is only through fantasy and play that the child learns to face painful reality. If denied the opportunity of such an evolution then, when the child becomes an adult, reality is evaded and distorted by psychical mechanisms explicated by Anna Freud in her seminal work *The Ego and the Mechanisms of Defence*. The relaxed parents help the child, step by step, to recognise and assimilate the facts of reality by entering into playful, consolatory games, sports with limiting rules which, within such boundaries, enable the child to indulge in fantasies which, in the end, give him the capacity to discard them.

We tell the small child 'what a big boy' he is and declare that he is 'clever as Mother', 'as brave as a soldier' or as 'tough as his big brother'. When we want to comfort a child we resort to the reversal of real facts. He is assured, when he has hurt himself, that he is 'better now' or that some food which he loathes 'isn't a bit nasty' or, when he is distressed because somebody has gone away, we tell him he or she will be 'back soon'.

We enter into fictions whereby children can transform painful reality into its opposite. There are, of course, conditions laid down which the child – given some rein – accepts, but the child who has just been an elephant or a horse romping on all fours with his teasing father knows, when called to eat at the table, that the trumpeting or neighing has to cease. The liontamer must, when appropriate, obey his parents, and the explorer or pilot must be ready to acknowledge, albeit initially, reluctantly, that his bedtime has arrived; because a pleasurable world of fantasy lies ready to the child's hand and is not prohibited he, in the end, achieves the resolution of the task of facing reality.

But if there is no fun in the household, if, even in the tenderest years, illusions are viewed with parental distaste, if no tiny sunshade or umbrella is available to help a little girl to be a 'grown up lady'; no walking stick or uniform to enable a little boy to ape manhood, if the attempt is made to outlaw imagination and impose a prosaic discipline on the little one, the result in terms of personal development can be maiming.

It is almost inevitable that the same arid ambience would have prevailed within the emotionally impoverished household when that same child was but a few months old and was going through the phase of development which Melanie Klein insists is crucial: it is the time when the baby recognises the mother as a whole person and then rapidly begins to recognise others in his environment, the father, the grandmother. Now the baby relates more and more not only to the mother's breast, hands, face, eyes, as separate objects, but to the mother herself. These are the moments of truth. Now the painful reality asserts itself. The splitting of the breast and the mother into a good and bad breast or mother becomes a failed stratagem. The continuing fantasies of the incorporation in the babe's interior psychic world of separate good and bad breasts falter: the same mother inexorably is at times good, sometimes bad, sometimes present, sometimes absent. Hanna Segal tells us, 'This recognition of his mother as a whole person has very wide implications and opens up a world of new experience. Recognising his mother as a whole person means also recognising her as an individual who leads a life of her own and has relationships with other people. The infant discovers his helplessness, his utter dependence on her, and his jealousy of other people.'[7]

The warm mothering mother can with soothing affection, lullaby and love, apply the balm to the wounded, frightened baby who can respond with gratitude and reparation, diminishing his fears that his anger against the withdrawn breast, the absent mother, will be so destructive that it will destroy what is now beginning to be acknowledged as one person. When the mother reappears after absence, bestowing love, care and attention, the infant's fear of the omnipotence of his destructive thoughts is gradually modified, as indeed is his belief in the omnipotence of his love. And with the discovery of the limits of his hate and love, the ego discovers more and more actual ways, not omnipotent magic, to face and affect external reality.

These intimations of reality are fitful and tenuously held. Repeatedly the often terrifying world of fantasy takes over, again and again the affectionate reassurance is needed, and still the attempt to find relief from reality by a retreat into fantasy continues, so that when the baby becomes the little boy or girl – if eventually, undistorted reality is to be courageously faced – the child must still have his temporary diversions into play and omnipotent fantasy when he is intrepid explorer or masterful liontamer; or, with bricks and cars, the controller of his world; and empathic parents by permitting this help the child to have the confidence to begin to see the world as it is.

But what of the fate of the child born into a bleak no-nonsense family? How then can the ego maintain its intactness when gripped with the apprehension that she is wholly dependent on the object that she is wishing to destroy. Somehow the utter despair felt when the infant grasps that her hostile, omnipotent thoughts may irretrievably ruin the mother and her breast has to be overcome. It is to cope with this awesome, depressive experience that the manic-defence organisation comes into existence: the precipitating causes of the depression must be wholly denied. Survival rests upon a denial, a denial primarily against any feelings of dependence: against the facts, the infant declares her independence.

Drawing on her clinical experience, Hanna Segal writes[8] of patients who have grown up bereft of early reassuring warmth and have survived only by using the armour plate of their manic denials, and identifies the pattern of their relationships: 'The manic relation to objects is characterised by a triad of feelings – control, triumph and contempt. These feelings are directly related to, and defensive against, depressive feelings of valuing the object and depending upon it, and fear of loss and guilt. Control is a way of denying dependence, of not acknowledging it and yet of compelling the object to fulfil a need for dependence since an object which is wholly controlled is, up to a point, one that can be depended on.'

Those of us who have observed Thatcher's demeanour in the House know well how redolent of control, triumph and contempt are her speeches and stances. The ablation of her mother which has been remarked, the contempt of her mother told to us by her fellow undergraduate, her unseemly rejoicing, when triumphing over her enemies, all present the syndrome which Hanna Segal delineates. The gloating quality of her speeches trumpeting her 'triumphs' do not express the joy and satisfaction of the completed creative task; shimmering beneath the surface of her stridency is denial of painful depressive feelings.

Manically denying that she ever valued and cared for the breast, or even felt guilt over her hostility to the mother, Thatcher's political and military victories proclaim her omnipotence to herself and the world. Thus she endeavours to demonstrate that she is free from the problems that arise from the primal dependency which she will never acknowledge. And all the crevices of her manic-defence mechanisms are sealed with the cement of contempt: for contempt of an object is, again, a direct denial of the object's value. An object of contempt is not an object worthy of guilt, and the contempt that is experienced in relation to such an object becomes a justification for further attacks upon it.

Here we are at the source of what has become known as Thatcherism: a fierce ideology repudiating the need for dependency; bristling with hostility at any thought of a region, an industry or an individual relying upon subsidy or succour from the State. Any policy, any suggestion which disputes the possibility of total self-reliance, endangers Thatcher: it is felt as an assault upon her personal defences. In 1988 her irrational hatred and fear of dependence drove her to make such an intemperate assault upon our social security system that even the Tory MPs could stomach no more and, fearful of the electoral consequences, insisted upon modification. Her retreat was reluctant and churlish, for care, never granted to her, must be rejected; compassion is seepage which may undermine the defence mechanisms protecting her ego.

Heedless of public and of medical opinion, her electorally reckless 1989 attack on the National Health Service can only be fully understood if we take into account her constant need to strengthen these psychic defence mechanisms: for it follows that, possessed of such a profound fear of dependency, she unconsciously perceives the NHS as a threat, not as a blessing. She does not yield when she is ill to succour from any carer. By paying privately, as she does, for her treatment, she can affect to remain in command, ordering care, not receiving it: and then, her mean private wishes overriding all departmental and Treasury advice, she orders Lawson to give tax relief to women of her age who pay premiums into private health schemes. By such mental acrobatics she maintains her 'independence' at the expense of the general taxpayer.

The traditional Conservative, priding himself on his scepticism and pragmatism, becomes increasingly embarrassed by her evangelism as she translates this compulsive need for independence and omnipotence into a doctrine imbued with fervour. She is for 'freedom', the free market, the free individual able to make choices untrammelled by any checks that come from acknowledgment of interdependence. But however manically we assert ourselves, we cannot step out of this world, and all of us, including Thatcher, are born of woman. Our biology demands that, of all the species on this earth, none remains utterly dependent for survival on parental nurturing longer than Homo sapiens, and that nurturing, good or bad, is etched upon our psyche and remains with us until we are dust in a few feet of soil.

★

There are moments, essentially transitory, in political life which can be poignantly illuminating for the participants. One such moment for me was when, having returned from abroad, I found the Shadow Cabinet had drafted me to speak on the front bench on the day assigned to the debate on Welsh Affairs, a debate which was bound to be dominated by the report just issued from the Select Committee on Welsh Affairs of which I was chairman. To the vexation of the government whips, the appropriate ministers, and Thatcher, I had succeeded in persuading the Tory MPs – who were in a majority on the Committee – to add their signatures to this well-researched and detailed report which, in effect, insisted that government policies to deal with unemployment in Wales were inadequate, and demanded changes which meant more state intervention and subvention.

Shortly after I had commenced speaking at the despatch box Thatcher came into the Chamber behind the Speaker's chair. For me, on that day, the body language of her awkward posture seemed especially eloquent. She was walking, as she often does, with one shoulder leading, as if she was pushing. She has received lessons from a physical training teacher to correct this revealing gait, but it has been of no avail.[9] It is a stance which she adopted as a child and the pushiness of the child has continued in the adult, a trait not to be corrected by physical education. She moved to her usual place, a few feet away, opposite me – and I immediately deflected my anger on to her. Freud has remarked, 'He who has eyes to see and ears to hear may convince himself that no mortal can keep a secret. If his lips are silent, he chatters with his finger tips; betrayal oozes out of him at every pore.' And on this occasion Thatcher's secret slipped out: even as I was speaking I became acutely aware of the pain expressed in her face. The eyes are not the only windows of the soul. Our frowns, tics and facial contortions are all part of the repertoire of emotions which are revealed not concealed, in our body language. Even as our handwriting is a seismograph tapping out the secrets of our psyche, so the creases that involuntarily form upon our faces are loquacious messengers and even the masters of histrionics, actors and politicians, cannot always dissimulate and mask their guilts and conflicts. On this occasion, Thatcher's eyes were not blazing with her customary indignation, the signal was not of vexation, not, as so often, of defiance: it was hurt. Doubtless such hurt has been revealed in public before and since, but the lineaments of her pain – perhaps because I was so near her and so directly involved – were at that moment startlingly clear to me. I'm certain it was not my thrusts that troubled her; she possesses a tough carapace which has withstood more skilled and much fiercer attacks than mine. It was not the external assault that troubled her; the whole issue – the need to acknowledge that help should be extended to the helpless; to the unemployed ex-miners and steel workers – had chipped a crevice in her manic-defence mechanism. An intimation of the interior psychic reality had slipped through and before she had sealed a crack, the glimpse of her denied primal dependency had caused a spasm of pain.

Academics in political science in Britain lack the advantage of such immediacy in their assessments of Thatcher, and their work too often reveals this handicap. However, it would be over-generous to extenuate on these grounds the work of those academics who, having set out to explore the relationship between Thatcher's politics and her personality, have presented their conclusions to their unfortunate students in the form of a panegyric to the lady. In a work on Thatcherism endowed with the insouciant and pretentious title of *Personality and Politics*[10] we are told by the Professor of Government at the London School of Economics that Thatcher's triumphs are due to 'realism' and her victories are the consequences of the 'unreality' of the causes of her opponents. The psychoanalysts following Sandor Ferenczi[11] have told us of the two ways, neither exclusive to each other, which enable man to make the attempt to adjust to reality: the alloplastic and the autoplastic.[12] We may strive to find our place by attempting to adjust reality to fit our needs, or we may strive to change ourselves to fit in with reality. The most dangerous politician is the one who denies psychic reality and then is driven to a mad attempt, Mao-like, to call the world to heel to suit his needs – though, doubtless, in Red China during the catastrophic Cultural Revolution, there were obsequious professors who described Mao as the great realist, even as does Professor Kenneth Minogue in his eulogy to Thatcher.

His co-editor, Professor Michael Biddiss, is, as becomes an historian, certainly more restrained in his enthusiasm, but it is a dismaying commentary on British academe that, having titillated the readers with the promise of a work on personality, all the editor offers is a superficial categorisation. Thatcher has 'an exceptionally forceful personality', she has her 'deepest roots in Grantham', she is influenced by 'a father with a conviction approach', she is 'a singularly forceful character'. These are characteristics we would expect to be attributed to protagonists in a novelette by a second-rate writer, not to be seriously presented by a distinguished historian presiding over the study of politics and personality by a whole range of academics. Inevitably, the failure to explore the psychodynamics and psycho-pathology of Thatcher leaves the Professor wrestling with what he regards as the paradox of her dirigisme on the one hand and her claims to be battling for personal freedom on the other. There is, of course, no paradox: Thatcher's compulsion to control and her neurotic need to be free from dependence are all of one piece. This, as has been noted, is Beatrice Roberts's legacy to the nation.

Professor Biddiss's diffidences do not extend to some of the other contributors. The Emeritus Fellow of All Souls, Professor S. E. Finer, knows no limits in his adulation: 'she radiates dominance', he trills masochistically, she is 'big', 'her courage intellectually, psychologically, and in the face of physical danger is quite out of the ordinary', she has 'towered over all her contemporaries'. This extravagant language telling of her size, stressing her height, is baby talk. His heterosexuality does not save him from the same excited submissiveness as Thatcher's praetorian guard at Cambridge. There, the homosexual intellectual Right now plays as sinister a role as did the homosexual Left of the 1930s. These class-ridden minor public schoolboys, dressed up as young fogeys, fortified by a corrupt network of academic patronage, eagerly prostrate themselves before

Thatcher, and wallow in the intellectual detritus of their journals.

Even when one turns to as serious and weighty a work as Professor Kavanagh's,[13] his attempt to use Thatcher as illustrative of the category of the mobilising leader – as distinct from the other group within his typology, the reconciling leader – leaves one with a feeling of profound unease. Thatcher is not a mobiliser, she is rather mobilised; driven not the driver; to attribute choice to her, to accept that she is in command, and voluntarily determines the options and the decision, is to fall into a trap. Professor Kavanagh authoritatively informs us that 'British political science has little or no literature in political leadership'; surely it is therefore important that if, however belatedly, a literature is to begin – and Professor Kavanagh is now making a valuable contribution – it should be informed by an awareness of the unconscious psychic forces that can determine a leader's decision-making. It is not quite as facile as it seems to say, as it often is said, that Thatcher relies on her instincts in making her policies: she has no alternative. It is her incapacity to negotiate an armistice with those instincts that really leaves her at their mercy, for her desperate psychic-defence mechanisms all reveal their inadequacy to save her from her predicament. A woman so propelled can scarcely be labelled a mobiliser.

No less can a genuine label of reconciler be attached (as Professor Kavanagh does) to Harold Wilson. I have elsewhere[14] told of Harold Wilson, the Walter Mitty in my political life, and his enveloping fantasy that the world was ceaselessly benevolent; the fantasy never permitted him to acknowledge that he was wrong in his optimistic assessments of the objective environment. As a method of avoiding the knowledge that he was facing antagonism, he would apply all his intellectual powers to prove that even the most mutually exclusive goals were not incompatible and, indeed, would often attempt to pursue all of them (and as a consequence would usually not properly achieve any of them). His attempts at reconciliation were not governed by rational considerations; he was under a compulsion, and his unconscious need was to play a considerable part in making his governments less than memorable. Professor Kavanagh is too trusting: he should not take politicians at their face value. Thatcher is no more a genuine mobiliser than Wilson was an authentic reconciler.

In fact, excellence in leadership languishes when a dichotomy between mobilisation and reconciliation exists. The politician should be a musical artist able to divine the rhythm in public events, and then use his conductor's skills to quicken or retard the pace. Timing is all: when to mobilise, and when to reconcile. This I have arduously learned in my own political campaigns. During the early 1960s when my bill to alter the archaic divorce laws was gutted by the Churches before it reached the statute book, I attacked the united theologians without restraint, but before the end of the decade, when the public opinion I had mobilised had eroded the Church's dogmatic approach, I was ready to initiate a reconciliation; a reconciliation which led to my 1969 Act – a very radical measure in its day – receiving the blessing of the Archbishops.

When Neil Kinnock and I led the campaign against devolution in Wales which, out of opportunism, Callaghan (a victim of his own professional and chronic conciliatory stances), was foisting on the Principality, I was, in and outside the House, intemperate and unrestrained in my invective, but having compelled the government to grant a referendum, and gained the overwhelming support of Welshmen and victory over the dangers of extreme xenophobic nationalism, it was immediately necessary to proffer an olive branch to the minority, which included so many romantic idealists, good men, who should not be further estranged. Consequently, I devoted two years to ensuring that a special select committee was successfully established to show, by example, that Wales could have a clear voice in Westminster, and that its claims could be recognised within a unitary state.

When the unselfconscious politician ceaselessly agitates in order to preserve the intactness of his identity, or when he is trapped by his psychopathy into being a compulsive, manipulative fudger, then his followers become slaves to his temperament, and consequently, only in exceptional circumstances does the nation benefit. It may be that Professor Kavanagh's typology of leadership has some descriptive validity but, if it has, then the lesson to be learned is that the nation should never yield either to an unbalanced mobiliser or reconciler.

9

Back to the Womb

THE emergence of a Thatcherite agenda, Professor Kavanagh asserts, is in some respects the outcome of failure. It certainly cannot be gainsaid that Britain's relative economic decline and the assumption of 'failure' has fed back into the political system. But that such an assumption should be so widely held, and that the prospect of a revitalising Thatcherite agenda has beguiled so many is due to a considerable extent to the failure of the political opposition. In no area of domestic policy was there a failure which had, in electoral terms, more catastrophic consequences than Labour's ambivalence to the sale of council houses; it gave Thatcher and her party the opportunity to assert that they alone were the champions of a property-owning democracy.

Because of its psychological significance the housing policy is one of the most sensitive issues in the whole field of politics. For five years before entering the Commons I was a city councillor representing the largest council-housing estate in Wales. During those years I learned to appreciate how the home tends unconsciously to symbolise the mother and her attributes – the womb and the breast – and that those who are responsible for making and enforcing policies about housing are always in danger of arousing the same feelings of hostility as does the interfering and authoritarian father who is bent upon disrupting the delicate and infinitely precious relationship which exists between the occupant and the thing which protects, encloses and comforts it.

At one time, when the Tory-dominated council was refusing my demands for the modification of an unjust, means-tested rent structure, I had taken the issue into the housing estates, speaking on the street corners, and had impressed upon the angry tenants the image of the tyrannical city fathers. At the head of thousands of tenants I marched to the city hall where the behaviour of the crowd indicated the depth of the emotions I had unleashed. It was with difficulty that we protected demonstrators from falling into the hands of the dangerous and illiterate paranoid leadership which arises spontaneously in every large mass agitation. The Tory city fathers, however, remained unyielding and, predictably, at election time, the electors committed the necessary parricide in the polling booth; for the first time my party took control of the city.

That was not the only occasion when events have prompted me to recall Freud's reminder that one of the first acts of civilisation was the construction of a dwelling, and that the dwellinghouse was a substitute for the mother's womb; the first lodging for which, in all likelihood, man still longed and in which he felt safe and was at ease. If a homestead is believed to be in peril, anxieties and passions quite disproportionate to the real threat can be aroused. In South Wales although, by an historical quirk, a very high proportion of the population has always owned their own houses, few owned their freeholds; the land upon which the houses stood remained in the possession of the ground landlords who received small annual ground rents. By the 1960s, the leases granted by landlords to the original householders at the time of industrial expansion in the last century were growing uncomfortably short, and Labour's campaign to give a statutory right to the leaseholders to purchase their own freeholds at a reasonable price received an enthusiastic reception. The issue dominated the subsequent election in Wales: anxieties had been so aroused that even Welsh Tory MPs who had huge and seemingly impregnable majorities, were to fall.

It was easier to arouse the passions than to implement the promises: Dick Crossman, then head of the Housing Ministry, found he had a sulking, over-burdened department who were reluctant to tackle the complex problems of leasehold enfranchisement. In exasperation he sent for me and Sam Silkin and made us a characteristically unorthodox offer of a small secretariat if we would undertake the task of preparing a leasehold bill. We were, in short, dragooned into being unpaid civil servants; but the passions we had aroused had to be assuaged, and we slogged away for months, finally producing a practical and reforming departmental brief upon which the Leasehold Reform Act 1967 was slavishly drawn.

The cold legal language of that Act concealed the passions which prompted its production. I had seen the complexity of emotions which had motivated my constituents' desire to be freeholders: their houses stood on mother earth, and they found it intolerable. For some, this was because their piece of mother earth was possessed by someone else; for others it was the dependency of their house upon a plot that was not tolerable; for they wished to dominate, not be dominated by, the mother earth beneath them.

Twenty years later Thatcher, in an unguarded moment, displayed the same syndrome as had gripped the leaseholders of Wales. Discussing house prices at a fund-raising cocktail party she said that she always really wished to live in Knightsbridge but, she claimed, the district was too expensive for her. She was then told by one of her listeners that for the £300,000 she had paid for her Dulwich house, she could, as he had done, buy a leasehold property in Knightsbridge. *The Times* columnist, with discernment, reported the response:[1] 'Allowing a rare and revealing glimpse of her innermost personality the PM retorted sharply, "I would never touch a leasehold property, not after having had freeholds."' The columnist had indeed had a glimpse of Thatcher's interior life and one which permits her to empathise with those wishing to own their own home.

Labour could have pre-empted Thatcher but the opportunity was lost by Tony Crosland, who could not respond emotionally to the widespread desire to own one's own house. While he was Minister for Housing the need to modify Labour's churlish attitude to home ownership was widely canvassed within the Labour Party, but although I made representations to Crosland, he lacked enthusiasm to embark upon the sale of council houses and his departmental officials were wholly negative. I always regarded Crosland as something of a vagabond; a gipsy who would have been content with a caravan. Indeed, when – during a Parliamentary recess – he called upon me in Italy he would be drifting around Europe like a young backpacker, and when he stayed with me in Wales I felt his dishevelment went beyond his rumpled clothes. He was a rootless man and although he was fortunate in his second wife, Susan, who got him together, he was certainly not the man ready in an inevitable battle to teach the Movement that whatever judgments may be made upon a man owning other people's houses, there was no breach of socialist doctrine in owning your own.

The initiative thus gained by Thatcher through Labour's default has had more than electoral consequences. The property-owning democracy has been born into a fevered world of profit making and the house has caught the current infection. The house is no longer a home: it is a commodity. In the south east prices soar as the building societies, banks and foreign mortgage companies – now untrammelled by government legislation or directives – release a torrent of credit. Those who have arrived late, and the homeless, gaze enviously into the huge casino of the property world; the more fortunate young become peripatetic, picking up their untaxed capital gains as they continuously move from one house to another. Conversation is dominated by the price obtained for a neighbouring property: and the householder relishes the conversation as he fingers his potential gains. The serenity and peace which should be captured within the enclosed space flees: the house becomes a counting house as impersonal as a bank. The slime of Thatcher's brew overflows across our thresholds.

This need not have been if Labour had listened to its own electorate and had understood and acknowledged the equivalent in the unconscious of house and womb. The yearning could have been met in an entirely different context, and house-ownership could have strengthened a home-centred society underpinning the family. To reach that goal Labour would have been required to practise preventative politics, the politics which, lamentably, are so often eschewed. Increasingly I have learned to despise the usual political methods of exhortation and coercion, methods which assume that the role of politics is to solve the conflicts when they have happened. Rarely do political demands which spring from such techniques produce permanent reductions in the tension level of society: the ideal of a politics of prevention is to obviate conflict by the reduction of this tension level in society, and this means an insistence upon a continuing audit of the human consequences of social and political policies.

My antipathy to instant politics is not merely founded on a personal prejudice against practitioners like Harold Wilson: it is because politics should be anticipatory, less to solve conflicts than to prevent them; less to serve as a safety valve for social protest than to apply social energy to meet deep-seated needs and to attempt to abolish recurrent strains in our society.[2] By such a yardstick, Labour's housing policy in the 1970s fell far short of the need; and that failure was Thatcher's opportunity.

The instant politics of the 1970s – played as a manipulative game with survival for its own sake as the objective – led to one other major failure which Labour is now in danger of rueing. The belated attempt by Thatcher, in 1988, to present herself as a concerned environmentalist would have been impossible if Labour had seized the initiative when in government. What are now known as the green issues were, but a decade ago, regarded in the Commons by all parties as so marginal as to deserve little attention: but by 1977, I had become seized of their awesome significance, and during the 1977–8 Parliamentary Session I devoted much of my time attempting to bring attention to the hazards implicit in projected nuclear energy installations, and to the threat that came with the uncontrolled disposal of toxic waste.

I forced a Commons debate[3] upon the Flowers Royal Commission

Report on the Environment, upon whose uncomfortable conclusions the dust was settling as both front benches, under the sinister influence of the lobbying nuclear industrial complex, avoided public discussion. I sought to alarm the House, canvassing support for my Early Day Motions, raised my concerns within the Parliamentary Labour Party and then compelled the reluctant government to give the House a further debate[4] on the Windscale Inquiry,[5] initiated a debate on the importation of toxic waste, and involved myself in the demonstrations organised by the splendid young scientists of the Friends of the Earth.

Together with Nobel Prizewinners and David Penhaligon, we led the first national march of the environmental groups through the West End to Trafalgar Square. It was, I think, when I stood on the plinth addressing the 15,000 demonstrators, so many of whom were apolitical young men and women who had never participated in a protest, that I first became acutely aware that, apart from rational argument, there were powerful, unconscious forces moving them, forces which would inevitably mean that environmental issues would come, as they have, to the forefront of national politics.

The personification of the earth, made explicit in the title of the Friends of the Earth, and the constant unselfconscious references made to mother earth in the pleas of environmental groups, tell us of the general identification of the earth with the mother. Even as this identification was made explicit in primitive cosmogonies, so again, as fears grow that our world is being laid waste, the assault by industry upon the earth is felt, at a subliminal level, as a rape of the mother.

The myths of a host of old cultures, from Greek to Polynesian, telling us of the creative mother goddess of the earth, are dormant, but not dead: indeed some of the most eloquent of present-day Greens have advocated that, as a matter of political strategy, a green myth should be deliberately reactivated.[6] They evidently believe such a myth would give hope and find resonances amongst a dispirited electorate. Such a viewpoint may not be as extravagant as first appears: for these green exponents are plugging into a highly-charged evolutionary current. As Flugel pointed out half a century ago, the very general identification of the earth with the mother has probably played an important part in the history of human culture, affording a ready means of rendering psychic energy for the practice of agriculture; 'the cultivation of the Earth's surface being, from the psychological point of view, a displacement of the original incestuous desires.'[7] This displacement was not always achieved: so close is the association between mother and earth that we have been told by the famed anthropologist J. G. Frazer that in some places this led to a reluctance to till the soil, such an act being looked upon as impious.

There is, therefore, in the present ecological debates, a background of underlying emotions, music to which the political protagonists are often supplying only librettos. That music was still muted when, a decade ago, I tried in vain to persuade my party to take environmental issues into mainstream politics: now only deaf politicians can ignore its presence. Thatcher, finding the clamour can no longer be ignored, shakes a limp fist at the greenhouse effect, but she is trapped by her commitment to grant unlimited freedom to incontinent industry, now dangerously polluting our world. At Labour's 1988 Conference Neil Kinnock forcefully emphasised the contradictions within her newly found concerns. 'How', he asked, 'does she think it would be possible to protect the local, the national, the international environment from the poisoning and pillaging which is now going on, by relying on the mechanisms of the market which she so much admires?'

Thatcher the environmentalist is ensnared too in another tangled skein which she is incapable of unravelling. The pathogen which is the dynamic and distorter of so many of her policies blatantly surfaces whenever she addresses us on the green issues. For her, the earth must be dehumanised: no association with the mother must come into consciousness. Contrariwise, the genuine, committed environmentalist is often one who, as a child, learned to decathect its love for the mother and spread it over the face of the world until its objects came to safeguard the child's sense of the goodness of life: as an adult, such a child, in gratitude, will protect nature.[8] Thatcher is barred from such an approach to the environment. For her, the earth must be regarded as a piece of property, to be managed as an estate; she speaks as a land agent or lawyer, of freeholds, reversions, trusteeships and leaseholders. She intends to control a piece of realty. She told the 1988 Conservative Conference, justifying her sudden interest in the environment, 'No generation has a freehold on this earth. All we have is a life tenancy with a full repairing lease. This government intends to meet the terms of that lease in full.' The language tells us of the strict limitations of her concern. The obligations that, as a leaseholder, can be enforced against her, she promises to honour: she will observe only the letter of the law.

The concessions she makes to the environmentalists are not to be made out of a passionate reparative concern for the damage done to mother nature. She resents the environmental fervour of the Prince of Wales whom, when winding up the 1989 Save the Ozone Confer-

ence, she impertinently admonished. Destruction not preservation is
more to her taste. Long ago, in May 1982, during the Falklands crisis,
she strikingly revealed her predilections. 'When you have spent half
your political life dealing with humdrum issues like the environment,
it is exciting to have a real crisis on your hands' she told the Scottish
Conservative Party Conference. Today, given the public alarm,
she grudgingly acknowledges environmental concerns, but they are
concerns that must be distanced, always expressed in the cold vocabulary of the counting house: nothing will be given to mother earth
unless something is obtained in return. Cleaning up your estuaries,
she defensively declared, is good housekeeping. 'Even though this
kind of action may cost a lot, I believe it to be money well and
necessarily spent because the health of our economy and the health
of our environment are totally dependent upon each other.'[9] The
ecological disasters, national and international, that threaten us will
not be averted by such curmudgeonly attitudes.

Thatcher, apart from her commitment to market forces, is, by
her ambivalences to our nurturing world, ill-equipped to meet the
challenges of environmental pollution. She is afflicted with a cluster
of emotional conflicts which singularly invade her decision-making
on green issues. As ever, whenever a problem arises, her first need
is to find someone upon whom blame can be thrust: her scapegoat,
in this context, is coal. The defence mechanism of projection, which
she is deploying, is always preceded by denial. In the psychoanalysts'
dictionary the sequence is explained.[10] First, 'one denies that one
feels such and such an emotion, has such and such a wish, but asserts
that someone else does. Sometimes the projected wish or emotion
remains directed at its original object – "I don't hate X but Y does."'
The dictionary explanation is apposite: the hate of the mother earth
is denied and here the guilt is loaded upon the mining industry. Coal,
of course, is filthy, and Thatcher's well formed reaction-formations
to detritus and litter, which have been remarked, are given full play:
now she can aim to wipe out the industry which contains so many
of her most bitter political opponents. 'Had we gone', she wistfully
remarked, 'the way of France and got 60 per cent of our electricity
from nuclear power we would not have our environmental
problems.'[11] The memories of Three Mile Point and Chernobyl
are blotted out: the terrible dangers of plutonium-escapes, and the
unresolved problems of disposal of nuclear waste are brushed aside:
she has, yet again, found her enemy.

Those who naively praise Thatcher for her clear-cut decisions
should hearken to the emotional turbulence reverberating throughout
all her partial and muddled environmental pronouncements: then

perhaps they would not laud her freedom from fudging, but would, rather, note the woman in chains, irrevocably bound to her infantile past. She is able today to make the claim, however spurious, that she is a Green because, a decade ago, Labour in its impatience for economic growth dismissed dissenters, like myself, as unrealistic romantics.

But if I can exculpate myself from some of Labour's failures, there are other occasions when I share responsibility.

However politically sophisticated the MP may believe himself to be he receives surprises when he canvasses at election time: then he finds issues that seem peripheral at Westminster are dominant in his parish. There were elections in more recent years when the gusts of anger I encountered against those who were fiddling their social security claims took me aback. These were not the outbursts of golf-club Tories but the fury of the respectable working class in my constituency who well knew how widespread were the abuses. Their anger offended our orthodoxies; my colleagues and I sought to relegate their vexation to the same category of grievance as we placed racism and we dismissed their complaint as based only on exaggerated anecdotal evidence. Apart from a botched-up regulation in 1968, curbing some payments for non-manual workers in a few designated areas, no response was made to the grievance. Our non-response meant confidence in the welfare state was, drip by drip, being eroded. Thatcher's attacks, although based on a neurotic fear and hatred of dependence, found resonances among large sections of the employed working class who believed that our social security system was excessively malleable. Thatcher would never have been able to attempt her total assault upon the social security system if we had not been so reluctant to acknowledge the widespread abuses that were taking place. It was one of our major errors, and still we are reluctant to acknowledge it.

One of the most perspicacious of our political correspondents, Ian Aitken, when insisting that Thatcherism is a state of mind not a coherent policy, gives his view that it is Labour's failure, not Thatcher's ideational content, which has so advantaged her. 'She does not so much offer a coherent and consistent body of intermeshed policies under the title of Thatcherism but bounces off various stimuli like a careering dodgem car. Thatcherism is an attitude of mind, a vision of the world seen from behind the Grantham grocery counter. Big idea it is not.'[12]

The task that the Labour Movement has now set itself: to rethink its policies; to listen to its electorate, should be undertaken in a spirit of confidence, knowing that it is not Thatcher's skills but our weaknesses that have given her victory. But the task will not be accomplished if we are content to steal Thatcher's clothes, for her raiments are misshapen, cut to the patterns of her desperate and unresolved emotional problems.

10

Miss Flag

FOR more than a decade the Gallup polls have, in their surveys on the personality images of various leading British politicians, confirmed that the overwhelming public perception of Thatcher is that of a strong leader. Whatever else may be thought of her by the public, 94 per cent in 1986 – either with praise or grudgingly – spoke of her as a 'strong personality'. Doubtless the Chinese at one time would have polled similarly if asked about their thoughts of Mao. The fact that strong ideological convictions are over-compensated doubts, and that a capacity to tolerate doubt is the hallmark of emotional maturity are contentions unknown and probably wholly unacceptable to an electorate longing for 'strong' leadership.

The British electorate's attraction to strong leadership is novel, certainly in this century; from Baldwin to Attlee to Callaghan, other characteristics, seen or imagined by the electorate, have acted as the charm of our prime ministers. Only in wartime was a 'strong' leader approved; and, thwarted before the war, Churchill was discarded immediately afterwards. Yet all of us who have been on the doorsteps know how powerful is the pull towards Thatcher because she is felt to be dominant and strong. How often the unemployed man, the deserted wife on supplementary benefit, the manual worker employed by the local council – impervious to our marshalled arguments – are determined to vote for her. These voters are like the true masochist who Freud told us always turns his cheek whenever he has a chance of receiving a blow. The eagerness of so many to vote for Thatcher and submit, against their financial interest, to her policies is a phenomenon which cannot be explained away by half-truths or overcome by the abusive relegation of working-class Tories to the lumpen proletariat. The intellectual temptation is to suggest that the alienation within our society leaves us with such confusions that, hot for certainty, the electorate desperately turns to a 'conviction' leader, but that is surely only a little less superficial a response than that given by the Tory MPs who state that it is self evident that it is the success of Thatcher's policies which has earned her the electorate's approval.

Those who deny the reality of that success, or who acknowledge the large numbers who have been disadvantaged not advantaged by the Thatcher government, must be prepared to probe deeper. There is clearly a particular relationship between Thatcher and the voters which has resulted in her extraordinary series of electoral victories. I believe that relationship to be essentially morbid, akin to relationships I have repeatedly witnessed in my professional work when dealing with matrimonial disputes. There are many marriages founded and maintained on dominance and submission, upon cruelty and hate – not love. Such a sado-masochistic affair exists between Thatcher and many of the electors: they are into bondage. We have a prime minister who, as I have already remarked, has a severe and punitive super-ego. And we have increasing numbers of our society who flounder in a slough of despondency. The coupling of sadism and masochism is not confined to the bedroom. Krafft-Ebing is distressingly relevant to our contemporary political scene.

The nation has been repetitiously alerted against those who excite or pander to the sadistic impulses in the community. There are so many who, like Mary Whitehouse and Lord Longford, endlessly protest against brutally erotic films and violent television plays; and there are not a few in the Commons who protest, on rational grounds or out of envy, about screen actors so uninhibitedly releasing the violence which the protestors so often imperfectly repressed in themselves. Almost all those who demand action against what I have elsewhere described as sexual fascism, are fearful lest viewers, stimulated by the violent and erotic fantasies, will live them out in real life. They lean heavily upon the Home Secretary, the BBC and the IBA, justifying their call for censorship by their concern that those seeing these spectacles may identify with the depicted savage 'heroes'. Rarely, however, does their concern extend to those who morbidly enjoy identifying with their *victims*.

They attack those of us responsible for bringing about legislation which they claim has been the precursor to a permissive society where the 'traditional' values have been subverted by Freudian doctrine, but their almost total failure to recognise or acknowledge the masochism afloat in our society illustrates how inadequately they have met the real challenge which has been set for us by Freud. My personal encounters with Mary Whitehouse and Lord Longford have always evoked for me the tale of the Greek philosopher who admonished a young man who, affecting humility while addressing a crowd in the forum, had dressed himself in bedraggled clothes. 'Your vanity', said the philosopher, 'peeps through every hole in your garments.'

Many of those voicing concern are monitoring every overt sexual act or display of violence on our screens: they are compulsive voyeurs. The mirror image of the voyeur is of course the exhibitionist, and the Whitehouse brigade can, by becoming well-publicised institutions, often obtain their Janus-faced satisfactions. But their neurotic pursuit distracts us from an awareness of the real threat that free-floating masochism within our society constitutes, a threat that becomes menacing if we have either a political leadership afflicted by a maso-chistic character-disorder or an authoritarian leader to whom the masochistic masses willingly submit.

The popular notion – encouraged by the would-be censors – is that we have become a society without sexual constraints. It is a naive proposition for although legislation such as mine, and the pill, may have brought about changes in our sexual mores – and brought some relief to those afflicted with appalling distortions of the spirit imposed upon them by former legal and societal taboos – nevertheless, the freedoms gained are often illusory. The widespread verbal disavowals of yesterday's condemnations should not mislead us; even in anony-mous responses to polls or questionnaires, the attitudes unconsciously presented by many are far different from those which they consciously affect. In his work, *Hysteria*,[1] my older brother, Professor Wilfred Abse, drawing on his investigative psychotherapeutic clinical experi-ences, stresses how in treatment the seemingly emancipated uncover their subjugation to persisting childhood attitudes. 'The archaic puni-tive core of the super ego must be reckoned with; this resists change stubbornly however readily the more conscious and evolved layers of the super ego or conscience undergo metamorphosis.' Conscious investment in the ideals of sexual freedom can be accompanied by a savagely puritanical but unconscious conscience that operates unceas-ingly and relentlessly beneath the veneer.

Many politicians can empty out much of their masochism, convert-ing the menacing, self-punishing elements of their nature into sadistic verbal attacks upon the evils which they claim to identify in society; and this of course is the projective technique of Thatcher whose severe super-ego would destroy her if it were turned in wholly upon herself. But the widespread incidence of frigidity among women and impotence among men reveal how far society is from being the liberated bordello the inflamed, over-excited Whitehouse brigade would have us believe. The vast sale of punitive pornography – like the demand for the services of the Miss Flags of Soho – and the widespread purchase of blue videos depicting bondage, reveal how psychically enslaved so many are in our society.

In 1984 I was invited to give a sermon on the disenchantments and hopes of the welfare state at the University Church in Cambridge.[2] I told the congregation, 'A few weeks ago I had occasion to walk down King's Road, once upon a time the fashion centre of the ebullient Sixties: it is now a sad sight. I looked into the shop windows. Bald female mannequins abound, usually clad in black rubber, eyeleted and laced, thigh-high gaiters supported by black suspender belts, matched by ferociously cantilevered brassières, sporting aggressively dark glasses and toying with a bullwhip. And around them stuffed rats nibbled at skulls amidst chains, manacles and other sorts of bondage gear. "Never before", a perceptive women's fashion editor in the *Guardian* recently ominously wrote, "not even in the Berlin of the Thirties, has masochism, sadism and fetishism had so strong an influence on fashion."' The fashions may each season take on different forms but the fetishistic emphases remain, reflecting the widespread regressive defeatism abroad.

The incantations of Nigel Lawson, the hype of the Confederation of British Industries, and the reality of increased prosperity for many may temporarily induce, until we move into the economic recession, a euphoria masking the underlying societal melancholia, but the shadows grow longer even as Thatcher boasts of economic growth. The increased alcoholism, particularly amongst the young; the huge number of drug addicts yielding to the oral masochism which will destroy them, the anxiety-induced widespread hypochondriasis which places still further burdens on the ramshackle, demoralised Health Service; the appalling incidence of child abuse and the increased practice of paediastry, all tell us of the ebb-tide dragging man back from maturity to dismal perversity.

Freud insisted that it is the death instinct which is the dark moon regulating that tide. The genesis of this strange compulsion in man to seek abasement, to welcome humiliation, to find pleasure in pain, is often contested, not least among psychoanalysts who have dared to follow clinically its convoluted manifestations; but whatever may be its origin, its actual existence is amply corroborated in our society and in our institutions. And if Freud is right and if indeed masochism is older than sadism, then it must be taken into account when we examine man's history of wars and violent class-struggles, for they may well be part of his frantic attempt to ward off his yearning for the ultimate delight of self destruction. By resisting the temptation of a still and lifeless Nirvana, and directing his erotically-loaded regressiveness outwards, away from the interior life, man may postpone, for a little while, the joy of his submission to death. The challenge Freud gave this century in illuminating the importance of sexuality in our lives has been only superficially met. Gripped with panic, we dodge the awful implications of an hypothesis which states that a biologically determined instinct, bathed in exciting sensuality, draws us to our nemesis, and that we can only advance the date of our masturbatory death by directing some of the force of this terrible instinct into sexually-inspired cruelty against our fellow man.

It is easier to avoid than to accept these forebodings. Yet the failure to see the need to create stations, stopping points where, at least temporarily, man can lay down his masochistic burdens, is a recent myopia; it has come about with the rapid decline of religious faith. Thirty years ago when I entered Parliament I was required by well established convention to attend the annual civic service in my constituency. The chapel was then packed and the hymns of the Cross were sung with fervour and commitment. Now not only the chapels of Wales are empty; churchgoing and religious faith withers throughout the land. The central myth of Christianity, the Passion – for so many centuries the great container of man's masochism – has within a handful of decades become utterly meaningless to millions. Unfocused, the free-floating masochism in our society has now become dangerously pervasive, and is readily available to be exploited by pornographers and politicians.

When Britain was a Christian society, religion gave some considerable relief to man's boundless masochistic desires. Contemplation of the agony of the Cross, of the ecstasy depicted on the faces of the tortured saints, can engage masochism therapeutically. But I am informed that within the Anglican Church the Passion is infrequently dwelt upon these days. Apparently, the Resurrection is more *à la mode* and doubtless superficially more comfortable. Christ risen, not Christ crucified, is the contemporary message. Good Friday slips out of view and, when Easter comes, the bishops, as in 1989, have their disputations as to whether the Resurrection is to be interpreted as a physical or spiritual awakening.[3] The focus is no longer on the Passion but on the empty tomb: ironically, at a time when there has probably never been more masochism at large, no conduit is provided between Man and the Cross. The certain knowledge that the nuclear powers can now blow up the whole world in thirty minutes presses down upon us and the likely spread of AIDS to millions result in man being oppressed by the same guilts as occurred in other times when plagues wiped out populations. The eschatological speculations that engulfed and depressed Europe as the year 1000 approached may have been irrational; similar speculations as we approach the second millennium may, unhappily, have a greater validity.

However unwelcome the introduction of such complexities may be to British politicians or political scientists, it is increasingly urgent that the insights hard-won from the therapy of individuals should be applied to political problems – for if political man now fails to make efforts to understand himself, none of us will survive. Puny politicians who wish to brush aside these complexities should note, when pondering their electoral successes and defeats, that in this century, exceptional leaders have been keenly sensitive to the consequences of man's masochism: it was observed with despair by Lenin and with delight by Hitler. Faced with having to examine the cause of the failure of the 1905 Russian revolt Lenin wrote,[4] 'The soldier had a great deal of sympathy for the cause of the peasant; at the mere mention of land his eyes blazed with passion. Several times military power passed into the hands of the soldiers, but this power was hardly ever used resolutely. The soldiers wavered. A few hours after they had disposed of a hated superior, they released the others, entered into negotiations with the authorities and then had themselves shot, submitted to the rod, had themselves yoked again.' But the submissiveness which Lenin bitterly regretted was the very element which Hitler welcomed; characteristically equating submissiveness with femininity, he divined the dimension which he was so success-fully to exploit. He contemptuously wrote, 'The people in their overwhelming majority are so feminine by their nature and attitude that sober reasoning determines their thoughts and actions far less than emotion and feeling.'[5] And the overwhelming majority of the 'feminine' German people yielded to the delights of humiliation and revelled in his domination.

[Just as the search for reasons to explain Thatcher's electoral victories is limited to socio-economic explorations, leaving the psychological ground uncovered, so in Germany the left-wing politicians and theorists faced with Hitler's growing ascendancy, feared to look into the dark abysses of man's psyche. There was but one important exception, the Marxist psychoanalyst Wilhelm Reich, and for his pains, he achieved the unique distinction of being expelled from both the German Communist party and the International Society of Psychoanalysis. During the 1970s, long after his death, Wilhelm Reich became a cult figure both here and in France, particularly among the young. Unfortunately, the works which were republished and the films they inspired were, for the most part, confined to his later publications where his incipient madness (which was to overwhelm him in the end) had already marred their validity. But in his earlier work he faced the psychological issues his fellow Marxists were evading, and in so doing angered both them and Freud who condemned his contributions as written in the service of the German Communist party.[6]

Reich was seeking to emphasise the disastrous consequences of certain social conditions that could tease out masochism. As a sanguine Marxist, he could not accept Freud's pessimism. He preferred to believe that reactionary political forces maintained the economic exploitation of man by way of a repressive religious ideology and a familial structure which ensured man could not enjoy the uninhibited sexual, orgastic experience which, if achieved, would liberate him both economically and humanistically. Such delusionary millenarian views, by suggesting that masochism was primarily prompted by external social forces and was not irredeemably indigenous to mankind, obscured the validity of some of his other contentions; yet he did recognise the fetishistic ethos of the Weimar Republic, and he did mock at his bewildered fellow Marxists' confusing socio-economic explanations of how the Nazis were being voted into power by the German people. 'Sexual inhibition', he insisted, 'changes the structure of economically suppressed man in such a way that he acts, feels and thinks contrary to his material interest.'

Wilhelm Reich's heroic attempt to understand Hitler's support displays a grandeur not matched by our left-wing academics as they seek to unravel the dilemma set by Thatcher's widespread popularity. Their theories fail to encompass the determinant of those many teachers, trade unionists, redundant steel workers, families of unemployed, and nurses who in 1983 and 1987 in my constituency, as in every constituency in the land, voted for Thatcher. Following the unfortunate example set by their counterparts in the Weimar Republic, these sociologists ignore the warning signals given by Durkheim, the founding father of their discipline, and so seek to explain the electoral success of Thatcher in reductionist terms, which seem drained of human passion. Even the most painstaking analyses of Labour's 1987 defeat, as those given by Dr Jessop and a concerned team of social scientists, submit unwittingly to Thatcher's vulgar version of the psychodynamics of mankind.[7] Infected by her belief that avarice and profit-seeking are the motivations waiting to be rekindled in Britain, they analyse Labour's defeats by asserting that two nations are being created; one increasingly affluent, belonging to the productive core of the market economy; the other marginal to, or living outside, that market economy and comprising the unskilled working class, poor pensioners, single parents and ethnic minorities, and the unemployed in and outside the favoured areas of the south east. Then upon a premise which is implicitly based on Economic Man, they seek to advise the Labour Movement on the best strategy for regaining the vote of the nation within the productive core. Dr Jessop and his colleagues appear to be attributing Thatcher's victories to the material concessions said to have been gained by the skilled working class and would have us believe that the task is to trump Thatcher by devising new areas for state intervention tempered by new decentralised, collectivised institutions which would result in yet more material gains.

Such diagnoses of the defeats are incomplete, and however well intentioned they can result in the pursuit of goals which are ignoble. Man needs to be viewed in his whole humanity – he is more than an acquisitive grub – and that means those who wish to elevate man above the station afforded to him by Thatcher must needs face both the life-denying and the life-enhancing potential of psychological man. These social scientists are in danger of reducing politics to a branch of economics; it is a danger which they share with some of Labour's young front-benchers. No diagnosis of Thatcher's electoral successes can be complete without an understanding of the willing submission by many voters to her authoritarian leadership. The force of the gale pulling many of Labour's voters from their traditional anchorage cannot be measured simply by financial yardsticks; abasement is a psychological not an economic condition. The redundant steelworker who knows he fought too long to be under-employed in his industry, the unemployed man who has failed to get on his bike and has heard Thatcher assert that his worthlessness is caused by his self-imposed immobility – these are part of the army of the defeated, and the defeated almost invariably feel guilty and deserving of their fate. They accept their punishment as deserved and will not use their votes to overthrow their admonisher. Thatcher has other allies besides the employed skilled working class who, the social scientists tell us, are voting out of newly found self interest.

The thinkers studying politics in the past, from Plato to Bentham and Mill, each had his own view of human nature and they made those views the basis of their speculations on government.[8] Now, however, the left-wing and Marxist theoreticians do not preface their treatises on political science by a definition of human nature. Yet, when they use their discipline to diagnose the causes of the Thatcherite advances and make their suggestions for a new Labour strategy, they tacitly take aboard obsolescent and naive definitions of human nature supplied by others. The influence upon them of the Utilitarians is clear; ignoring masochism with superb insouciance, they thought they had found the key to man's behaviour in the hedonistic principle of his seeking pleasure and avoiding pain; and, curiously, the influence of the classical economists with their Homo oeconomicus, desirous to obtain additional wealth with the least sacrifice, is also not lacking. Like these earlier writers, too, many of those in the universities and in the Commons who are seeking to rid Britain of Thatcher's dominance, are basing their investigation into past defeats and their suggested future programmes on the assumption of the essential rationality of man, a rationality which will cause him to vote in his own financial interest. It is a dangerous assumption as the historian Sir Lewis Namier pointed out more than thirty years ago when disapprovingly he quoted Macaulay's dogma, 'When we see the actions of a man we know with certainty what he thinks his interests to be.'[9] Namier knew history could not be so interpreted and stressed that 'unconscious promptings combine with rational thought and in every action there are inscrutable components. Undoubtedly one of the most important lines of advance for history, and especially for biography, will be a thorough knowledge of modern psychology.' If, heedless of such advice, Labour politicians and left-wing social scientists misinterpret recent history, they are unlikely to devise a strategy which will determine the future history of political leadership in Britain.

It was with the declared principles of the 1688 Glorious Revolution in mind, but with a comment that is pertinent to the so-called Thatcher revolution, that Namier wrote, 'So far we have hardly reached the fringes of the field of mass psychology, the most basic factor in history . . . One inevitable result of heightened psychological awareness is, however, a change of attitude towards so-called political ideas. To treat them as the offspring of pure reason would be to assign to them a parentage about as mythological as that of Pallas Athene. What matters most is the underlying emotions, the music, to which ideas are a mere libretto, often of very inferior quality; and once the emotions have ebbed, the ideas . . . become doctrine or . . . cliches.' Unhappily, the application of heightened psychological awareness to political ideas which Namier thought was 'inevitable' has not taken place in Britain; even the most acute analyses of Thatcher's victories, such as those by Professor Eric Hobsbawm, are flawed.[10] They are locked in to Marx's pre-Freudian psychology which was content to identify workers who voted and acted against their own interests as being possessed of a 'false consciousness' shaped by external cultural factors; to use such an unsophisticated nineteenth-century psychology, to throw away the armoury that contemporary depth psychology makes available, results in faulty political diagnoses and prognoses.

It is not that Hobsbawm takes up a vulgarised Marxist position; he is not content to rely on a claimed historical determinism which will restore the forward march of British Labour which he believes began to falter forty years ago. On the contrary, he quotes with approval Marx's affirmation that 'Man makes his history in the circumstances that history has provided for him and within its limits – but it is he who makes history.' But the Hobsbawm man is man at his factory, office or laboratory, or at Marks and Spencer. Hobsbawm argues that Labour's difficulties have arisen because the working class is no longer homogeneous and he identifies a growing tendency for workers to divide into sections and groups, each group pursuing its own economic interest irrespective of the rest, and all of them discouraged from maintaining their former political consciousness by a media which drenches them with the values of 'consumer-society individualism'. This view only tells us part of the story. Hobsbawm appears to see man as worker and consumer, but man is shaped in his cradle as well as in the workshop or supermarket. To emphasise the particular importance of Thatcher's personal relationship with the electorate does not mean one lapses into the Great Man interpretation of history, but it does focus on the crucial interplay that can come into existence between a political leader and the masses in particular resonating social conditions. After three successive Thatcher victories, it is ostrich-like behaviour to exclude that major consideration from a political analysis of Labour's defeats.

Yet despite the innumerable essays and articles by British Marxists, and despite their prolonged debates, they remain coy about anatomising Thatcher personally. It is always an abstraction, Thatcherism, which is elevated to a coherent, conscious, well thought out ideology, which they purport to explore and to which, with marked ambivalence, they attribute such 'power' that, in defeatist mood, they counsel the Labour Party (to which they have never belonged) to enter into alliances with other political groups to gain victory. These genteel revolutionaries, although describing Thatcherism as an 'authoritarian populism' shrink from the bad taste of examining the fundamental dynamics that prompt people in particular circumstances to enjoy submitting to authoritarianism. The most Professor Stuart Hall and Martin Jacques, the editor of *Marxism Today*, will venture when acknowledging the popular support for Thatcher is this:[11] 'The whole shift towards a more authoritarian type of régime has been grounded in the search for "order" and the cry for "law" which arises among many ordinary people in times of crisis and upheaval and which has been dovetailed into the imposition of authority from above.' Thus the 'crisis' is blamed for the popular response, and the relationship between Thatcher and the electorate is explained, if at all, in non-psychological terms. Their avoidance of the personal confrontation with Thatcher reveals their anxiety, for so great is their overvaluation of the 'power' of their construct of Thatcherism, that they evidently fear confrontation would mean seduction. No New-Right theorist fascinated by Thatcher would write more glowingly of the triumph of her administration than Professor Stuart Hall.[12] He informs us, 'When, in a crisis the traditional alignments are disrupted, it is possible on the very ground of this break to construct the people into a populist political subject: with, not against, the power bloc; in alliance with new political forces in a great national crusade to "Make Britain 'great' once more." The language of "the people" unified behind a reforming drive to turn the tide of "creeping collectivism", banish Keynesian illusions from the state apparatus and renovate the power bloc, is a powerful one.' The grammar of the professor may be shaky, but the apotheosis of Thatcherism is clear.

He is far removed from his mentor, Antonio Gramsci, who, whilst acknowledging the social forces carrying along the fascists in Italy, mocked at Mussolini as a 'carriage fly'.[13] Hall shrinks from such a belittling of Thatcher. And, in the same mode, his Marxist colleague, Professor Andrew Gamble, in his latest work, cowers before her and instructs us that 'She has been an exceptionally dominant and powerful Prime Minister.'[14] These British Marxists lack the intellectual courage possessed by Leon Trotsky, who, even when assessing Hitler, made no such concessions: he asserted that the temporary political success of Hitler was not to be found in himself. 'Naive minds think that the office of kingship lodges in the king himself, in his ermine cloak and his crown, in his flesh and bones. As a matter of fact, the office of kingship is an interrelation between people. The king is king only because the interests and prejudices of millions of people are refracted through his person. When the flood of development sweeps away these interrelations, then the king appears to be only a washed-out man with a flabby lower lip.'[15] Our political Marxists, however, stand in awe of Thatcher and, in their defeatist political tracts, are forever treating her as 'king': indeed she usually is the personage whose name they dare not speak.

It is not surprising that the irreverent Alan Watkins, too shrewd a Welshman and too experienced and sophisticated a political correspondent at Westminster to indulge in absurd idealisations of politicians, has included these Marxist theoreticians in his roll call of Thatcher fawners. Writing in the *Observer* he commented:[16]

Since the election there has been a tendency to bow down before Mrs Margaret Thatcher. This collective self-abasement extends from most of the Conservative Party, through Dr David Owen, the *Independent* newspaper and Mr Peter Jenkins, to Mr Bryan Gould and on to Dr Eric Hobsbawm and the savants of *Marxism Today*.

It is not that these people and papers wholly approve of what she is and what she has done (although some do). It is rather that they attribute extraordinary powers to her . . . As Mrs Thatcher has now won three elections, people are somehow reluctant to regard her as the same as any other politician. There is supposed to be both a magic ingredient and a coherent body of doctrine called Thatcherism. In reality there is neither . . . In all this adulation of Mrs Thatcher as a person, Thatcherism as a force, there is an unwholesome whiff of the worship of power for its own sake.

These defeatist Communist Party theorists, fascinated by the nimbus of power, reveal how subtly masochism, under a mask of opposition, can command abnegation. They are wrong to believe they are far removed from those publicists, like my former Labour colleagues Brian Walden and Woodrow Wyatt, who attempt, by prostrating themselves before their goddess, to be redeemed from their sins of past allegiances to the community values of the Party which Nye Bevan had taught must have as its goal the creation of a serene society. Their repudiation of their political past is total. Once in other days these men with wit and considerable intelligence lightened for me not a few of the leaden hours, the longueurs, which can fall upon us in Parliamentary life. They both have a seductiveness often found in fantasists who, with little embellishments of truth, capture amused audiences who then reflect and enhance their false self-images, making them feel real. Fundamentally both always lacked self esteem, concealed – in Wyatt's case – in an absurd display of bravado and make believe; self disgust leads to self abuse and they have squandered their rich talents in the service of a vulgar icon. Walden heralded in the 1988 New Year with a declaration of his current political view: 'In my opinion governments exist to do all in their power to make ordinary citizens as materially prosperous as the circumstances of the time permit. Prosperous you note, not happy. Happiness is an elusive state best left to the judgment of individuals.'[17] Money is all: government must become a magical one-armed bandit returning the insertion of a token vote with a shower of gold.

This repentance of their Labour past is of an extravagant, Russian order, and some of their travail comes from the same source as that which poisoned the life of the gambling Dostoevsky, ever punishing himself at the tables for his terrifying, unresolved Oedipal desires. Their political abasement is of a similar nature; it is indeed an irony but not a coincidence that both men have had heavy flirtations with the bookmaking and gambling industry, an affair which in Walden's case contributed to the sad wrecking of his Parliamentary career, and which led to Tote Chairman Wyatt, as a Thatcher ennobled peer, to reach the apogee of his political career by persuading the Lords that betting-shops should be opened at midday on Sundays. Teachers in my former constituency lamented that, if Wyatt had his way, the one occasion – in these days of working wives, continental shifts and tele-snacks – when the whole family sit down for a meal together would no longer exist: that, however, is a finale which would be unlikely to trouble the so far four-times-married Wyatt.

Both the communist theoreticians and those of the Walden/Wyatt ilk are congregants of the same temple. By grouping together so many seemingly diverse groups, Alan Watkins identifies the communion binding them together as they genuflect in professed or tacit adoration; all of them succumb to the incense surrounding the shrine. The worship of power and all representing it on earth is a placatory theology, for, of course, it is prompted by fear: and those subscribing to the doctrine are resorting to a defence mechanism well explained in psychoanalysis – the overcoming of fear by the stratagem of unconsciously identifying with the frightening aggressor.

In Anna Freud's seminal work on the syndrome she presents children who use the mechanism to overcome anxiety as simple illustrations of the phenomenon.[18] A child who was always making uncontrollable grimaces in class and who, when reproved, would react with abnormal behaviour was in fact found to be making grimaces which were simply a caricature of his teacher; when the boy feared a scolding he tried to mask his anxiety by involuntarily imitating the feared teacher. Similarly, the little girl found to be making all sorts of singular gestures in the dark was seeking to overcome her dread of seeing ghosts, and her magic gestures, representing the gestures she imagined ghosts would make, were helping her to surmount her anxiety; she became the ghost she feared would otherwise meet her.

The defence mechanism is not only to be found in children's idiosyncratic behaviour or indeed in their games where they impersonate a dreaded object and, by the metamorphosis, quench their fear; nor is it only to be found in primitive tribes who use the technique to evoke and exorcise spirits in their religious ceremonies. It is a defence mechanism to which all, during certain stressful occasions, can resort. I am certainly not surprised that it is so often and so ostentatious a ploy of political traitors who have deserted my party for I have seen it in its most florid form, as I recounted elsewhere, among not a few of the spies I have encountered.[19]

Will Owen, one-time MP for Morpeth, was a text-book example. In 1970, although acquitted by a credulous jury of spying, he was compelled to admit he had received payments from the Czechs. After his consequent resignation from the House, he came to me complaining that, despite his acquittal, the security service was harassing him – obviously wishing him to 'sing' – and he asked me to protect him. I knew the man to be a cunning rascal; on one occasion, having won in the annual Parliamentary ballot (which give him priority in introducing a bill), and knowing that I wanted to put through a reforming measure, he offered to *sell* me his place! Still, he knew that whatever distaste I had for him I would, as a lawyer, acknowledge the legitimacy of his complaint as an 'innocent' man. My subsequent intervention led to the request that I help to persuade him to talk and I co-operated, although I found the role of intermediary unpleasant. Owen ultimately agreed – provided I obtained him immunity and that I sat in with him during the interrogations – requests which the security service willingly granted. The following sessions gave me full opportunity to understand the unconscious motivations which had driven Owen into his shabby role – no clearer indication of a man using the defence mechanism to overcome anxiety by identification with a feared powerful personage is likely to come my way.

Will Owen, the son of a miner, was the oldest of ten children who came from a poverty-stricken household where love, like money, was thinly spread. He felt keenly the displacement he had endured as a succession of new brothers and sisters arrived, and his cloying, sentimental recollections of his mother did not disguise from me the wrath he felt against her: he could not forgive his submitting, ever love-making mother. Owen, in fantasy, allied himself with the Russian conquering enemy, thus identifying himself with the all-powerful father he hated and feared. He fitted exquisitely into the picture of a traitor presented to us by Ernest Jones who wrote, 'Treachery, by allying oneself with the conquering enemy, would seem to be an attempt sadistically to overcome the incest taboo by raping the Mother instead of loving her. Perhaps that is why it is generally regarded as the most outrageous and unnatural of crimes, since it combines disloyalty to both parents.'[20]

Certainly Owen did his puny best to rape his motherland. But although being a traitor to your country and being a deserter from your Party is clearly conduct of a very different order, nevertheless it is not difficult to discern that some of the articulate protagonists who have left the Labour Party and today identify with the 'powerful'

Thatcher and forever laud her are, as they attack the party which once fathered and mothered them, and placed them on their public platforms, acting out similar unresolved Oedipal problems as beset Will Owen.

Woodrow Wyatt's recent autobiography richly illustrates the predictable syndromes presented by those so ensnared.[21] Ingenuous as ever, he spells out the history of his many infidelities before he became unfaithful to the Labour Party. The pattern of his wantonness shows a repetitiveness, and an involuntariness, that springs from deeper sources than the particular individual circumstances which he would claim occasioned his conduct. His adulteries which he advertises in his book are matters for him, and if it were not that he so determinedly and ostentatiously displays them to public view, it would be tasteless, and an unforgivable intrusion upon his privacy, to deploy them as part of the case that he lacks a capacity for sustained fidelity in public affairs. In any event, I believe that many of his liaisons have taken place only in his head: I have always found him, when we have talked together, scarpering quickly away from any Freudian interpretations I may place upon current controversies or the behaviour of our fellow politicians. He is a prim man and his silly prurient accounts remind one of the tales of an uncertain adolescent boasting to his peers of his conquests and rebuffs. Perhaps a man who, by his own telling, has had the experience of three wives in succession leaving him, needs to publicise his machismo.

More relevant to this study is the scrutiny of Wyatt's ambivalence to authority. During his war service his successful attempt to undermine his incompetent commanding officer led to Wyatt being tossed out of his regiment. Later, when serving as personal assistant to Stafford Cripps (who was leading a Cabinet Mission to India in 1949), he sought to undermine Cripps's negotiating efforts by privately carrying tales to the other side. When this behaviour came to light it so shocked Cripps that he reported Wyatt to Attlee who severely reprimanded Wyatt and kept him out of any office for years. Indeed, Attlee only rehabilitated him after Wyatt, whilst enjoying confidences unwisely given to him in the Commons Smoke Room by Nye Bevan and while working on the left-wing *Tribune*, privately distanced himself from the Bevanites and wrote to Attlee telling him how moved he was by his 'patent loyalty to the Party he has served so long'. Evidently impressed by Wyatt's new expertise in 'loyalty' Attlee rewarded him with a minor junior ministry.

All these, and many other such incidents, were premonitions of his ultimate apostasy; when he renounced the Labour Party he was already a well-seasoned recidivist from whom political stability could never be expected. He has not, he insists, become a Tory but a Thatcherite; and there is some validity in his insistence, for it is power, not policies or principles, to which he is fatally attracted. It was ever thus. As a young MP in the 1945 Labour Government his thrill was not belonging to a splendid reforming Parliament but to be sitting in the same Chamber as the 'powerful' leader, the ageing Winston Churchill, whose manner and speech he deliberately, as he concedes, took as his models. He could, if he chose, present the same apologia for his desertion of the Labour Party as Kim Philby used when attempting to deny his treachery. 'To betray', Philby said, 'you must first belong'; and Wyatt never really belonged to the Labour Movement. His account of his sad childhood tells us, unwittingly, the origins of the perpetual estrangement which afflicts him: he never felt that he belonged to his own parents. He was forever frightened of his elderly, dominating father who treated the young Woodrow as someone to be despised, and his mother ridiculed him even when he became an under-secretary of state, and later cut him out of her will. From the first he experienced neither real love nor recognition. It is not surprising that in his private life he has so desperately sought for love, nor that in his public life he has submitted so obsequiously to Thatcher to obtain the recognition so cruelly and unfairly denied him in his childhood.

Now in his autobiography he complains that Michael Foot, with whom he was once friendly, regards him as a 'traitor': and he will be no less surprised that he is here treated so harshly since, until his defection, as next-door neighbours in London and in Tuscany, we saw each other frequently: his very fluidity can sometimes mean he is possessed, even if only temporarily, of less than orthodox views, and when his subversions are exhibited in their mildest form – as mischievousness – he can, if one yields to the poignancy that lies behind his efforts to recreate himself in a grandiose image, be a beguiling companion. But he was brought up neither knowing nor learning from his parents the music of love, and consequently he now lacks many of the notes in the gamut of human emotions. Whole octaves are dead, though he tries to fake them, and the melody of allegiance is outside his range. He will never understand how outraged those like Michael Foot and I feel when we read his column in a tawdry tabloid, and witness how he regularly savages his political past and delivers himself up to what, at seventy, is doubtless his last mistress.

*

Freud tells us there are two broad groups of instincts:[22] the life instinct, Eros, and the destructive instinct, Thanatos, directed towards the breaking down of living matter to a previous inorganic state. There is in our instinctual manifestations usually a fusion of the two; and in our sexual and personal relationships, although a destructive sadism and masochism enters, Eros can normally overcome its eternal adversary. But in the individual, as in society, disease can cause instinctual defusion; then, split off from the life instincts, Thanatos reigns and our aggression is no longer constructively employed in the service of our ego. It is in danger of turning back from the external world on to the ego itself, producing self-punishment: an extraordinary rage is thereby turned against the self. And in an increasingly lonely and loveless society, too often Eros is unavailable to temper the consequent excesses.

A politician has the dangerous capacity, even unwittingly, to ally himself with this death instinct and to create a condition or an ethos when the dormant masochism in the community becomes awesomely manifest. There was one occasion when my carelessness led me to feel its ensnaring pseudopodia slimily reach out to me. During an abortion debate in 1966, for the first time in the history of Parliament, I raised the issue of vasectomy. I scoffed at those colleagues of mine who were using the debate as an arena in which to wage the class struggle; the wealthy had abortions, they argued, so why should the workers be denied them? I insisted there was no need to incite the workers to commit the folly of the hated bourgeois, and that it was droll to proffer abortion, however compellingly necessary in some circumstances, to a pregnant, poverty-stricken wife who had already had half a dozen children and was living in squalid overcrowded conditions. If she aborted the foetus, the indifferent husband would, within months, undoubtedly impregnate her again, so it seemed to me more rational to sterilise the man, and I suggested that the law relating to the performance of vasectomies should be clarified and facilities made available. I was conscious as I broached the then unfamiliar subject of vasectomy that the Members wriggled uncomfortably in their seats; whatever views they had on an assault on a woman's femininity, they had other views on what could be interpreted as an attack on their maleness.

But, however coolly the House received my suggestion, the reported comments on my speech provoked a different response outside. I was astonished to find myself deluged with prurient letters from men in all parts of the country. I recalled, when reading them, the anathematisation by Justinian of the second-century martyr, Origen: all the Synod's condemnation of the early heretic had clearly not influenced twentieth-century semi-Christian England. Judging by my correspondents' fervour, they had been gripped by Origen's heresy and wanted a vasectomy as a penultimate step towards the self-inflicted sacrificium phalli, the course followed by the great scholar. My postbag taught me the need to be wary, for many of the letter writers were clearly young, lonely, unmarried men. Nevertheless, I still felt that there were special circumstances when it would be wise to encourage a vasectomy and six years later I co-operated with Phillip Whitehead, a splendid Member of Parliament lost too soon to the House by a capricious electorate, in putting through a Vasectomy Act.[23] I was careful to insist that the Bill included safeguards which ensured that state aid would only be given after skilled counselling, and only to mature couples with completed families who were prepared to regard this contraceptive method as potentially irreversible. I had learned of the need for sophisticated screening if we were to distinguish between those who seek sterilisation as part of a voluntary programme of planned parenthood and those who erotically desire self-abasement.

Although on that occasion I persuaded the government to my view, the House almost always is averse to acknowledging the pervading influence of the death instinct: it can be unnerving to peer down the abyss of despair. Still, I have always, when opportunity arose, sought to focus on its power for we will not overcome it by denying its existence. Such an opportunity arose when, in 1983, the demand arose for hanging to be reintroduced, this time in response to IRA terrorism. I found myself trying didactically to instruct the new Parliament on the significance of a memorandum circulated to Members of the British Council of Churches which stressed how capital punishment may positively excite a potential killer. I said:

> I do not dismiss the experience of the Churches in putting forward the proposition that, far from being a deterrent, in some cases hanging is an attraction. That accords with my experience of dealing with those charged with murder while hanging was still the ultimate penalty. I, with many of my professional colleagues, discovered that those bizarre men, who do not possess the rationality that Hon. Members sometimes attribute to them, continually resisted our legitimate attempts to save them from the rope. The more we adumbrated the reasons why we could persuade the court that a man had acted with diminished responsibility, the more the killer's resentment grew. It became clear that he resented the attempts of his legal advisers to deny him the ultimate victory, as he saw it, which was to have the major part in the macabre theatre of the gallows.

I am not surprised that the Churches seized upon that aspect of the matter, because we must take into account the fact that our community has great difficulty in dealing with the problem of masochism. However, in days gone by, because of the identification with the Passion, many would claim that masochism was dealt with therapeutically. Identification with the Crucifixion meant that masochism could be dealt with in a way that did not bring about far more miserable consequences. If some Hon. Members doubt that masochism is widespread they should look at pornography, where they will see spread forth for them the various, although monotonous, details of bondage. The yearning for punishment is extraordinarily deep-seated. If some Hon. Members deny what the Churches say, or dismiss as extravagant the suggestion that people could yearn for punishment and seek it – those who kill to die – I can give them some statistics. One third of those who commit murder then commit suicide, which means they pre-empt the gallows or any other punishment. Those who are naive enough to believe that those people would be deterred by the rope are denying the facts. We would be presenting something to a band of murderers that is likely to excite and encourage them and which, far from containing murder, is likely to increase it.

Thanatos is a cunning adversary, and can insinuate himself into the hearts of politicians as well as murderers. When, in the guise of masochism, it turns inwards upon the political leader, the private and the public consequences can be shattering. Both the heroes of my adolescence – Stafford Cripps, who became Labour's Chancellor of the Exchequer, and John Strachey who, during the 1930s, long before he became Labour's Secretary of State for War, inspired a whole generation by his ceaseless efforts to give British socialism, up to then always a ragbag of pragmatism and evangelism, a real and driving unitary theory – lost their battles with their enemy. Their death certificates record that they died from natural causes, but the truth is they killed themselves even as, before their deaths, they had killed their hopes and the hopes of so many who had found a fraternity in their teachings.

It is probable that a monitoring of the life of Stafford Cripps would provide us with more clinical material about the role and dangers of masochistic leadership than could be gleaned from a study of any other single British political figure; but I am too disadvantaged to attempt such a scrutiny, for I did not know him personally: he belonged to an older generation and his influence upon me as a boy and youth came only because I attended so many of his evangelising

meetings. But in those early days my admiration of him was boundless: his role as a great lawyer, playing Robin Hood, plundering his
rich clients to aid the poor, fuelled my own ambitions, and his
expulsion in 1939 from the Labour Party precipitated the one occasion
in my life when, disenchanted for a while, my commitment to the
Labour Movement faltered. Yet, after the war, on my return to Wales
from the RAF, I clashed with him at conferences on more than one
occasion: I formed a distaste for his sickly religiosity and his clear
enjoyment of the austere economic policies he was imposing. Professor Ben Pimlott in his monumental biography of Hugh Dalton[24]
has described Cripps as a dazzling, destructive and uncompromising
personality, and in the immediate post-war years it was the destructiveness I sensed, a destructiveness that ultimately he was to turn in
on himself. In anorexic mood he imposed upon himself a diet of
strict and ill-balanced vegetarianism, excluding the cyanocobalamin
present in liver, kidney, milk, eggs and mussels and which he
evidently needed; and which was further exhausted by the detox-
ification of cyanide in tobacco smoke, for Cripps at conferences was
a chain smoker, ringing the changes on cigarettes and pipe tobacco
and, in the evenings on cigars too: there can be little doubt that the
troubles of his spinal vertebrae which led to his death stemmed from
dietary insufficiency. It was said that the tireless Chancellor of the
Exchequer had sacrificed his health for the sake of the nation but that
was only a partial truth. His yearning for sacrifice was morbid, and
in the sealed envelope he left on his death for his wife, he made it
explicit. 'I want my effort to live on and to inspire others to work
for the eventual salvation of mankind which we all look for.' Politicians are more healthy and effective if they are more modest in
their objectives. Whatever may have been the value in first-century
Palestine of redeemers, in our party conference and in the twentieth-
century Westminster they, if possessed of the brilliance of Cripps,
became a menace to themselves and to the nation.

If I saw Cripps only from a distance, it was otherwise as far as
the three other significant masochistic figures of this century are
concerned. Strachey was a friend of mine and I served in Westminster
for decades with Keith Joseph and Enoch Powell. Of Strachey I have
written elsewhere:[24] he was a man who, by his writings and lectures,
first gave faith and hope to so many and then, having fed them with
illusions, brutally divested himself and his followers of a multitude
of wonderful dreams, leaving them dispirited while he, yielding to
his despair, with deliberation, proceeded to embrace his own death.

Thanatos, however, does not skip a generation and, relentlessly,
he continues to make his selection. In more recent decades the chosen

ones have been the 'mad monk', Keith Joseph, and the sombre Enoch Powell, the two men who, above all, prepared the way for the coming of Thatcher. A glance, therefore, at these two political leaders, and at their iconoclastic eloquence which has been their armoury, may help us in our enquiry, and unravel a little the perplexities which otherwise ensnare us as we witness the sado-masochistic relationship between Thatcher and a large section of the electorate. An understanding of these two men may provide at least a partial explanation as to why so many, panting for dominance, welcomed Thatcher's arrival.

11

The Harbingers: Keith Joseph
and Enoch Powell

THERE is no place on earth where the fierce force and courage of a masochistic leader can sear one more than at Ephesus, the city dedicated to the celebration of sexuality. Here, amidst the temples and shrines built to acclaim fertility first in the name of Cybele and later to her successors, Artemis and Diana, came the great adventurer, one of the most extraordinary men ever produced by my people:[1] Paul of Tarsus, the myth maker and founder of Christianity, the harshest disparager of the flesh the world has ever known.[2] And down these marble roads, unintimidated by the grand temples affirming the joys of sex, the zealot declaimed the turpitude of the worshippers, subverting their confidence as he inflamed the dormant guilts that forever lurk beneath the ecstasy of the reveller. He was the great converter of self disgust into spirituality, and his message finds resonances thousands of years later in these contemporary leaders miserably discomfited by their own sexuality. Paul's utterances are often echoed in their speeches: 'I know that nothing good lodges in me – in my unspiritual nature . . . I bruise my own body and make it know its master . . . In this present body we do indeed groan . . . We know that as long as we are at home in the body we are exiles from the Lord . . . We are not better than pots of earthenware to contain this treasure.'[3] Paul's words may afford contemporary masochistic leaders some temporary solace, but he cannot save them; to gain relief from their own agonies they must publicly exhibit them and be their own missionaries.

The language of Britain's modern ascetic political missionaries, Keith Joseph and Enoch Powell, sometimes matches the awesome grandeur of Paul's rhetoric; they are certainly no mean practitioners of the word, and they too still rail against fertility. It has proved their undoing. Joseph in 1972 and Powell in 1968 both forfeited their strong claims to the premiership because men and women more

confident in their sexuality recoiled from their apocalyptic decla-
mations against the copulation habits of other groups. The statistics
Joseph used to demonstrate his belief in the dangers of the breeding
habits of the disadvantaged, and Powell's preoccupation with the
birth statistics of blacks, were seen by many as a prurient inquisition
into the lovemaking of those whom Joseph and Powell evidently
felt were menacingly vigorous in bed. The reaction to the prolific
disadvantaged and the fertile blacks came from two men who appear
to have a yearning for celibacy. Indeed, in a television appearance
which he shared with his wife and daughter, Powell displayed breath-
taking insensitivity when, in the presence of his family, he told of
his wish to be a monk; and Joseph earned the soubriquet of the 'mad
monk' as a consequence of his self destructive speech on the 'stock'
of the nation. As Peter Jenkins has stressed, his pronouncements
ruled Joseph out of the successorship contest in the Conservative
Party, even as Powell's notorious 'rivers of blood' speech set him on
the path to the political wilderness. But their involuntary slaying of
their own ambitions as they extravagantly, in Pauline fashion, warned
the nation against the dangers of potency, does not mean these
eloquent and brilliant men ended their Commons careers without
having influenced and, in Powell's case, polluted the political environment of Britain.

Powell's oratory is considerable and compelling, and much of his
inimical influence stems from his rhetoric, but rhetoric has gone out
of fashion in the House of Commons. Already in the last Parliament
Powell and those of us oldies still insisting upon its use were only
deferentially tolerated by the younger MPs. We were soon to die or
retire and were therefore not felt to challenge them as they frenetically
compete with each other. Their vocabulary is poverty stricken, and
their style, if it exists at all, is anti-style. Their language is that of the
sociological and economic text book. Their contributions are well
researched, delivered fluently but unimaginatively. The accountant
has taken over and, ironically, nowhere is Karl Marx's Economic
Man more triumphant than in our monetarist and post-monetarist
period. Not man, but the desiccated calculating machine is in charge,
and, inevitably, with humanity denied, the computer blunders.

The speeches of the MPs become passionless, no longer inspirational, and part of the cause is that they do not now come to the
Commons versed in the classics or with the resources of the Bible at
their disposal. In the schools few are now taught Latin or Greek:
even lawyers can now qualify without knowing a word of Latin.
And the churches and synagogues are empty in our faithless Britain.
As Professor George Steiner has pointed out, the acquisitive reach of

the Hellenic and Hebrew articulation after so many centuries seems to have reached its limits. The vitality that informed the speeches of Disraeli and Gladstone or, in this century of Lloyd George or Churchill, seem spent: the greatest orator of my lifetime, Aneurin Bevan, determinedly secular as he was, entranced his audiences with concrete imagery which he had captured in the chapel culture, now dying, of the Welsh mining valley in which he was cradled.

The loss is grievous. It is not simply an aesthetic loss; it is a severe deprivation for our society. It cripples our capacity to shape the future (which Keith Joseph when he was Education Minister foolishly believed now lies only with our illiterate, numerate scientists), for the future, if it is to be created, requires political leadership with the capacity to provoke a metaphysical scandal. It requires, even as did the grammar of the prophets in Isaiah, the enforcement of the future tense, the extension of language over time. It requires prophecy of the type encapsulated in the United States more than twenty years ago by the Reverend Martin Luther King: 'I have a dream that one day this nation will rise up, and live out the true meaning of its creed: "we hold these truths to be self evident, that all men are created equal"'. And such a visionary metaphysical scandal cannot only defy time but, as we see in the turmoil in South Africa, it can transcend continents, and defy geography too. But, unhappily, in the Commons, the European Parliament and the United States Senate, the responses to the contemporary human predicament are miserably muted. All that is offered are words worn threadbare, filed down; too often words have become phantom words, the carcase of words as the politicians drearily chew and regurgitate the sound of them between their jaws. Mrs Thatcher takes elocution lessons and is tutored in humming, an artifice which it is claimed makes her speak more deeply and slowly, and so sound more statesmanlike[4] as unconvincingly she recites the words given her by failed playwrights: and as the president of the most powerful nation on earth looked at the banalities on his teleprinter, we became embarrassingly aware that a second-class cowboy actor had a Hollywood script to match his histrionic talents. We found no inspirational dreams there but only the nightmare of star wars.

Of course the new technology enabling the inarticulate deceptors to take by stealth the words of another has consequences other than the dissonances arising from the inauthenticity of the speaker's authorship. The arbiters of television, tutoring the politician, can gut him; for no orator can change the world without verbal violence. The speaker has always depended upon his aggression. Indeed, the aetiology of his rhetorical capacity reveals his oratory as a defence against his rages; that is why Freud taught us civilisation began when man first hurled abuse, not spears. And bearing witness to Freud's insight is the fact of the well-loaded myth that from Moses to Demosthenes to Churchill and Bevan, the eloquent stammerers have always been amongst the most violent of men. God punished the stutterer Moses for his ungovernable rage by refusing to permit this greatest of man's leaders ever to reach the Promised Land. Nye Bevan was to share a similar fate, for his oral aggression was feared by foe and friend, often in political terms proving counterproductive as it recoiled on him. His stammer was, at least in part, an unconscious attempt to regulate his intemperate attacks, but although his verbal aggression denied him the leadership to take Britain to the socialist millennium, it nevertheless gave us the magnificent result of a National Health Service that became a model for the world.

Orthodox television will have none of this; its ideal is the chat show. The producer slyly counsels the politician to tread softly, to remember he is speaking to 'the little old lady in the parlour'. He must simulate a false intimacy, speaking as to one although he knows he is talking to millions. Despite her elocution lessons this is not an act which Thatcher can successfully perform. The novelist Angela Carter, mocking at her attempts, has written, 'Of all the elements combined in a complex of signs labelled Margaret Thatcher, it is her voice that sums up the ambiguity of the entire construct. She coos like a dove, hisses like a serpent, bays like a hound . . . It is a voice from the past, a form of "toff speak" now reminiscent not of real toffs but of Wodehouse's aunts.'[5] But Thatcher is not the only politician who fails in her efforts, at television's behest, to convince the viewers that they are confidants, not part of a huge audience. Now, in a bid to escape the straitjacket, the fashion is to televise the conference or public meeting and then the political leader's attempt to confirm the prejudices of his immediate adulatory followers tends to disrupt his efforts to communicate with the millions of uncommitted viewers: the medium indeed becomes the message. There is little hope from such a platform that the orator will give us the Ciceronian union of wisdom and eloquence that teaches delights and moves men to virtuous living. Indeed, the more honest the man, the more likely the conventional television canons will ensnare him. His aggression mortified, his spontaneity suppressed in the service of these meretricious advertising techniques, he becomes stricken. On becoming leader of my party, Michael Foot – a superb, bellicose Parliamentary orator in his day and his moment – was trapped by his integrity. On television, his freedom forfeited, he became dumb; that we lost the election and now endure Thatcher is due in some little part to his inhibition. The orator must release not choke back his rage against stale establishment values if he is to move the people, but now, yielding to political opportunism and to their narcissism rather than a weighty evaluation of its full consequences, the MPs have taken the decision to bring television into the Chamber. If the potential of the men is less than the potential of the technology, the result could be a diminution not an enhancement of our democracy.

There are, however, some who will, with justification, sing hallelujah that politicians, partly through technology, may be deprived of their charisma. The use of demagogy at mass meetings in Germany and Italy this century has had awesome consequences that my generation cannot forget. Mussolini's short speeches were praised by his contemporary sycophantic journalists as comparable to Julius Caesar's. Veni, vidi, vici; a triadic affirmation ran through the arias of his operatic performances which were to encourage many to accept as reality his fantasies of a rebuilt Roman empire. And the demonic eruptions of Hitler, sweeping away a whole nation's conscience, engulfed millions in hell. The orator can move men to evil as well as good. In Britain no single speech in my lifetime has caused more continued havoc than Powell's pronouncement on immigration when, abusing his skills and knowledge, he gave his warnings in terms inevitably interpreted by many as legitimising racialism.

When the personal, the sexual, problems of the orator become enmeshed in the public domain, when his or her problems are acted out in socially resonating conditions, the results can be catastrophic. Despite the masculine display of uniform, big boots and spurs, Hitler certainly did no more than fumble in private with the pathetic Gelli, who shot herself in despair, and though Eva Braun also tried to shoot herself for love of Hitler, he never proved to be a fully potent lover. Consolation for private impotence can be found by politicians in multi-potence or in the omni-potence to be derived from the highly charged, introactive group situation of the huge public meeting or large conference where the orality of the orator can bring temporary balm to his deeply wounded self esteem and win him the full response which he has vainly sought to give and receive from women.

Such men often cannot bind flesh and the spirit into one. They frequently make a virtue out of their affliction, and acting as the scourges of their fellow men, they call on all mankind to suffer their dichotomies. Though they may deny it, they belong to the dualists, the campaigners for the Good against Evil, against Satan. Heretical Manichaean doctrine pervades their absolutist political philosophies and, if they are scholars, their intellectual rigour insists that they too must submit to the flagellation which all must endure. There are no more dangerous political leaders than those uncomfortable in their own sexuality. They have a capacity to displace their private and ceaseless battles against their turbulent instincts on to the public stage and, as producer, director, designer, and often superb scriptwriter, they create a play peopled with protagonists who act out for them all the facets of the Demiurge in whom they really believe. Not for them a god of love or justice but rather a belief that at the beginning, Darkness had invaded Light, and Adam, from whom we are corruptly descended, contained the sordid flesh as well as the spirit, always contending with each other.

What those influenced by the gnostics, with their claims to special knowledge and their explicit attachment to dualism, light and darkness, God and the devil, declared to be the true religion eighteen centuries ago, is now presented to us in political terms. In pursuing their fanatical heresies, our contemporary, life-denying leaders are no less insistent than their gnostic forbears for they suffer the same psychic fracture: body and soul are for them never one. There are public consequences of their personal fissures. 'How nicely does doggish lust beg a piece of the spirit when denied a piece of flesh!' declaimed Nietzsche's Zarathustra. And their monkish self-denials come to us in political doctrines possessed of vertebral refusals to compromise and ever scornful of consensus. The political heirs of the Encratite gnostics, who fanatically strained after a spirituality empty of all sensuousness, are to be found in the hard left and the hard right; among the followers of Benn, Powell and Joseph. If only these political ascetics would desist from presenting us with prescriptions to save society, and work through their internal conflicts *internally*, instead of externalising them in the political arena. But that is a vain hope, for there is one prescription they are ill-equipped to observe: for them charity can never begin at home.

★

Few in politics fit so appositely into Carl Jung's typology[6] than Keith Joseph, for Joseph displays almost all the characteristics which Jung labels as belonging to the introverted, thinking type. These are men forever intellectualising, overvaluing thought processes, searching for intellectual solutions for what are properly emotional problems. Their thought processes can become highly libidinised, and their predominant mode of self expression is not in relation to other people but in the world of thought; ideas tend to become substitutes for feelings, and intellectual values for emotional values. They are doubtless splendid Fellows of All Souls, but they make imperfect politicians, for, always faltering in any attempt to relate to others, they are forever creating misunderstandings, and then, with an air of bewilderment, apologising for their gaffes. Jung has written, 'Courtesy, amiability and friendliness may be present but often with a particular quality suggesting a certain uneasiness which betrays an ulterior aim, namely the disarming of an opponent who must at all costs be pacified and set at ease lest he prove a disturbing element.' The other person in reality may in no sense be an opponent, 'but if at all sensitive he will feel somewhat repelled, perhaps even depreciated. Invariably the other person has to submit to a certain neglect . . . Thus it happens that this type tends to disappear behind a cloud of misunderstanding . . . '

They also have other vulnerabilities; however subtle their intellectual propositions may be, there can be an astonishing infantilism displayed in their personal relationships. Jung observes, 'If he should have a chance to be understood, he is credulously liable to overestimate. Ambitious women have only to understand how advantage may be taken of this uncritical attitude . . . to make an easy prey of him. He lets himself be brutalised and exploited in the most ignominious way, if only he can be left undisturbed in his ideas.' Of such stuff are the Keith Josephs of this world made. Who but a high-minded intellectual of Keith Joseph's calibre could so absurdly tell us how stricken he is by Thatcher. 'My eyes light up at the sight of her, even though she is hitting me about the head so to speak.' Doubtless his eyes light up *because* his goddess hits him over the head; but not all of us pine for such masochistic pleasures.

His yearning for punishment seems to be boundless: his public recantations are notorious. As the minister responsible for the accursed high rise council flats, he was later to wallow in his blunder, never missing an opportunity to confess publicly his error: unfortunately the buildings could not be dismantled as easily as his original support for them.[7] Joseph may have enjoyed his lamentations but they brought little comfort to those attempting to live in them.

These *mea culpa* attitudes of Joseph are particularly familiar to me. For over thirty years he was my regular, punctilious and scrupulous pair, each week arranging, as far as our Whips would permit, our absences from the House to meet our outside political and social commitments. If through inadvertence, forgetfulness or sudden change of Parliamentary business, by error, one of us recorded our vote, Joseph was until the last days of the 1987 session, when both of us quit the Commons, disproportionately grieved and always determined to accept responsibility for the minor contretemps. Since he so evidently enjoyed blaming himself, and was so well-meaning a man, I rarely denied him the pleasure.

However, talking to him almost every week for over thirty years does not mean that I knew the man and I doubt if anyone else in Parliament established an intimate relationship with him. I can recall only two conversations in which this upright and honest Parliamentarian ever lifted to me the curtain behind which he lives. The first was when he screwed himself up to approach me to be his pair a few days after I had entered the House. Not surprisingly, though he had already been in the House for some years, his painful diffidence meant that he had established no link with any Labour MP and, consequently, had no pair. On that early meeting he must have felt compelled to present his credentials in order to obtain my agreement to his request, and I found this strikingly handsome, gazelle-like man – then very much what was later to be described as a 'wet' Tory – talking to me at great length on the Terrace of the Commons. And thirty years later, on the last day before we quit the Commons, both of us now old, and the stresses and ravages of our political lives showing all too plainly on our faces, he talked to me again.

He was not the only prominent Tory MP who approached me during that week. Leaving the Commons, for those who have served for decades, is a painful premonition of death and has the same finality. These men who so often had played a prominent part in the counsels of their party and of the nation were seeking solace; some knew they would be going on to the Lords but that was little consolation, for although the Upper Chamber may be fulfilling for those who enter it directly, for those who have been active MPs for years, it is seen as an ante-chamber to death. For a little while after they have been elevated, they nostalgically return to the Commons tea room or cafeteria but, no longer able to participate in the conspiracies and group projects of their former colleagues, they soon become even more aware of their estrangement and drift back into their limbo. Those proud Tory MPs who turned to me perhaps felt I had a little more resource to deal with our common predicament and wanted comfort. What we were experiencing was the crisis that has to be met by most others earlier in life: we were suffering our mid-life crisis in our old age.

The psychoanalysts[8] speak of the mid-life crisis as one taking place after our adolescence and early adulthood have been left behind, after we have emerged from that period of activity dominated by the development of our sexual relations, career, and family. All that intense outgoing activity defends us from the necessity of acknowledging the katabolic forces operating upon and within us, of the death instinct, and of the inevitability of death. But then there comes a time when the recognition can no longer be postponed and with the recognition comes the depressive anxiety of loss of youth, of opportunities and of more than half one's life. The resolution of the consequent crisis requires that the lost years of the past must be mourned, and only a mature love can foster a successful mourning. Love of oneself is needed, and acceptance of our badness as well as goodness, and a similar acceptance of our loved ones and their badness and goodness. And if we are fortunate to have adolescent children, the resolution of the crisis can also be facilitated by providing a mature love for those children, a happy counterpart to their own adolescent crisis. Professor Michael Allingham, one of the rare social scientists in Britain who, with the advantage of a personal analysis, is ready to deploy applied psychoanalysis, has succinctly explained, 'the adolescent crisis erupts because of the increasing force of the life instinct through emerging sexuality, and the mid-life crisis because of that of the death instinct through the recognition of mortality.'[9]

At Westminster, ageing and dying are not matters for discussion. If a prime minister tactlessly reshuffles a cabinet in a bid to present a more youthful party, an extraordinary wave of resentment sweeps through the House; for at the Royal Palace of Westminster life is held to be eternal. In a sense, indeed, this is true literally as well as metaphorically, for no one is permitted to die upon the premises. Members may collapse there but they always die outside. So intricate and elaborate are the inquest rules of a Royal Palace that medical co-operation can always be relied upon to ensure that nobody is pronounced dead within its precincts. And when a Member's death creates a by-election, the discussion immediately centres upon the size of his majority not upon the merits of the man: obituaries are left to *The Times*. No one is more determinedly blotted out than the Member who has died or retired; to speak of him would be too intrusive, and an unacceptable reminder of the fate from which no one can escape.

Given a supportive working culture of this order, the Member can ward off, by his constant frenetic political activities, the passing years; and these days other stratagems are permitted without comment: as my hair became increasingly white I observed the hair of so many of my colleagues, Reagan-like, became increasingly black. But when the day of reckoning comes, as come it must, it means it comes brutally and abruptly; for the Member stretches himself to the last day of his working life, avidly clinging on to his public acclaim, preferring to believe that the dissolution of Parliament will be later rather than sooner and that he still has ample time to adjust and ponder on his retirement. In the last Parliament a larger group of older MPs retired than at any time since 1945, and the customary anxieties of MPs fighting for election jelled with the depressive anxieties of these older men as the Prime Minister announced an election earlier than had been anticipated. In the last whimper of that Parliament, those retiring leaned on each other; for they feared the dissolution of Parliament meant their own dissolution. Inevitably, as Keith Joseph and I made our goodbyes to each other, the future had to be mentioned, and I attempted to reassure him, since it was clear to me he was not exempt from the apprehensions that beset all those about to leave the Commons after a lifetime's political service. I tried to intimate that the disorientation we both felt could be essentially healthy and constructive; that out of the temporary disintegration there can emerge a new configuration, and I hoped I could achieve it. I could see from the grimace on Keith Joseph's face that the fact that I was expressing hope and not certainty caused him hurt and surprise. His reaction was genuine (he is incapable of simulation), and he began to protest painfully. 'But', he expostulated, 'it is different for you.' Perplexed, wondering why my predicament was different from that of the man who, in his own terms, could look back at his ministerial successes and his role as *éminence grise* of the Thatcherite Tory Party, I clumsily asked him what advantage I had over him. The lonely, divorced man uncharacteristically released a strangled cry, 'But you, Leo, have your family.' Immediately embarrassed as we both were by his self-revelation, we entered a short awkward silence and then, perfunctorily, said goodbye knowing that after thirty years of pairing our contractual association had ended and we would not be in touch again.

Of course, in a sense, he was born into the loneliness he betrayed during that farewell. He was an only child but certainly not a mother's boy, for he has, at least by implication, rebuked his mother by asserting the improbable: that she had no influence on him. Nor could he have had, as a child, any sense of belonging to his own people, for his father denied him a barmitzvah and sent him off to Harrow, experiences not likely to mitigate a sense of estrangement. He inherited a baronetcy and considerable wealth, but such benefits can be poor substitutes; the glow of being brought up in a large, rumbustious, turbulent family and in a community full of wondrous myths and magic ceremonial is a richer inheritance. That was denied him.

Persistent, if not desperate, strangulation of affect – so visibly revealed on the sad occasion of our parting – inevitably has public consequences in the life of a public man. The over-controlled, self disciplined, ascetic public man, like all such men, finds that emotion cannot be extinguished by repression: they hit back, sometimes dramatically. Keith Joseph has often been described as the John the Baptist heralding-in Thatcher, a description congenial to those who, at least unconsciously, endow the Premier with the powers of the deity. But although Joseph was indeed Thatcher's precursor, a no less revealing comparison would be one made with Paul, whose repudiation of sensuousness made him a vulnerable candidate for a dramatic conversion. The sudden revelations of the Truth and extravagant repudiations of past sins are usually associated with religious, not political, experience, but Keith Joseph illustrates how politicians can take the road to Damascus. The outcome of inner struggles can find political as well as religious expression: for in each case the conversion is a bid to still unacceptable illicit passions.

We all know the date of Keith Joseph's blindingly dazzling conversion: he has pinpointed it himself. 'It was only in April 1974 that I was converted to conservatism. I had thought that I was a Conservative but now I see I was not one at all.'[10] He had found the true Light and the Way. Peter Jenkins claims that 'In conversations at that time he compared himself with a prophet come down from the mountain. Indeed there was an Old Testament ring to his cries of woe from the wilderness as he urged repentance from the wicked ways of socialism and beat his breast in immolation for his own part in the betrayal of the ark of the Conservative covenant.'[11] Even as Paul renounced the Torah as shit, so, in similar terms, did Joseph denounce past governments with which he had been associated, and declared, 'the reality is that for thirty years Conservative governments did not consider it practicable to reverse the vast bulk of accumulated detritus of socialism.'

In Freud's delightful essay, 'A Religious Experience', he tells with delicious irony of the reproachful letter he received from a fellow physician who had heard an inner voice which had brought him back to a belief in the Bible as God's Word. Freud politely explained to him that God had not done so much for him. 'He had never allowed me to hear an inner voice; and if, in view of my age, he did not make haste, it would not be my fault if I remained until the end of my life what I now was – an "infidel Jew".' But although Keith Joseph has on at least one occasion sought to invoke Freud in aid to justify his philosophy, that was a case of the devil quoting scripture for his purpose; I do not doubt that just as Joseph would never identify himself, as I do, as an 'infidel Jew', so too Joseph would find highly unacceptable Freud's explanation of the particular Oedipal conflicts which can precipitate sudden conversions accompanied by intemperate repudiations of past sinfulness. Freud emphasises how, for the adult, a particular event in the present can reawaken aspects of the

child's Oedipal struggles, and how those conflicts can be displaced
into the sphere of philosophy. Even if one could hazard a guess as to
what were the particular personal external events that acted as the
precipitate for Joseph's exhibitionist self-flagellation and fervid conversion, to explore them in excessive detail would no doubt be an
intrusion into the very limited rights of privacy a politician can claim.
Nevertheless, the public consequences of that conversion were indeed
to be far reaching. Keith Joseph's suffering and agonising were
unloaded on to the nation, and many in the Conservative Party and
in the nation were ready to accept them and to hearken to the
self-proclaimed prophet, for there were confusions abroad and it is
in such seasons that those who claim new visions and certainties are
given deference. In more confident times, the political fanatic, the
psychopathic and severely paranoid leader is treated with disdain, or
in a mental hospital. The ravings of Hitler would, in a healthier
society, have qualified him for the madhouse, not the leadership of
Germany. But even in Britain's milder political climate where our
crises are not as severe as those of the Weimar Republic and our
leaders not so aberrant, there are, nevertheless, societal conditions
which give rare opportunities to the prophet-politician.

Keith Joseph and I belong to a people who have a history of a high
turnover in prophets and messiahs. Most of these characters were
totally spurious but the rabbis have always had great difficulty
in coping with them, from Jesus down to the extraordinary seven-
teenth-century flagellationist and self-proclaimed Messiah, Sabbatai
Zevi of Smyrna. He attracted tens of thousands of Jewish followers
who ranged from the merchant princes of Amsterdam to the poor of
Asia Minor. Faced with the problem of having rejected Christ but
still maintaining that the Messiah was yet to come, rabbis always
had the wisdom to insist whenever a new Messiah emerged that he
was a false one. They were faced with a dilemma, however, because
since ancient times, it has been a commonplace amongst the rabbis
that the Messiah would come to redeem his people at the darkest
hour before the dawn, when conditions seemed to be at their worst.[12]
As the darkest hours of our Jewish history are legion, so are our false
messiahs.

The admonitory lesson to be learned is when the framework of
society is dangerously rusted and catastrophe threatens, beware the
prophet-politician. It cannot be disputed that by the mid-1970s,
confidence in Britain had ebbed. No one has more thoughtfully
delineated the nature of this bewilderment than David Marquand.[13]
He believes that by this time, the set of commitments, assumptions,
and expectations which transcended party conflicts, and was shared

by the great majority of the country's political and economic leaders, providing the framework within which policy decisions were made, had collapsed. Successive governments had found their implicit, neo-Keynesian economic doctrines were not providing the desired and expected results. Their failure had left political and economic leadership dispirited, and imprisoned by their tacit acceptance of long established utilitarian philosophy, and having become little more than unsuccessful technocrats, they were without intellectual or moral resource to overcome the mounting problems.

Marquand's presentation has considerable force; no one in the Commons during the 1970s can forget how repeatedly at Westminster it was said that Britain was ungovernable. The political leaders of the period characteristically sought to exculpate themselves from their own incapacity by projecting it on to their electorate. At such a juncture, when long-held illusions have been shattered, the time is ripe for the coming of the prophet-politician: with his lamentations he brings the Truth, and calls upon the truly faithful to follow him. Whatever personal precipitate occasioned Keith Joseph's revelation of April 1974, his arrival was awaited by a multitude who were lost, bewildered and hopeless. He had found the Way and lemming-like they followed him down the well-worn path away from illusion and disillusion towards delusion.

The nation, Joseph preached, needed 're-moralising': we must repent for if we do not 'the nation moves towards degeneration' and, like all old-time evangelists, first he had to induce guilt and shame – acknowledgment of sin was the prerequisite to rebirth. 'The worship of instinct, of spontaneity, the rejection of self-discipline is not progress . . . ' Then, abandoning the burden of intellectual rigour, the academic – in an orgy of self-indulgence – offered us the inspiration of the second of his *femmes fatales*. 'Let us take inspiration from that admirable woman Mary Whitehouse . . . a shining example of what one woman can do. She has mobilised and given fresh heart to many . . . ' The banality of Whitehouse and her lashing of Britain's concupiscence appear irresistible to the guilt-laden, submitting Joseph.

Perhaps most significant of all was the inevitable comfort and strength he received from her because she had 'set out to protect adolescents against the permissiveness of our times'. Child psychiatrists have pointed out that at the time when a man's children become adolescents, he can experience what is described as 'decompensation in retrospect'.[14] The adolescent child prompts the reactivation of the father's own adolescent struggles with auto-erotic, homosexual and Oedipal conflicts. Few fathers are likely, when faced with their adolescent children, to be unmoved by the reverberations which echo their own struggle to cope with the threat once felt to their own authority as a clamorous sexuality assailed them. The classic defence used by the adolescent to cope with his newly aroused sexual impulses is to deploy the defence mechanism of projection, to work out the sexual revolution against his father and against all the institutions of his father's generation. Adolescence is the period of rebellion and it befits the adolescent: but it is not fitting for influential middle-aged men, on becoming fathers of adolescents, to over-react to their own reawakened adolescent passions by imprisoning themselves, by condemning adolescent 'permissiveness', and by calling upon the nation to wear hair shirts.

Economic theories, however, can, although apparently sophisticated and rational, often be little more than psychological prejudices. The critique of post-war Conservatism that Joseph developed in 1974, and which became the blueprint for Thatcher's government, is replete with Joseph's self-chastisement. Stern monetarist doctrines were needed, cuts must be ruthlessly made in welfare expenditure, spendthrift policies and departments must be outlawed, unemployment must be endured and we must shed the feeling that 'somehow the lean and tightlipped mufflered men in the 1930s dole queues were at least partly our fault.' Only through suffering can a nation ultimately find strength and joy. The Centre for Policy Studies set up in 1974 by Joseph and Thatcher to serve as their 'think tank' was less cerebral than it claimed; instead, by way of highly refined rationalisations, Joseph's masochism was institutionalised. And with such backing, when the battle for leadership came, Joseph – the sole front-bencher to give Thatcher full support – found that the bewildered backbench peasants were ready to respond to his masochistic pleas; and together, with exquisite relief they submitted to She.

★

No less a herald of the coming of Thatcher was Enoch Powell. No single man did more to promote what Peter Jenkins has perceptively identified as 'the general angst' and which Jenkins sees as the societal condition which led to Thatcher's emergence and, I believe, to her dominance. Powell's significance, therefore, cannot be overestimated: he is both a cause and a symptom of the ethos which provided Thatcher with the opportunity to gain power. An attempt to divine the public consequences of the particular psychodynamic and psychopathology of Thatcher would indeed be incomplete if, out of distaste or disapproval, we evaded a scrutiny of the man who was

her precursor: his dark moods cast the shadows from which, to his
chagrin, the intellectually inferior Thatcher, not he, emerged.

Enoch Powell is a man whose antipathy to me is matched only by
my antipathy to him. Only once in the last twenty years have I spoken
to him, and that is an occasion I regret. His public proclamations were
always, of course, intended to mark his entry as the hero, and that a
heroine should upstage him was no part of the scenario. That unfore-
seen result was mourned by Michael Foot in his seductive elegy on
the demise of Powell.[15] He regards the notorious race speech of
Powell as a bewildering aberration, and that it led to Powell being
barred from the premiership is regarded by Michael Foot as a 'tragedy
for all of us'. That massive misjudgment springs not only from
Michael Foot's most serious flaw – his generosity – it also comes
about because he shares some of Powell's dominating obsessions.
Both men are besotted with the Commons and their delight is to be
from afternoon till night in the Chamber; both are entranced by
the magic and sanctity of the British Constitution; both abandon
themselves shamelessly to the wondrous sovereignty of Parliament;
and both would jealously guard their beloved institutions against the
dictates of the bureaucrats, technocrats and all those Edmund Burke
berated as 'sophisters, economists and calculators', particularly, in
Powell and Foot's case, if they come from foreign lands.

But there is one dangerous obsession with which Michael Foot is
happily not afflicted, and that is the most dangerous of all Powell's
obsessions, and the one which tells us most of the man. Indeed,
although Powell in his speeches and writings totally eschews the
autobiographical, his commanding rhetoric in no way camouflages
his most personal compulsions: on the contrary, his exotic language
illuminates them. There is no major contemporary political figure –
although the simple may think otherwise – who possesses a career
trajectory so lacking in enigma and mystery, for Powell's very
articulateness makes him, unlike lesser politicians, painfully and
pathetically self-revelatory. No politician has so dramatically advertised his vain efforts to emancipate himself from his most fearful
obsession: and that obsession is with birth.

Obsessional behaviour always tells us of desperate efforts to cage
and contain anxiety; our word 'anxiety' has Sanskrit roots signifying
an association with narrowness or restriction. Tracing the source of
anxiety, Freud made the connection between fear and the act of birth.
With its attendant profound changes of physiological environmental
conditions and its manifold dangers and discomforts, birth becomes
the prototype of all situations of a threatening or disquieting nature,
or in which life itself is threatened. Our anxieties may have their

origin in our initial fears as we made our passage through the narrow vagina; our ears are linked with pressure and shortness of breath which constitute the most menacing and terrifying aspects of the birth process.[16] No man born of woman can escape the trauma: and indeed politicians and journalists possessed of the vanity that they are the great opinion-formers should glance at our modern astrologers who in almost every journal in the land tell millions of their eager readers how to face their destiny for the month. Astrology, of course, is the first doctrine of the birth trauma, teaching that the entire being and fate of man is determined by what occurs at the very moment of birth, and what occurs during those crucial moments can, the astrologers claim, be discovered by the reading of the stars. Although Ronald and Nancy Reagan think otherwise, their claim is fanciful, but the validity of the belief in the determining influence on every individual of his own particular parturition is rationally unchallengeable.

There have been pioneer psychoanalysts (now unfashionable) like Otto Rank, who insisted that so overwhelming was the influence of the birth trauma, and so seductive was the call to return to the trouble-free safety of the womb, that anxiety at birth forms the base of every anxiety or fear, and every pleasure has, as its final aim, the re-establishment of the intra-uterine primal pleasure. Only the fear that the way back to total bliss would mean enduring yet again the terror of birth inhibits us from attempting the retreat. But we create in our myths our consolations. All the tales of the heroes,[17] recounted in so many different cultures, from Sargon the founder of Babylon, to Moses, Cyrus, Romulus and Jesus, bestow upon us similar compensations. We identify with these heroes, whose births are magical, whose real fathers are not those who tended them, but kings or divinities. In our worship of such heroes we are not only expressing our hostility to our fathers and seeking to deny them and ennoble ourselves, we are engaged in an even more cunning strategy: we are also seeking what Rank described as the cancellation of our own birth, and trying to erase all the terrors associated with our parturition.

Rank wrote *The Trauma of Birth* more than sixty years ago but its perception in one form or another resurfaces again and again. That influential guru of the 1960s and 70s, the anti-psychiatrist, R. D. Laing,[18] taught that we are haunted by and re-enact our conception, foetal life, and birth, and the loss of the cord and the placenta; and, he believed, our birth experiences, in the same way as our pre-natal experiential patterns, function as templates for some of the patterns woven into the complex knit of post-natal design. Rank always insisted that the later traumas: the shock of weaning and – during our Oedipal phase – the intense fear of undergoing castration, have the benign purpose of absorbing some of the original, fatal anxiety-affect forever threatening us; and that the genital trauma of castration should be regularly fantasised in the history of an individual is an obvious consequence, since 'the female genitals, being the place of the birth trauma soon again becomes the chief object of the anxiety-affect originally arising there.' It is not, therefore, surprising that those whom we note are fated to be forever struggling to overcome their primal anxiety are men uncomfortable in their sexuality and monkish by temperament. The vagina is to be feared: for them, it is not an object of desire.

Powell's outrageous race speech, wholly based upon a comparison of the birth statistics of immigrants with those of the indigenous population, was most certainly not the demagogy of a vulgar popu- list. That coarse interpretation fails to understand that Powell's maso- chism is more likely to prompt him to court unpopularity than acclaim. Nor, as Hailsham alleged, was it an elliptical challenge to Heath and the Tory leadership, for there is no deviousness in Powell. On the contrary, his existential need is to obtain constant reactive responses which act as corroboration for him of his personal identity, and he teases out such responsiveness not by a sly politician's trick but by open and ceaseless provocative confrontation. I do not understand why Michael Foot in his essay on Powell expresses bewilderment and searches in vain for the reasons for Powell's devastating eruption. Powell, although blind to his own predicament, is an honest man and we should take him at his word. His speech was explicit: it was about Birth and Anxiety – he was overwhelmed by an anxiety which he wrongly believed sprang from his cold, pitiless mathematics. Its real source was in a more menacing undergrowth.

This need and this capacity to convert his private anxieties into public anxieties is striking; the personal terrors, loaded with grim forbodings, are translated into alarmist jeremiads warning the world in apocalyptic terms of the coming disasters. Warding off his own private devils, he sends them scurrying into the world of public affairs. Powell was against the excesses of a spending, profligate society and he became the first great ascetic prophet of monetarism – long before Keith Joseph or Nigel Lawson were champions of that creed. In flawless English, he spelt out the tortured doctrines of Hayek and Schumpeter. He preached what Michael Foot describes as 'his suffocating economic theory' and, subliminally, Foot's choice of words intimates the unconscious source of Powell's irrational bid to choke the industrial economy of Britain. His private trauma, as he gathered disciples, was to become the trauma endured by our manufacturing industries.

His speeches are always suffused with anxiety: the implication being that the consequences of ignoring his warnings will be utter disaster. He defended his British Constitution with inspired xenophobia, telling us of the woe the Common Market must bring. For Powell, 1992 is Armageddon. When his anxiety is put into the service of his formidable intelligence, it can result in the most challenging of analyses. His scoffing of Britain's retention of the bomb falls into that category. But more usually, the anxious-affect drenches the argument, leaving it distorted and exaggerated. In the notorious race speech there was no conscious political calculation, as his enemies have often suggested. On the contrary, Powell was out of control; his anxiety drove him over the top. As he, in a rare unguarded moment, revealed, 'In 1968 I did not know there was a precipice. It was an elephant pit . . . '

His excitement over birthrates are, I believe, reverberations of a birth trauma, reverberations which are also echoed in his publicly expressed yearning to be a monk (a vocation for which he is indeed temperamentally suited). Powell's persistent fascination with the birthrates of blacks – the subject continued to dominate subsequent speeches – is surely essentially prurient: he fears the blacks' sexual and progenitive capacity. But men and women more comfortable in their sexuality do not forever act as calculating-machine voyeurs, adding up the congresses of their fellow citizens.

Infuriated by the havoc his speech and his subsequent apologies caused, and indeed continue to cause, twice in the Commons I have said that if there were fewer eunuchs in this country there would be fewer Enochs. The responsive laughter my comment provoked ensured that Powell would never speak to me again, but that is a deprivation I have borne lightly, for I believe no forgiveness should ever be extended to Powell for those merciless speeches – speeches which even twenty years later he continues to justify.[19]

I have, I admit, my special prejudices on the issue. Even as I write this essay in my study, I am overlooked by a large coloured photograph taken some 110 years ago in Swansea of my great grandfather on his arrival, penniless, from the Russian Pale. But he arrived carrying proudly and confidently with him the ethics that have acted as one of the main civilising influences of Europe. The blacks have brought no such baggage. They have not the lineage of the people belonging to the Book; their research into their genealogy comes to a full stop with a bill of sale. The most rabid anti-semitism is more forgivable than attacks on the blacks: understanding may make it possible to forgive irrational attacks on the strong; but such charity must never, never, be extended to attacks, however unselfconscious, on the weak.

The actual precipitate for Powell's speech was not, of course, the immigration of blacks from the West Indies, but the coming to Britain of the Asians from East Africa. Powell was fighting against their entry from Kenya despite past pledges given to them at the time of the granting of independence to Kenya. This incensed me still further, for a sojourn in Kenya with the RAF during the war had taught me how the worthless white settlers ensured that the Asians, originally brought by Britain to Kenya as indentured labour to build the East-African railway, suffered severe discrimination. They were given no option but to become small traders, and survived only too often by exploiting the Africans. I had seen them suffering the same dilemmas as afflicted the Jews in Russia of whom I had heard so much at my favourite grandfather's knee as he recounted to me his experiences as a boy in the pogroms of Tsarist Russia. These memories were powerfully evoked when I witnessed Powell seeking to block the escape route of the Kenyan Asians from the pogroms threatening them.

Powell has, however, always insisted that he is without racial prejudice and that the point his speech made was that 'numbers were of the essence'. He maintained all he had talked about was numbers and that it was the 'present trend' of births that prompted his alarums. And indeed the imagery he employed to put his case lends corroboration to his defence that it was births not colour which aroused his concerns. He deduced from the number of projected births the dangers which would arise, and then left the consequences to the imagination. The central image of Powell's speech was his quote from Virgil of the Sibyl's vision of the Tiber foaming with blood. The river, as psychoanalysts have long explained, is a womb symbol, and the association of blood with birth is well illustrated by Rank – in any case, it hardly requires Freudian insights to divine its relevance. Powell's language speaks without dissimulation; the tremors of the birth experience reverberate throughout the fateful speech.

Yet one is left with unease: many have found it difficult to accept his disavowal of racialism, however severely insistent he may be in rejecting the charge. Prejudices are not always conscious and known to those who peddle them. As the practitioners of the curious theology of the Dutch Reform Church of South Africa make clear, those possessed of a profound belief in original sin can easily believe a special curse falls upon the sons of Ham who must now pay the price for their alleged ancestor's mockery of Noah's nakedness. For those Boers, the black is forever associated with wrong-doing and evil. And none of us escape from describing the dark passions: we do not speak of white as sin but of black as sin. The more the spirit and the flesh are severed, the more becomes the hostility to what are felt as threatening dark passions: sin is black and sex is black and dirty.

Antagonism to and fear of the dark man's sexual endowment finds its ultimate expression in laws and taboos against miscegenation. They have been created by white men to ward off the fantasised threat of a black man endowed with a more vigorous sexuality luring the white woman; and the prohibitions against sexual coupling between black and white reinforce the restraints of the white men. Torn by their ambivalences to sex, feared as joy, suffered as agony, they need the protection from temptation which anti-miscegenation laws or social conventions afford them. Embedded within many of the various creeds of Protestantism, particularly those with puritanical emphases, are notions which can be speedily triggered into hostility against the black man. Powell has his own special interpretation of Christianity, one that has brought him on not a few occasions in conflict with Church leaders. For my part, I always find he reminds me of the Cathars, the courageous thirteenth-century heretics of Languedoc, who to become 'parfait' advocated celibacy and suicide, both ideals negating the physical side of our nature. Powell also feels guilty in living, and has more than once expressed his dismay that, unlike many of his comrades, he survived the war. And it is indeed the life-negating not the life-enhancing moods of his politics which make them so dangerous and seductive: such politics can carry with them pernicious prejudices.

Powell was not, however, always a Christian. As a younger man he was a declared and committed atheist, and doubtless affirmed his disbelief with his customary display of dazzling logic. But disbelief and faith are not necessarily mere cerebral creatures; it would not be excessively reductive or speculative to trace his oscillations between godlessness and belief to the formative influences of his early familial life. For Powell was not born into a kingdom but, as his admiring but painstaking biographer Roy Lewis tells us, he entered into a family which was 'a republic of three persons'.[20] And within that republic his biographers agree there was an intense alliance between the young Enoch and his school-teacher mother.[21] The father played a decidedly lesser role, leaving his wife to shape the gifted child into a mental athlete; and to perform her task the mother gave up teaching and made the child her single pupil.

Predictable consequences can flow from such an austere, intense family unit in which loyalty is not ceded to the father and whose foundation rests upon a coalition of mother and child. The narcissism of the child can be excessively corroborated by the admiring mother and then, insufficiently mortified by a strong containing father, the child is left to grow up permeated by a haughty grandiosity. This trait, although often successfully borne by Powell's formidable intellect, is nevertheless one of the least engaging elements in his make-up, and has been a severe handicap throughout his political career. In addition, the elimination of the father in the early years of the child from any claim to priority can lead, in adolescence and later, to a pronounced bias against father-asserting surrogates or philosophies or religions perceived as surrogates. God the Father was clearly not tolerable to Powell as a young man and in his atheism he denied Him priority as his own father had been denied.

God the Son was to prove another matter entirely. The isolation of the only child growing up in a literary, non-gregarious family, overvaluing the word and seemingly deficient in human relationships outside the books, could not be sustained. The atheist must walk and die in his own footsteps, his eternity limited to his work and his children, and although Powell has said 'unless one is alone one is unimportant', he lacked the resource to maintain that position. He turned to, and identified himself with, his Saviour, ready to emulate his Redeemer and to sacrifice himself for what he believed to be the true word. The political sophisticates who are astonished by Powell's renunciation in 1974 of his safe seat and power base at Wolverhampton, rather than fight under what he believed to be Heath's false banner, do not understand their man. He was acting out his needs; and lacking, as ever, subtlety or pretence, he made this explicit to those attuned to listen. After briefly announcing his decision not to participate in what he described as 'a fraudulent election', he remained silent for two weeks except for one public intervention, and that was his little noticed sermon entitled 'The Meaning of Christian Sacrifice; the Road to Calvary'. Powell was indeed with masochistic relish on his way, enjoying every moment at the stations of his cross. To those who accused him of being a Judas he retorted, with full justification, that he received no reward for his services. His critics misunderstand his role; his mimesis was no fringe part in the drama. His grandiosity, always teetering on the edge of omnipotence, insisted he was the central figure and as such he endured his political crucifixion.

The heroic stance, always requiring a smudging of the relationship with the natural father, is the corollary of the specially intensive relationship between mother and child; and Powell is no exception to the general rule. Indeed, the consistency of his political views shows how little elasticity is at his disposal. His emotional ties to his mother keep him firmly on track and first the British Empire and later Britain were his supreme mother surrogates. The issues in which he has played an heroic part have always been a defence of his motherland. Once he belatedly grasped that entry into the European Community was not merely a commercial transaction but had political unification as its goal, the notion of his motherland being usurped by foreign elements was found to be intolerable; and no one fought with greater stamina against Heath and those of us supporting entry into Europe than Powell. He believed he was rescuing his mother from a fate worse than death. When he lost his fight he taunted the British with having enjoyed the 'rape of their national and parliamentary independence'.[22]

He has a singular weakness for mother surrogates and if they can be so constructed as to be congruent to Britain, then his political judgment deserts him. His romantic imperialism was part of this behavioral pattern. His language when he wrote of India was of a lovesick swain: 'India claimed me almost from the first moment there. I started to love and learn thirstily. I bought and read omnivorously anything about India I could lay hands on.' There are more than shades of the instructing teacher-mother as he learns from India, and practises his Urdu among Indian villagers. His love, of course, was blind. His failure to see the realities of the situation is clearly revealed in the crazy plan which he put to Churchill in 1946 to take and hold India with ten divisions.[23] His most recent biographer[24] suggests that the tale of this desperate plan is a canard, but Rab Butler, not given to such fantasising, always insisted on its existence; and Butler's affirmations have the ring of truth. Powell could not bear to see his loved one wrenched from him, and fumed against the grant of Independence, but when he had mourned his loss, he saw it as it was. He was helped by a psychoanalytical insight to free himself from his fixation to Empire and India, for he has written: 'So the psychoanalysis through which lies the cure for Britain's sickness has to be two-fold: first, we must identify and overcome the mythology of the late Victorian Empire; then, we must penetrate to deeper levels and eradicate the fixation with India from our subconscious.'[25] But this attempt, at one remove, to examine his own motivation, is incomplete. It gave him the intellectual courage to discard his whole concept of a world role for Britain but then, when he began to re-think Britain's national status, he still remained locked into his compelling need for some mother surrogate. The boundless passion he had bestowed on the British Empire was now concentrated upon

Britain itself, and from then on he was to devote a lifetime to defending his motherland with a xenophobic fervour.

When the devolution issue arose, our political paths crossed. Powell saw the government's attempt to placate the Scots and Welsh nationalists as a further step towards the dismemberment of the nation-state to which he owed total allegiance. It was as a supreme British nationalist, jealous of any interference with our existing, carefully evolved Parliamentary institutions, that he commenced battle against the government's Devolution Bill.

My opposition to the Bill had a quite different source. It was founded upon the internationalism of the South Wales socialist movement in which I was cradled. The fundamental allegiances of the miners' leaders whose teachings had so influenced me were expressed in their call upon workers of all lands to unite. In my youth I had recoiled from the Welsh Nationalist leaders who, in those pre-war years, had had heavy flirtations with French fascism; and although in post-war years their leaders' approach had different emphases, their policies beckoned Wales into a cul-de-sac.

One of the important strands of Welsh socialism was its anarcho-syndicalist tradition. The essential sense of locality; the small pit or forge where all worked, when work was available; the comparative isolation of valley villages or townships; the central role of the local miners' lodge; the cinemas and breweries owned by the miners; and the local health schemes which were to become the prototype of the National Health Service, all created a world – now sadly slipping away – where an intense loyalty was made to the immediate community. The commitment did not end there: there were miners' leaders who in the early days of the movement had taught communities to have international links with syndicalists in other lands, and those attitudes were implicit in the South Wales Labour Movement. It was the rhetoric of the miner-novelist, Lewis Jones – the man who would attend the Comintern conferences in Moscow and who, alone of all the world-wide delegates, would refuse to stand up when Stalin arrived – and the fervour of the sensitive Arthur Horner, president, during my boyhood, of the South Wales miners, that took me into the Labour Movement. These men, although declared communists, were in constant conflict with the Communist Party machine; although Moscow detained Horner for many months in an attempt to 'correct' his attitude, they could never cast him into the Stalinist mould. He was not the man to yield priority to Stalin's fatherland even if it claimed to be a socialist country; such an exclusive patriotism was not part of the ethos of the Labour Movement in Wales. Our allegiance was to the locality and to the world, and nationalist flag-waving, Russian, Welsh or English, was anathema to those of us shaped in such a society. A proposal to limit centralised power and initiate more participatory forms of local and regional government throughout Britain would have dovetailed into a syndicalist socialist tradition: but what, out of political opportunism, was intended to be imposed on Wales was an institution which I believed would fall prey to ugly chauvinist and divisive nationalist prejudices. So it came about that, ironically, on the issue of devolution, I found myself as a cosmopolitan in alliance with the great British patriot: in politics one learns that it is possible to choose one's enemies but not one's allies.

Yet, at the end of the day, none of the main protagonists in those fierce Parliamentary battles over the Devolution Bill determined the result. Neither Powell, brave Tam Dalyell or myself can claim the victory. Nor can John Smith, Michael Foot or John Morris, all of whom so persistently and persuasively attempted from the Front Benches to put the Bill through, blame themselves for their defeat. The man who primarily stopped the major and fundamental change within our constitution is an unrecorded and unsung anti-hero. Although a brief telling of the untold tale may shift attention from this theme of the role of Thanatos, through his intermediaries, in our contemporary political life, the recounting of the story for its own sake may be justified. Perchance it will puncture some of the portentousness with which we politicians are afflicted, and mock at our belief that it is the magic of our words that moves mountains; and it may be an admonition to those who, afflicted with one form or another of historicism, would, in their historical tomes, as they claim to divine the forces operating within past or present societies, unwisely dismiss the strength and frailties of individual human beings as unimportant irrelevancies.

There is one further justification for telling the story in this study of Thatcher. It was in the aftermath of the collapse of the devolution proposals that the shabby Parliamentary alliance between Labour and the minority parties wore too thin to endure, and the Callaghan government fell. A major political event always has a multiple causation but it is one of the ironies of recent political history that, even as Christine Keeler played her part in bringing down Macmillan's government and elevating Wilson to the premiership, so, no less, another inadequate played a significant part in precipitating the election of 1979 which was to bring Margaret Thatcher to power.

★

A year or two before the Devolution Bills came before the House, the Whips' office telephoned me and asked if I would talk to Dan Jones, the MP for Burnley. Such a request in itself was not unusual; an inexperienced Member needing help on some drafting detail or one requiring guidance over a Private Member's Bill, or wanting legal advice to reply to a constituent's query, often found his way to me on the suggestion of the Whips; but this was different, and I knew immediately it meant Dan Jones was in serious trouble. He would swallow hard before he approached me, for he bore me a long sustained grudge and had always shown it in his demeanour. As the organiser in Wales for the engineering union he had been the firm favourite when, in 1958, the seat in Pontypool fell vacant and a selection conference was called. He had a limited intellect but an unlimited guile which he effectively used on behalf of his union members but which failed him, despite his legitimate stratagems, at Pontypool, when, to his surprise and dismay, I was selected. Although he shortly afterwards gained the Burnley seat he never forgave me, for his heart and roots were in Wales where he had been king and with which he always maintained his connections. In Lancashire, although he worked hard for his constituency, he always felt a displaced person.

My premonition was soon fulfilled; full of anxiety he reluctantly, and with considerable gaps, spelt out the dismal convoluted tale in the usual self-accusatory, self-justifying manner of the guilty man, so familiar to those of us who have been criminal lawyers. There was no novelty in the ignoble story; in one form or another I had heard it many times before in Wales. There, out of extended family ties, within the community a system of kinship can grow and favours are given and returned by those able to exercise them which can go beyond the bounds of propriety. There is value in a widely spread kinship-system giving, as it did, supportive help in a South Wales once so severely stricken by economic deprivation. But it has its dangers. The favours and patronages of those with a little influence working within such a kinship-system can move from kindness and concern to corruption, and Dan Jones had crossed the boundaries. Already the underground press was nibbling away and, indeed, shortly after he first saw me, *Private Eye* began publishing its version of events; and I realised as he spoke to me that if it had not already commenced, it would not be long before a police probe would begin.

It was not easy to protect poor Dan from himself for his religious fundamentalism made him ashamed of his conduct and I feared that he might, out of guilt, blurt out some fatal confession to the authorities. And I also had to protect myself, for he indulged in no exegetical or anagogical interpretations of the Bible: he believed literally, and he thought that the least he could do in return for my help was to save me from my disbelief – I was more concerned that he should avoid judgment in this world than that I should suffer in the next. Twice in my Commons room the police questioned Dan, where, under my tutelage, he gave replies and signed carefully drafted statements. Although he was no client of mine, I was engaged in the chess game which is the role and duty of the defending solicitor: in the end the police, thus balked, gave up and concentrated their attentions on others involved in the affair. For a while this brought dangers of blackmail and I had to help Dan Jones skate over very thin ice. But in the end with more guarded statements given to his local press, which had begun to carry the story, he reached safe land. His travail had lasted some twelve months and when it was over he remained embarrassingly grateful, ever seeking me out to see if there was anything he could do to help me. There was nothing I wanted from him – until the coming of the second Devolution Bill.

The government had lost the first Devolution Bill, largely through filibustering. But to survive, the precariously poised government made its shabby deal with the Nationalist and Liberal Members and were determined to bring in a second Bill and this time, if necessary, to use the guillotine to put the Bill upon the statute book. It was clear to me that only the people of Scotland and Wales themselves could stop what I regarded as a massive act of opportunist folly. I decided to put on the Order Paper what is described as a reasoned amendment to the second, and vital, reading of the Bill to call upon the House to refuse its passage unless the government first agreed to a referendum which would be conducted on the issue in Scotland and Wales. Such reasoned amendments when sponsored by a Private Member are very occasionally used as an expression of opinion by Members, but are rarely called to be debated and voted upon: it is within the absolute discretion of the Speaker whether to permit debate, and convention meant that the calling by the Speaker of a backbencher's amendment on such a momentous second reading was almost an impossibility.

Now I started to play my cards. I called Dan in, for I knew as an old-time Welsh trade unionist he would have no sympathy with nationalist sentiments. I told him I wanted a hundred signatures to the amendment I intended framing, and that it was his onerous task to get them, half at least from Labour members with whom he must begin. I have rarely seen a man so delighted: in some curious way he was to regard this difficult duty that I imposed upon him not only as an expression of thanks to me but as a massive act of reparation for the unseemly conduct which had initially brought him to me. He was of course ideal as a Welshman to circulate quietly among his English colleagues, cajoling, flattering, wheedling, scoffing at any notion that every signature added was a nail in the government's coffin, for he was the supremo of the tea room, forever whiling away his time, gossiping with those of his kind.

There was always a substantial number of Members, many trade union war-horses, whose ambitions rested when they became MPs. They diligently looked after their constituencies where they enjoyed esteem but lacked the will and usually the capacity to become distinguished Parliamentarians: they were, to be unkindly blunt, the reliable lobby fodder. Those who thirst for the Front Bench diligently woo these men's votes for the annual Parliamentary party election and so have some acquaintanceship with them, but since this had never been my aspiration I was on but nodding terms with most of them; and I was aware they treated me with respect but with suspicion. I lacked the capacity to approach them with success; and I am sure Dan's inconsequential, illogical persuasions, laced no doubt with tales of yore and a dozen other excursions, were far more effective than any principled, logical argument I could have put to them.

All Dan's communications, even when he was talking to one or two, were to an audience and were indistinguishable in manner from his occasional speech in the Chamber where, with a fine Welsh voice and flailing arms, he poured out a jumble of sentences lacking coherence and syntax, leaving his listeners bewildered but giving him, as was quite clear when he sat down, great satisfaction. When as a union organiser he had addressed his mass audiences of shop stewards and workers at the factory gates, he must have left them bemused, but satisfied to leave matters entirely in the hands of one so evidently fluent and confident. And I had the same confidence in him when, out of the corner of my eye, I saw him assiduously laughing and joking with his union colleagues determined, in the end, no matter how long it took, to get their pen to his paper. Dan may have lacked intellect but certainly not intelligence and he possessed an empathetic quality which enabled him, usually by flattery, to gain his victory. Each night as I was leaving the House he would triumphantly come up to me reporting his progress but I doubt, in his preoccupation with his task, whether he really had any appreciation of the consequences that could flow and did flow from his assiduity.

While he was at work I tackled Francis Pym, who was leading the opposition to the Bill, telling him of my intended bid for a referendum and urging him to give it support. But, not surprisingly, Pym was hesitant: his attachment to Parliament had a proud lineage; his ancestors were in the House centuries ago and I do not doubt that like myself he has a distaste for referenda, which by their nature diminish the role of Parliament, making Members mere delegates not representatives. Pym has no cunning: he is an honest gentleman, direct, courteous and sensitive to others, possessing, in short, all the qualities which marked him out as a future victim of Thatcher who is more at ease with political ruffians like Tebbit. And my scheme had, too, many complications for someone more used to taking to the uncluttered high road than reaching his destination by devious, circuitous routes. But I did not leave him empty-handed: he agreed to tell his Whips that if individual Tory MPs wished to add their names to my amendment there would be no official disapproval.

Thus helped, I told Dan Jones now to go after Tory signatures. I knew he had his own lines of communication with religious Conservatives, for I was sure Dan was a powerful performer at the all-party prayer meetings he regularly attended. And so it proved to be, for he was soon producing Tory signatures and, when I looked at them, I knew I had the Lord on my side. It must have emboldened me to break my silence with Enoch Powell and invite him too to support my amendment.

I could not be sure of his response. He had supported the Common Market referendum, the first ever held in Britain's history, because he believed the people would save his beloved country from Europe's embrace. The result had severely bruised him, and I thought he may have no stomach for another similar encounter. Moreover, my proposition was a constitutional abortion, suggesting as it did that the people of Scotland and Wales would decide their future with, in effect, the people of England being given no chance to participate. It would, I feared, not stand up to Powell's over-logical scrutinies and scrupulous protection of constitutional niceties.

However, I sought him out in the Commons Library where he was always to be found working, and always in the same seat. He placed himself at a small hexagonal table with his chair close to the bookshelves so no one could pass or stand behind him, and it was a position where not only was his rear covered but from which he could command a view of all who came into or left the library. It was a paranoiac placing; and I had learned of his need for that particular corner when one day, by chance not design, I had pre-empted him and he found me working on his territory. He silently sat down right beside me although I had piled around me hefty law books which I was researching. I was half conscious of the oddity of his crowding in on me since there was ample seating and desk space available elsewhere but I was at first too much involved concentrating on my own task to be aware of his mounting anxiety that I would remain there, frustrating him perhaps for hours. When my work was completed and I had become conscious of the tension I had inadvertently precipitated, I moved away. Within seconds the anxiety-ridden man rearranged his papers and with relief moved into the safety zone his seat so evidently afforded him.

On this occasion when I entered the library he was just moving away from his desk. As he became aware I was approaching him, even before I spoke, I could feel the frisson of dislike. He did not deal with my request but instead responded curtly by recalling the exact debate in which, years ago, I had made what he regarded as an insult and then, turning on his heel, he left me literally standing; and much vexed with myself that thanks to my wish to obtain a broadly based set of signatories to my amendment (which would enable the Speaker to put it to the vote of the House), I had fruitlessly thrown away my lawyer's caution. I was, however, mistaken. No sooner had I put down the amendment and the names of my first batch of supporters than Powell added his. His action reflected the honesty of the man; principles were more important to him than people. His antipathy to me was irrelevant to his conclusion that my proposition was one to be supported.

Now I could draw my trump cards. There were two people who were in a position to determine whether Dan's efforts were to succeed: the Speaker, George Thomas, and the Prime Minister, Jim Callaghan. There were no men in the House with whom I had had a longer acquaintance. In the early 1950s – long before I had come into the Commons – when I was Chairman of the Cardiff City Labour Party, they were the two Labour MPs representing the city, and it was often my difficult task to try to get them to ride in tandem.

George Thomas, of course, was a man of the Welsh valleys. He knew and understood every nuance of the special quality of the political life in Wales. His sustained attacks on parish-pump nationalists and their fellow travellers and their attempts to politicise the Welsh language had, while he was the Secretary of State for Wales, the approval of the overwhelming majority of the people of the principality. James Callaghan thought otherwise. He no doubt counted the votes but his calculations with regard to Welsh issues were often awry, for despite his years of commitment to his own port constituency he was, and was felt to be, an outsider. Moreover, he certainly could not learn very much about Wales and the Welsh from *his* electorate. His constituency was idiosyncratic; substantially composed of deracinated descendants of Irish immigrants who were brought to South Wales to build the port and steelworks. As George Thomas has now revealed in his autobiography, Callaghan – despite ostentatious protestations of undying friendship – was never free from ambivalence to George Thomas. He secretly went to Harold Wilson and insisted George was estranging the Welsh electorate and should be removed from his position. Wilson yielded to the pressure, demoted George Thomas, and although the move was ultimately to lead to George becoming Speaker, that certainly was not then Callaghan's anticipation.

George Thomas is a man with the longest of memories; he never forgets the smallest slight or kindness. His role of Speaker meant he could show no outward favour or prejudice, but the wound he had received from Callaghan, and which was inflicted precisely because of his personal hostility to devolution and separatism, meant the Prime Minister knew he could expect no favours when the Speaker's discretion was to be exercised one way or the other on my referendum amendment. And I well knew if I was seen to have sufficient support that George Thomas's private views and his long sustained friendship with me, which still endures, would mean he would never lean backwards against me.

As the fateful day of the debate came closer and I was daily adding Dan's collection of signatures to the referendum amendment, I went through the charade in the Chamber of drawing the Speaker's attention to the amendment and inviting an intimation as to whether he would call it for debate. There was no need for me to be a supplicant behind the Chair asking the Speaker for his favour or to take tea with him in his rooms in an improper attempt to influence him. There was a total but tacit understanding between us: George's replies to me in the House, though seemingly equivocal, were in such terms that even the unsubtle government whips had no difficulty in deciphering his short comments and ran to their masters as the bringers of bad tidings.

If I had an understanding of the Speaker's likely reaction to my move, I had no less doubt about how the Prime Minister, when assessing the developing situation, would respond. I have written elsewhere[26] of the probable source of Jim Callaghan's Parliamentary skills and of his lack of a fixed philosophy. His fluidity is his strength and weakness; sometimes it enables him to be a superb negotiator and reconciler, but too often his excess of facility can lead him adrift: when the gales really blow, his lack of anchorage in principle shows. It would be excessively complimentary to his intellect to describe him as too clever by half; but it would be accurate to depict him as too labile by half. This acted in my favour, for he had no genuine

commitment to the principle of devolution. His unassuaged narcissism, which was never satisfied despite his extraordinary political
successes (and which always revealed itself in his envy of the strong),
meant that his first priority was the continuation of his premiership,
a conceit which ultimately led him to postpone the election, suffer
the winter of discontent, and ensure Thatcher's reign.

The Prime Minister was well aware that if my amendment was
called and – despite the government's opposition to it – this led either
to its acceptance by the House or the failure of the government to
obtain a second reading of the Bill, then the government would fall.
It was a government already balancing on a knife's edge. I had no
genuine belief that, faced with the crunch, Dan's signatories, so many
of whom were traditional Labour loyalists, would have dared to
come into the Lobby with me when they saw the full consequences
which could arise. But that was a qualm I kept to myself; Jim
Callaghan was not the man to play poker with me when the stake
was his premiership – that is not the type of courage he possesses.

On the eve of the second reading of the Bill the Prime Minister
called a Cabinet meeting. He had no difficulty in obtaining the
decision to which he had sulkily reconciled himself, particularly as
there were fifth columnist members of the Cabinet, friends of mine,
who had no affection for the Bill. They respected my judgment and
I had assured them that if I obtained a referendum then, despite the
misleading current opinion polls in Wales and Scotland, devolution
would never see the light of day. I was speedily informed of the
decision: there was no need for me to press my amendment as the
government spokesman in introducing the Bill would announce, as
he did, that the government would conduct the referendum demanded and devolution would be subject to the approval or veto of
the vote.

All the rest of this story has been frequently told, the shaping of
the procedures governing the referenda and the campaigns which
were waged. But without the near criminality of Dan Jones no
referendum would ever have been wrested from the government.
Britain, constitutionally, would have been dismembered and the
kingdom no longer united. Of such is the stuff of history.

*

With the devolution issue closed I was relieved of my temporary
alliance with Powell. But before our Commons lives ended we were
to be engaged in fierce combat. Like a moth around a flame, he was
programmed by his primal anxiety to be lured into the *in vitro* birth
controversy. In 1984, to the astonishment and bewilderment of most,

Powell, having drawn in the ballot the right to introduce a Private Member's Bill, announced his intention to introduce one which would ensure that *in vitro* fertilisation, and research into improvements in the techniques of the fertilisation, would be severely restricted. The Bill was greeted with acclaim by the fundamentalist lobbies. But Powell's move was nevertheless perplexing to them – as it was to the rest of the House – for his religion had subtleties and flavours far removed from the vulgarities of these lobbies; he had no history of a formal association with them and such little contribution as he had made when what is now known pejoratively as permissive legislation was passing through the House, would certainly not have been approved by them. Instead, he had supported me in the lobbies when I organised the final end of capital punishment[27] and also when I extinguished the criminality of private adult homosexual conduct. The House, wondering why he should voluntarily and unnecessarily throw himself into the tumult of the controversy, therefore cynically concluded that he was wooed by political opportunism. It was a shallow conclusion.

It was true that he was a septuagenarian politician whose frenetic political activities and ceaseless speechmaking displayed the politician's usual manic denial of the ageing process; it was clear that with a wish to fight yet again in his Northern Ireland constituency, his age disadvantaged him. As an outsider in Ulster he had an uneasy relationship with his constituency where, as was later proved to be the case, his majority was more than precarious, depending as much on past divisions in the Catholic vote as upon the Unionist voters; and he was undoubtedly well aware that he could sink at any time in the treacherous bogs of Irish politics. To be the champion, therefore, of the movement against *in vitro* fertilisation afforded him a singular opportunity to gain the support both of his Catholic electorate and those stricken with Ulster's primitive brand of Presbyterianism.

Yet to attribute such motivations to Powell, a man who had so determinedly thrown away his safe Wolverhampton seat, is to misrepresent him. Though it is often difficult for his conduct to be understood by equivocating mean politicians who judge others as themselves, Powell gave the explanation for his intervention honestly and without trimming: he said that his instinct determined his stance. He made no claim to be moved by religious conviction or by logic or reason. Repeatedly he declared when defending his intention to stop defective-embryo research that his was a 'gut reaction'. And certainly it was not an intellectual response, although I would identify the bodily response as being situated a few inches away from the gut.

It is predictable that the less sexually robust feel *in vitro* fertilisation as a subversion of their own virility. The macho man, over-determined in his bid to assert his maleness, finds the suggestion he may be dispensable terrifying. Powell's anguish over the black population growth, as over embryo research, reveals something of the same psychopathology, and it is one shared by so many of the new puritanical campaigners in contemporary Britain.

Powell's move endangered years of effort on my part. As early as July 1978 I had specifically put to Shirley Williams, the Secretary of State for Education and Science in the Labour Government, that her appointed Genetic Manipulation Advisory Committee, then super-vising the development of recombinant DNA, should be enlarged to enable the ethical, legal and social aspects of the innovatory techniques to be reviewed and I drew attention to concerns over research involving *in vitro* fertilisation and embryo transplants. It was clear to me that wondrous possibilities were within the grasp of the doctors and scientists; the desperate needs of the infertile could perhaps be met, the anguish of miscarriages relieved, and some terrible inherited diseases might be conquered. I knew that these possibilities would be under threat if uncontrolled embryo research provoked alarm and panic; and unless the preparatory educational work was done, the fundamentalist anti-abortion lobbies, never prepared to appreciate that abortion was concerned with the destruction of life and *in vitro* fertilisation with its creation, would do their worst.

My request to Shirley Williams to have the issues reviewed without delay was dictated by my belief in the necessity of a politics of prevention, a form of politics which, as I have observed, has, unfortu-nately, gone out of fashion. In fact, the continuing *in vitro* fertilisation controversy is an exquisite paradigm of the incapacity of contempor-ary British politics to anticipate and transmute, to prevent rather than to react. Inevitably, an unanticipated and unassimilated challenge for which the nation is unprepared results in feelings of helplessness and panic: with political groups, as with individuals, such a circumstance can lead to the making, in both psychological and historical terms, of regressive choices. In 1978 I wanted the issues immediately re-viewed to avoid that possibility.

But Shirley Williams turned me down flat. She insisted the Genetic Manipulation Committee was unsuitable in any event: it was con-cerned only with bugs. And to bolster her refusal to take action, the Minister pleaded the conservatism of the Medical Research Council who, she informed me, 'retain the view they took some time ago that they could not support research in these fields until there was satisfactory evidence from work with animals of the safety of the

techniques'. The sulking medical establishment had given encouragement to the Minister and her bureaucracy to sweep the problem
under the carpet.

The Minister's reply had barely been given when, doubtless to the
embarrassment of the Medical Research Council, the first British 'test
tube' baby was born, healthy and without blemish. News of Robert
Edwards's breakthrough came by happy coincidence on the morning
I had forced a debate in the Statutory Instruments Committee[28]
relating to genetic manipulation regulations, and I repeated my
demand to set up an inter-disciplinary reviewing committee. I carried
with me all my committee colleagues except Margaret Jackson, the
Under Secretary of State for Education and Science, who had been
told by Shirley Williams to deny me my request.

From then on for four years I found myself treading a lonely path,
continuously making my demand. As late as February 1982 the Prime
Minister gave me a dusty procrastinating reply when once again I
urged the formation of a comprehensive inter-departmental, inter-
disciplinary committee to review the issues. I pressed the demand
again in the House of Commons in an adjournment debate in March
1982, and then for the first time the government began to falter.
Hesitatingly, they admitted the need for some enquiry. In July 1982
the formation of the Warnock Committee was announced; four years
had passed since I had first demanded it.

The Committee's work now needed to be done immediately and
the Members clearly were conscious that events would overtake them
if they were tardy. If a committee had come into existence four years
earlier it could have proceeded at a more leisured pace. It could have
followed the wise practice of the Law Commission, the group of
judges and lawyers appointed by the Lord Chancellor, and issued
a public and tentative interim report inviting all the institutions,
organisations and individuals likely to be impinged upon to give their
views upon the document. This practice enables the Commission
not only to identify weaknesses in its own report but to see where
compromise may be needed to obtain consensus. The technique also
has, as has been proved, wide educational effects since the interim
report is publicised by the media and is mulled through at scores of
meetings. It identifies, too, the strength or weakness of those who
will sustain unremitting hostility to the Commission's proposals and
alerts those who wish to support the interim suggestions to the nature
of recalcitrant opposition.

The Warnock Report, however, was sprung upon the public
without any such preliminary forages into mined territory. The
Department of Social Services (the department primarily involved),

had still not grasped how little weight an authoritative and rational report carries today in our ragged society. The unsuspecting medical establishment, accustomed in the past to a cosy relationship with the department, and aware that with Kenneth Clarke as Minister for Health there was ministerial sympathy for the recommendations, sat back anticipating that government legislation would soon follow the Warnock recommendations. But although establishments may exist within departmental bureaucracies and professional organisations, the old homogeneity of yesterday's Establishment has gone. The old lines of communication – the old boys' network between a minister and his department, *The Times*, the judiciary and the leaders of industry and the professions – have long since been torn to shreds. Irreverence is almost compulsive and the new populism of Britain has not only brought much needed democratisation in some areas, it has also brought malignant side-effects – one of the most lethal has been the decay of party and the growth of lobby.

No longer can the political parties act as the sole containers of a wide spectrum of opinion; the special interest groups are impatient of the inevitable restraints which must come with the membership of a party and, indeed, all the political parties are finding it difficult to maintain such unity as they possess and to prevent further fragmentation. Interest groups with tunnel vision proliferate; and although few would dispute that many of them, by directing attention to the disadvantaged, are salutary in our yuppie society, there are others pursuing their goal with a fanatical zeal quite alien to our more traditional and relaxed democratic tradition.

Of all lobbies, the fundamentalist lobby is unsurpassed in its commitment and, more relevantly, in its organisational skills. The conjunction of Powell and the fundamentalists made certain that the Bill would be passed in principle on its second reading. Enoch Powell had the temporary advantage of speaking from his 'guts'. His reaction mirrored the panic reaction of many; it expressed their fear of the unknown. The direction that the Warnock Report proposed to take and the cool pragmatism with which it proposed it were too abrupt for the legislators and for much of the electorate. Both the novelty of the challenge and the answer to it had not been metabolised; legislation which impinges upon human relationships – as I know from my experience of steering such legislation on to the statute book – cannot be precipitate. The buried fears and anxieties have to be explored, expressed, at least partially acted out, and finally worked through; otherwise the resistance is as strong from the legislator as it would be from the patient of a bungling psychoanalyst who impatiently and over-logically seeks to impose his explanation of the cause of the neurosis: timing is all. Like the patient, the legislator must be prepared and a congruence established between the proffered resolution of the problem and the needs of the anxious electorate. Only when the correct moment comes can legislation then be felt to be a redemption and not perceived, as many perceived Warnock, as a threat.

I have published elsewhere[29] an account of the battle which followed. What became most evident, however, in the ensuing debates was how profound was Powell's commitment to the irrational which he unabashedly and fluently claimed was the moving agent of his cause. Given the nature of his allies, it was therefore inevitable that the debates became musty, soaked in the vocabulary of medievalists. In and out of Parliament we conducted no pristine colloquy: rather, we witnessed the re-enactment of the old struggle between religious zealots and science. The physicist of the skies, Galileo, daring, by his advocacy of an heliocentric cosmology, to obliterate the distinction between the celestial and territorial was condemned as an heretic by the Pope. The Catholic Church ensnared Galileo by charging him with 'necessitating' God, for he was possessed of unforgivable hubris by imaginatively usurping God's place and telling Him how He must have created the universe. Huxley, in his famed debate with Bishop Wilberforce, recalling the sage when defending Darwin against the onslaught of the churches, asked who could number the earnest and ancient seekers for truth from the days of Galileo until his time, whose lives had been embittered by the mistaken zeal of Bibliolators. And Freud was later to endure the self-same prejudices compelling him to refrain from publishing some of his works in Catholic Vienna; exploring the psyche was seen as soul searching, a monopoly to be preserved by the Church. Enoch Powell, by threatening the medical and scientific community with the stigma of criminality if they dare in future to pursue their embryo research, was aligning himself with a long and dishonourable tradition.

In the event, Enoch Powell's Bill was frustrated in its final stages. The battle to protect the rational Warnock recommendations was largely fought by the 'oldies', those of us who had battled in the 1960s for social reforms which would create what we believed to be a more civilised society. A generation ago there would have been packed Labour benches when a momentous social issue of this kind was being debated, but Thatcherite attitudes have also infected the young Labour MPs. Too often they become preoccupied with establishing that our party's economic programme will bring greater wealth to the desired materialist Britain of the future, and debates about more profound human needs are considered peripheral to the central argument as to which party will shower more consumer goods on the electorate.

However, my opportunity came when the Bill returned intact from the committee reviewing the proposals to the Chamber for its final report stage. A minor technical Bill which slightly amended the rule relating to the production of motor-car licences was due to precede the consideration of Powell's Bill. It was anticipated it would last but a few minutes, but I had other thoughts. Using my knowledge, as a solicitor, of case law I spoke for hours on that Bill and the fretting Deputy Speaker, despite pleas from Powell's supporters, could not halt me since I was, with the material in my hands, too experienced a Parliamentarian to stray from the rules of order. When Powell's Bill was finally reached, I had put down an amendment which the procedural rules required to be called first, and having dallied with that amendment, despite Powell intervening to indicate his readiness to accept it as he tried desperately to save his Bill, my supporting colleagues then had no difficulty in consuming such little Parliamentary time as was left to his Bill. The Bill ran out of time, and thus fell. My pact of animosity with Powell was well and truly sealed.

Yet Powell has not wholly failed. The recommendations of Warnock remain in suspension, unimplemented; and all the anxieties that, in my judgment, cluster around the initial trauma forever haunting Powell and are now part of the continuing debate involving *in vitro* fertilisation, will spill over into debates that are yet to come. The concerns surrounding *in vitro* fertilisation, as with the new concerns relating to the use of brain cells of a foetus to alleviate the cruel disabilities of Parkinson's disease, only presage further controversy. As yet we have seen only the tip of the iceberg; human genetic engineering is around the corner and as advances proceed at a terrifying pace, it is certainly no less pregnant with triumph and hazards than embryo research. Instant politics and reactions will not cope with the awesome societal challenges human genetic engineering presents. The need for wide-ranging assessments of the possibilities and consequences of such engineering is overwhelming. Unless the government takes the initiative now to set up or co-ordinate the needed enquiry, once again, as with *in vitro* fertilisation, events will overtake the politicians and they will find that their miserable preoccupation with the minutiae of politics will leave them totally unequipped to present informed options to the nation. Powell's forceful intervention, which stirred up so many unnecessary anxieties, will make it even less likely that the necessary initiative will be taken by this government to enter into what will now be regarded as highly

mined territory. Thatcher's government will remain more concerned
with the poll tax than with the future of the human race. Yet the
capacity of Parliament to mediate between the scientists – now
wresting spectacular secrets from the gene – and the bewildered
layman, will ere long be measured; it will be tragic if the challenges
contemporary science bring prove too large and the politicians too
anxious and too puny.

Over those coming debates Powell's shadow will linger, for he has
that rare capacity, as few have, to provoke the metaphysical scandals
that are the gifts of true rhetoricians: the capacity to command the
future belongs to eloquent visionaries who possess the grammar of
the ancient prophets and Greek sibyls able to enforce the future tense,
the extension of language over time. But not all are like Martin
Luther King who, in his famed address, by proclaiming his dream
of inspiration, can help to bring about its consummation. There are
other grim prophets who can provoke what they fear, and rivers of
blood can indeed flow from their jeremiads. Just as today (as all
Labour candidates who have fought in the Midlands know to their
cost), Powell's speeches of 1968 continue to have their inimical effect,
so in the future, the anxieties of his birth trauma will bedevil the
resolution of the problems that will be released as the secrets of the
gene are unlocked.

No doomsday man did more to promote what Peter Jenkins has
perceptively identified as 'the general angst' and which Jenkins sees
as the societal condition which led to Thatcher's emergence and, I
believe, to her dominance. Now Powell has been rejected by his
electorate and his capacity to infect us all with his despair has at last
been curtailed. But his obtuse electorate, no doubt careless of the real
consequences of their rejection, have done a disservice to the nation,
for Parliament is diminished by his departure. Eros, the god of love,
needs Thanatos as his eternal adversary if he is to remain strong and
powerful. With no battle of the Titans, no struggles will take place,
only squabbles. The Commons needs grandeur and there is so little
left there that it can ill afford Enoch Powell's involuntary departure.

It is reported that in his enforced retirement he intends to set his
intimidating scholarship the task of revising the accepted chronology
of part of the history of my people. His fascination with virgin and
other births will be at his and our service in his review of the history
of the New Testament's tales of the Annunciation and the Virgin
mother. Now that we are both old men, rancour should cease: I
genuinely wish him some serenity in his constructive task. And since
he is, unlike me, a Christian, it may be that he will extend forgiveness
to an unbeliever.

12

St Michael and the Dragon

T HATCHER may threaten to go on and on but yet, mortality cannot be defied: in politics the intimations of age and physical degeneration are cruelly exposed, and nowhere more than in faulty decision-making. Bevin's heart block, Cripps's spinal infection, Churchill's strokes, Macmillan's prostate, all influenced their decisions. Eden's inflamed bile duct and Nasser's diabetes made a grim contribution to the Suez débâcle even as Roosevelt's affliction at Yalta played a dangerous part in determining the destiny of Eastern European states. And in the 1970s the German Chancellor Helmut Schmidt's troublesome thyroid acted as a catalyst for many of the strains and stresses that occurred in Europe's relationship with the USA. Showing all the classic symptoms of thyrotoxicosis, the German leader failed to conceal his irritations and was constantly irascible with the slower-thinking President Carter. The fate of nations and political parties may be determined by the physical pathology of their leaders.

Yet so clamorous is the demand for magical leadership that recognition of flawed decision-making caused by age or disease is only grudgingly made. How else can we explain the acceptance by the peoples of China, the USA and Russia (until Gorbachev), of geriatric leaders all maniacally denying their mortality? At the age of eighty, Deng claimed to be swimming non-stop each day for an hour (no doubt emulating Mao who claimed to have swum across the Yangtse River). And Reagan has demonstrated, on and off horseback, his physical prowess and his resistance to cancerous growth.

Thatcher's boast, therefore, falls into a familiar genre: nowadays she denies her need for any real holidays although formerly she would visit the home of the Glover family in Switzerland. That I would have thought was not a holiday but an endurance test. The late Sir Douglas Glover, a successful northern draper, was the greatest bore in the House. His claim to political fame was that he could, on rising to speak, empty the House with greater speed than anyone this

century. One terrible week, as part of a small parliamentary delegation, I was entombed with him on a ship in the Indian Ocean. The
other member of the delegation was an amiable Tory MP and with
him I devised multiple stratagems to conceal our whereabouts. It was
to no avail and I still hear him booming as with delight he found our
hideaways. Margaret Thatcher, with other tastes, evidently found
him an engaging companion but now she appears to have renounced
such delights and limits herself to a few days on the south coast,
ensuring that the brevity of her holidays is amply advertised as
a tribute to her relentless capacity for work, and, of course, her
indispensability.

This display of extraordinary physical stamina and of constant
activity yet again spells out a determining deprivation. Long ago
the psychoanalyst, Guntrip, wrote of the hyperactive personality,
'Activity is forced, tense, strained, an attempt to compel an insecure
personality to carry on as a "going concern". This may become a
manic or obsessive compulsive activity for the "mind" cannot stop,
relax or rest because of the secret fear of collapsing into non existence.
It is the individual's incapacity for experiencing a sense of "being" that
is primarily dissociated, left unrealised at the start of development. He
cannot get at his capacity to feel real, because at the start of his life
no one evoked it. His mother gave so little genuine relationship that
he actually came to feel unreal.'[1] She cannot take a real holiday, for
that would be an intermission, and she must continue to act in a
never-ending play without interludes, for if the lights came up the
woman as well as the actress would disappear. Her need to keep on
stage now rivals that of an absurd, ageing opera star.

At this late hour of her political life, desperation has taken over:
now she makes the final belated bid to live out the childhood fantasy
which she once wanted to believe would be her escape route out of
the cribbed prohibitory terrain of the Roberts family. 'At one stage
I really would have liked to be an actress' she has unguardedly
revealed.[2] Wistfully she has recalled a rare childhood event of going
to a cinema, and her enjoyment of her amateur acting at school. The
film, the stage, was the yearned-for glamour, so removed from the
bleak reality of her childhood. And, although she now seeks to
mitigate her disappointment by telling herself 'No one I know of has
a glamorous life', the more time slips by, the more avid and extravagant are her desires to give world performances. When, after enduring
a heavy session, more rational MPs greeted with relief the rising of
Parliament in 1988, she, eschewing a rest, immediately plunged into
a world tour. The surprised prime minister of Singapore, Lee Kuan
Yew, greeted her at his dinner table by telling her she was 'crazy' to

be engaged at her age upon such an itinerary: and no sane person would gainsay him.

But Thatcher, increasingly, does not dare to be alone. Thirty years ago Donald Winnicott wrote a seminal paper, 'The capacity to be alone', telling us of the positive aspects of a capacity to relish solitude. Winnicott suggested the capacity to be alone in adult life originated with the infant's experience of being alone in the presence of his mother. If the child's immediate needs, physical contact, food and warmth had been satisfied and there was no further need for the mother to be concerned with providing anything, nor any need for the baby to be looking immediately to the mother for everything, then, at such moments there was a blissful stillness. This relatedness between mother and child is the basis of a capacity to be alone. The paradox, Winnicott indicated, 'of "the capacity to be alone" is based on the experience of being alone in the presence of someone and without a sufficiency of this experience the capacity to be alone cannot be developed.' This capacity was never one to be bestowed upon little Margaret by her remote mother, and the consequent emotional shipwreck is increasingly illustrated as Thatcher embarks on her desperate world tours. The psychiatrist Anthony Storr in a recent work complains, with justification, that too many psychotherapists have omitted to consider the fact that the capacity to be alone is an aspect of emotional maturity.[3] And, drawing on Winnicott's thesis, he declares, 'the capacity to be alone thus becomes the link with self discovery and self realisation; with becoming aware of one's deepest needs, feelings and impulses.'

This is the capacity Thatcher lacks: as Francis Pym, bearing his scars, has ruefully commented, 'She is not able to sit and ruminate for an hour or two alone.'[4] Such voyages of self discovery are not ones on which Thatcher can dare to embark. She would prefer the soft option: never has there been such a peripatetic premier. Running non-stop away from herself at our expense with increasing acceleration, since she became Conservative leader she has made 165 visits to 53 countries. In the first six months of 1988 she had wooed her acclamations in Kenya, Nigeria, Brussels, Paris, Toronto and Hanover and, after her world odyssey prompted further invitations, the United States. By the spring of 1989 she was off again on a regal tour of Africa. Such a thirst for acclamation is morbid, but it is a condition known well to historians reciting tales of disintegrating monarchs. The grovelling journalists accompanying Thatcher justify these expensive trips in paeans of praise of her talents as a supreme huckster, selling Britain to the world. Moreover, the accompanying *Times* correspondent told us, 'With her own country in reasonable order, as she sees it, she wants to sort out the world.'[5] Some of us, however, see such delusions of grandeur as part of the ageing process when, so often, early characteristics can become grotesquely enlarged.

Thatcher, however, makes the arrogant assumption that time for her stands still, and that she will be leading her party into a victory for a fourth term. At the October 1988 Conservative Party Conference she was again affirming that age could not weary her, and that, at sixty-three, she was far too young to go. She is inviting retribution from the gods. Inexorably the body wears out. I recall a duel I had with her on the floor of the House in the 1963 session of Parliament when, as a junior minister, she was in charge of the family allowance and national insurance Bill. Then, spirited though the clash was, even when on the attack I was inhibited by her charmless good looks. But, despite all the artifices, the bloom of those days has inevitably faded, and today she can no longer command gallantry.

Growing older brings its penalties, as I well know now that I am a septuagenarian. Thatcher has had the wretchedness of an eye operation to correct a detached retina, another operation to correct the condition known as Dupuytren's contracture and so prevent a deformity and loss of function of her hand, and yet another to deal with her varicose veins. More, she has had warnings, hailed in the psychosomatic disorders, precipitated by her lifestyle, which will probably end her political ascendancy. Her faint at the Palace at the end of 1987 took place on the evening of a day which included a long audience with the Queen which, judging by the Commonwealth Conference encounters, is unlikely to have been a relaxed occasion for Thatcher. Moreover, as the medical correspondent of *The Times* commented, 'Even worse than the political stress is having problems superimposed on it from home.'[6] She was 'having to withstand one of the periodic and unjustified attacks on the business life of her son.' The Oedipal disturbances, reactivated by her relationship with the Queen, like the guilt and anger which her son's indiscretions provoke, are, as she grows older, less capable of being controlled: part of the price of the ageing process is a diminishing capacity to contain our anxieties.

In the week preceding her faint other burdens of guilt had pressed down upon her. She had courageously attended the memorial service for those massacred at Enniskillen, a visit which would have poignantly recalled the slaying in the Commons car park of her faithful aide, Airey Neave, a friend whose organisational skills had played not a little part in securing her the leadership of her party. Enniskillen would also have prompted the memory of the IRA's failed attempt to assassinate her in Brighton, an attack which led to the death or maiming of others of her supporters. Survivors always feel guilt; it is a guilt which may be dealt with by the notion that they have been especially chosen and lead them to believe that they belong to the Elect who will be saved at Armageddon – a delusion made explicit by Reagan in his final election campaign. But such delusions of invulnerability cannot be sustained. The fatigued, ageing woman could not maintain the pretence, the blood failed to reach the brain and she had an intimation of the inevitable. For Thatcher, like all of us, is subject to the ills to which the flesh is heir, and Ayerveda electric baths and the hormone replacement therapy which it was suggested she was having during the last election campaign can only ward off temporarily the encroachments of time.[7] The younger Tory MP aspirants have always been well aware of this and as Thatcher was seeing off all the leading contenders among her contemporaries, they submissively waited, initially content to be held in her thrall but nursing the thought that where there was death there was hope.

Michael Heseltine's rebellion, nominally over the Westland issue, broke the spell, as the Tory MPs' revolts of 1988 were later to prove. Someone within the Conservative Party had at last challenged the phallic woman and she had been found vulnerable. Heseltine's defiance was an initiation ceremony for the pre-pubertal Tory MPs. Now they were encouraged to be men, to face and overcome the castration anxieties which have recurred in so many disparate forms in Western myth and legend: Samson whom no man could conquer but was robbed of his strength by Delilah; Judith beheading Holofernes after giving herself to him; or Salome carrying the head of John the Baptist on a platter. But castration anxieties have in history had other tales to tell: thousands of witches, those perceived to be wearing phallic hats and riding on their phallic broomsticks, have been burned alive in the western world. Heseltine's revolt brought Margaret Thatcher many steps nearer the stake.

This is not a fanciful prognosis: it is unfair but the woman leader must walk even more warily than does her male counterpart. During the period of the emergency in India when Indira Gandhi imposed a near dictatorship, I travelled to India and met – under the scrutiny of the security police – those leaders of the opposition who had not been jailed, and I had, too, the opportunity of discussing events with dismayed High Court judges. I was shocked to find that a daughter of Nehru could be so imperious and inevitably, when we subsequently met, my distaste showed and my short encounter with Indira Gandhi ended in mutual antipathy. But Mrs Gandhi was to go too far: her imposition of compulsory vasectomy aroused all the latent fear of castration which so dominant a woman provokes, and she was consequently swept out of office despite the poor calibre of most of the leaders of the opposition. She needed all her very considerable resources and the renunciation of her vasectomy campaigns to claw her way back to power.

Rarely do events present us with so overt a demonstration of the responses that can occur between a dominant woman and her followers as occurred in India. But subliminally similar psychodynamics have been at work in Westminster. Throwing down the gauntlet, and surviving – as Heseltine has – is far more significant than when 'Tarzan' Heseltine displayed his manhood by picking up the mace. He has bestirred the Tory backbenchers and they are no longer content to be political eunuchs in Margaret's court. When that indispensable MP, Tam Dalyell,[8] described Thatcher as 'a bounder, a liar, a deceiver, a cheat and a crook' during the Westland affair, he was articulating the view silently held by not a few on the government benches. As an Old Etonian, Tam Dalyell placed top of his list of epithets the 'bounder'; and his subsequent valuable book[9] and temporary expulsion from the House similarly revealed that his indignation was that of a public schoolboy outraged that the public school ethic – which states that if you are found out you must own up to your culpability – had been breached by Thatcher.

For my part, however, I doubt if I could subscribe to Tam's roll-call of opprobrium. The consequences of Thatcher deserve the harshest of condemnation, but the woman herself is fundamentally a tragic figure; her destiny was shaped by her mother even as her mother's was by the grandmother. There is an essential involuntariness about her conduct, and it is she, not the nation, who has no alternative. Her psychic defence system is characterised by her dissociations; a phenomenon in which two or more mental processes co-exist without being connected or integrated. This capacity results in the charges of deceit but, nevertheless, she genuinely believes in her own denials. She is as much of a victim as those she victimises. The mitigation I have pleaded so often in court for those accused of grave offences cannot be withheld from her, and those who would protest that the criminal is in the dock and Thatcher is in Downing Street should not be aggrieved by her apparent triumphs. Her visible agonies as she thrashes around in a sea of denials leaving so much public tumult in her wake, tells us there is no serenity within the woman: she illustrates yet again that nothing fails like success.

No such extenuation will be granted by Heseltine. He will never accept that her aides, Bernard Ingham and Charles Powell, during the Westland affray, fearing their mistress's fall would end their power and patronage, were solely responsible for the leak from Downing Street of the Solicitor General's famed letter: that leak was intended to destroy Heseltine, and will never be forgiven by him. There are no statutes of limitation on the laws of the talon. Stalin is reputed to have declared, 'Revenge is best eaten cold', and Heseltine is the kind of politician who would approve of Stalin's culinary tip. His 'grand remonstrance of protest' – as the *Observer* leader described Heseltine's resignation – may have been presented in its public dimension as a dispute about Cabinet procedure, but essentially it stems from Heseltine's longstanding bid to found a personality cult.

Originally Heseltine had plans to mount a grand rescue operation of the inner cities. Informed by his ministerial intervention in Liverpool he canvassed support from other departments to enable him to have Whitehall support for his bid in Cabinet. But all his assiduous wooing and dining of permanent secretaries was of no avail. Thatcher, aware of his gathering support, moved in: public money was inevitably involved, so she would have none of it, and with the help of the Chancellor she killed off Heseltine's proposed bold rescue operation. He did not forgive her and Thatcher knew it. Ere long, to isolate him, she switched him out of the Environment Ministry to Defence. But even there he fought his rear-guard actions. Still nostalgic for his 'vice-royalty' of Liverpool, in the comparative privacy of the Cabinet he battled with Thatcher and, against her wishes, placed an important order for frigates with Merseyside shipbuilders. His biographer tells us 'His hostility was private but deepseated.'[10] When his defiant resignation came, Westland was the catalyst, not the cause. The bewildered Tories who protested it was absurd that so puny a matter – the future of a small and shaky company – should be allowed to cause such an upheaval in their ranks, were blinkered to the real causes of the storm, causes which go even deeper than Heseltine's frustration over his inner-city programme.

On the political stage, no one is more likely to upset the whole production than the man who decides unilaterally to cast himself as his own hero, and Heseltine is such a man. At Oxford he had diligently rehearsed his future political role. It was not only his dyslexia and his disinterest in academic learning that took him away from his studies. He was forever lured to the cinema, for there he found the cowboy heroes with whom he could identify. His passion for old-time Westerns led to the more avant-garde film-buff undergraduates renaming him Michael Philistine. Gary Cooper was his name. *High Noon* was his favourite film and his favourite hour. When the clock strikes, Tarzan Heseltine swings into action, holds up the mace, and, fearlessly, before the cameras, strides out of the Cabinet.

In a modern idiom he recalls for us the old legends and tales which tell of a totemistic monster that terrorises the people: someone – the hero – has to emerge to liberate the intimidated people, usually by freeing a captive maiden. The story has a particular resonance in England where St George is the patron saint. It appears in many guises but always the hero steps out alone, unaffected by the apprehensions of the group, to slay the monster. Although this tyrant is usually envisaged as a dragon – as the younger Tory MPs often call Thatcher in private – it is evidently perceived as an oppressive parental figure. In my political lifetime I have seen not a few men who yearn to play the part of their own hero. They are men who take unkindly to group commitment and seek and find a reason to march out of the group, determined to lead, no matter where – determined to slay the dragons. Mosley, Enoch Powell, David Owen and Heseltine – whatever different political beliefs they may have espoused – have all displayed themselves as compulsive heroes: the stance comes first, the political justifications follow.

The politicians with the self image of the hero are always possessed of fantasies of rescuing, fantasies that are sublimated, often imperfectly, in political policies they claim will save the nation. Indeed, it perhaps may not be coincidence that the public clash-points between Thatcher and Heseltine both involved rescue operations; one of the inner cities and the other of an ailing company. The source of the rescue fantasy has long since been clearly marked by Flugel in his psychoanalytical study of the family:[11] 'Since the thought of the sexual relations of the parent is, both on account of jealousy and on account of the repression of the incestuous cravings, one which is exceedingly distasteful to the child, the latter often likes to imagine that the loved parent enters into such relations unwillingly and under compulsion. Such a belief can arise most easily in a boy's mind as regards his mother: it then in its turn gives rise to the idea of rescuing the mother from the unwelcome and tyrannical attentions of the father; a fantasy which has found expression in the many stories and legends of which that of Andromeda and that of St George are perhaps the most widely known examples in which a distressed and beautiful maiden is delivered by young knight or hero from the clutches of a tyrant giant or monster.'

There is another characteristic which is common to the heroes in the tales of yore, of Moses, Perseus, Oedipus, Romulus, Christ and Siegfried, all of whom in the end are revealed of noble or divine parentage: they reveal how the antagonism to the father can not only give rise to rescue fantasies, but can prompt the heroes to deny their fathers as their real progenitors and to claim they have received a divine endowment. The politician 'heroes', not surprisingly, have similar messianic pretensions. For some, like Powell, it can lead to a yearning for political martyrdom; for others, blinded by their belief in their special charisma, to their staggering, as Owen, into a political wilderness: but in Heseltine's case, possessed though he is of the 'heroic' aura, his outside commercial successes show he retains his grip on reality. Now in the Commons he moves with stealth, and around the adoring constituency Conservative Associations with panache. Carefully he chooses his weapons for the final assault; interlacing ostentatious displays of loyalty to his party and measured rebellions against the most unpopular of Thatcher's policies, with deadly precision he prepares for his glorious heroic challenge. This is a St George whom the ageing dragon has good cause to fear.

13

Margaret Thatcher's Jews

WITH the embarrassment of Christmas 1987 over, Peregrine Worsthorne, using his ever-pristine eye, joyfully welcomed in the new year of 1988 with a *Sunday Telegraph* editorial headlined, 'Judaism is the New Creed of Thatcherite Britain'. The editor evidently believed Thatcher had performed the greatest single act of proselytisation in history, one indeed only to be matched by the command of the pagan king of the Khazars who in one ukase in the eighth century converted all his subjects to Judaism. 'For months,' Worsthorne reveals, 'the Chief Rabbi has, in effect, been the spiritual leader of Thatcherite Britain. By putting him in the House of Lords, the Prime Minister has publicly and formally recognised the enormously important role he has come to play, more than amply filling the vacuum created by the blank refusal of the Christian Churches to make any constructive contribution towards the crusade for the regeneration of Britain. Judging by the language of the Christian Bishops, Catholic as much as Anglican, this Government is bent on doing the Devil's work. Only the Chief Rabbi, in his pronouncements, makes any attempt to suggest that what she is trying to do might be pleasing to God.'

Worsthorne's belief that the Chief Rabbi thought of Thatcher as God's agent was fully justified by the Chief Rabbi's public pronouncements. But less than two years before his ennoblement, stung by an article I had written deploring his stances, he had initiated a correspondence with me in which he sang a different tune.[1] 'To dub me a "Thatcherite" is certainly without foundation . . . I am in fact quite critical of some policies pursued by the present government and particularly the apparent lack of concern and compassion,' he assured me. But now we await in vain the public castigation of the policies which he claims to deplore, and certainly no disclaimer came from this Lord denying Worsthorne's assertion that he thought God delighted in Thatcher's works.

My quarrel with the prelate is no new one: it extends over twenty years and it does not grow stale. The cause of the quarrel lies in an issue which is presently causing unprecedented tensions between the diaspora in the USA and Israel. Lord Jacobovitz recalls its origin in his book *If only my people . . .* ² when he tells of the controversy that arose when the Israeli Supreme Court, refusing to yield to the racialist doctrine of the orthodox rabbis of Israel, affirmed that the children of a war hero married to a woman not born a Jewess, and not converted according to orthodox rabbinical law, had the right to be registered as Jews. Lord Jacobovitz, outraged, sent a cable to Prime Minister Golda Meir, purporting to speak on behalf of Anglo-Jewry and demanding a legislative overruling of the court's decision; in his book, Jacobovitz recalls my response to his impertinent intervention. He wrote:

> Typical of the action of those aggrieved was an irate letter from Mr Leo Abse MP which appeared in *The Times* on 7th February 1970: 'The Chief Rabbi of a section of British Jewry, with extraordinary presumption, has sought to interfere with the ruling of the supreme court of a sovereign state. He is reported to have cabled the Prime Minister of Israel asking her to reverse the ruling of the Israeli Supreme Court that the children of a non-religious Jew and a Scotswoman may, at the choice of the parents, be registered as Jews.' He then denounced these 'racialist doctrines' and continued: 'Dr Jacobovitz should be made to realise that Israel is not a colonial outpost of his group of synagogues . . . As Ben-Gurion once remarked, a Jew is someone who calls himself one; and I shall call myself one as long – to quote another secular Jew, Ilya Ehrenburg – as there is anti-Semitism.' He could not have put the case for the secular Jew more bluntly – or more honestly, quite frankly admitting that not Judaism but anti-Semitism made him declare himself a Jew, and would continue to determine his Jewish identity so long as it existed.

He could have added that he thereupon engaged in a broadcast debate with me on the issue when, at a time when I was involved in Parliament in attempting to end the legal disabilities of the illegitimate, I told him that one of the differences between us was that I was seeking to make illegitimate children legitimate whilst, contrariwise, he was attempting to render legitimate children illegitimate. After that broadcast his political advisers told him to stop going on the air with me. But of course the fundamental issue between us was, and is, that I believe he has lost his Jewish heritage and he believes I have forfeited mine.

In other days the rabbis had certain powers of enforcement against those, including some of the greatest of Jewry's sons, who scoffed when the rabbis sought to snuff out the intellectual adventure and enquiries which are the very stuff of Jewish history. Upon Baruch Spinoza they placed the dreaded 'cherem', chastising him physically and excommunicating him from the community. Such enforcement procedures are happily denied the orthodox rabbinate today, and perforce they return to other techniques. To deal with Jews of my ilk places them in a difficulty: bound by their blood theories, which affirm that a man born of a Jewish mother is irrevocably a Jew, they seek, as the Chief Rabbi sought with me, to stigmatise the non-orthodox Jew as one possessed of a negative identity, a product of anti-semitism not of the Jewish tradition. The irony and wry humour of the great Russian journalist, Ilya Ehrenburg, who, with extraordinary skill, courage and cunning survived Stalin, is lost upon Jacobovitz whose heavy German background shows, for he is no son of the Pale. Ehrenburg's oblique comment carried with it the pessimistic view and criticism that anti-semitism in Russia is there forever, and that he will therefore assert his Jewishness unto eternity.

The dispute between secular Jews like myself and this Chief Rabbi is no mere existentialist one: it arises because we make the accusation that there has never been in Britain a more brazen Jewish exegete, one ever ready to provide from the Old Testament a defence of all the 'values' that Thatcher preaches. In 1986 he was telling the world:[3] 'The key to true contentment in the Jewish view can only be found in economic self reliance and self sufficiency.'

Judaism 'never frowned on gaining wealth as such, nor demanded that wealth be shared or distributed to equalise rich and poor by some artificial balance, unrelated to skill and effort.' 'The poor cannot be compensated for monies others earn.' And to make his prejudices yet more explicit he raged against 'the crippling effects on the economy of strikes which paralyse entire industries, or other coercive measures which sometimes result in pricing whole businesses out of existence, thus directly swelling the unemployed ranks,' and condemned as 'morally indefensible' 'the selfishness of workers in attempting to secure better conditions at the cost of rising unemployment and immense public misery.'

Indeed this Chief Rabbi outflanks Thatcher in his views on unemployment: he would be content to reduce the workless to Pharaoh's slaves. 'Cheap labour is more dignified than a free dole, and industriousness generates greater wealth than increased wages for decreasing hours of work.' 'Any job is better than paid idleness', and proffering sanctimonious advice and comfort to the disadvantaged worthy of a rapacious nineteenth-century mill-owner or sweatshop employer, he affirmed it would be 'salutary to remind those presently enduring much hardship and despair that others have faced similar trials before them and that self-reliant efforts and perseverance eventually pays off, turning humiliations into dignity . . . ' This humbug doubtless well satisfied those who in the boardroom of a large shop-owning public company originally appointed Jacobovitz. It certainly brought him acclamation from hundreds of Tory MPs who, deserted by the bishops, put on the Order Paper of the House of Commons a treacly congratulatory motion applauding the new religious champion. I do not doubt many of them would have rushed to the Chief Rabbi to become proselytes if it were not that they knew the Chief Rabbi's precondition to a conversion is circumcision.

Jacobovitz's bizarre exposition of the Jewish tradition which so pleased the Tories was occasioned by the sage report of the Archbishop of Canterbury's Commission on the inner cities. An eminent group of theologians, scholars and social workers who had written the Report had, to the Chief Rabbi's evident chagrin, correctly identified the essential core of Jewish ethics, and expressed their view that the Church must free itself from a nineteenth-century obsession with individualism. The Report stated:[4]

> It is against the background of the excessive individualism of much Christian thinking in the nineteenth-century that we must place the Marxist perception that evil is to be found, not just in the human heart, but in the very structures of economic and social relationships. This perception is also found to a notable degree in the Old Testament (from which, in fact, Marx may have derived it), where there is explicit recognition of the inevitable tendency of the rich to get richer and the poor to get poorer unless some constraint is imposed to limit the freedom of individuals to profit without restraint from a market economy. Most ancient societies were aware of this tendency . . . But the Old Testament is unique in attempting to impose a number of controls upon society to check the inevitable increase of social and economic inequalities . . .

Such a reading of the Jewish tradition was the one spelt out to me by my Talmudic grandfather when, at his knee, I was taught to translate the five books of Moses from Hebrew into English. My maternal grandfather, I hesitatingly claim, was the first man to speak Welsh with a Yiddish accent; but there were more significant accentuations in his tutoring. Although respected for his Talmudic learning by the small fanatical orthodox Jewish community in Cardiff

in the 1920s, he was looked at askance by many of his local co-religion-
ists because of his commitment to Zionism; they felt he was presump-
tuous and should wait for the Messiah to come down via Paddington
to South Wales to lead them back to Palestine. His Zionism, however,
was not a political commitment: his regard for Theodore Herzl, often
regarded as founding father of Zionism, was not boundless. My
grandfather had come in his teens from Russian Poland to Wales, and
the Zionism of the Viennese Herzl was too much a product of the
rebellious nationalism growing within the decaying Austro-
Hungarian Empire to be comfortably accepted by him. Rather he was
at ease with the spiritual Zionism of the Russian Jewish philosopher,
Ahad Haam, Herzl's opponent, who mocked at the vapidity of
nineteenth-century nationalism and affirmed the absolute necessity
for the Zionist movement to be permeated by the morality and ethics
which he believed, as long as the Bible was extant, proved the special
genius of Jewry.

Ahad Haam and his teachings are, of course, unknown to Jewish
Tory MPs now in the House of Commons but his influence throughout international Jewry was for decades enormous and his memory
is honoured and commemorated in present-day Israel. The spiritual
teachings of this great Hebrew scholar, the most unorthodox champion of Jewish religious orthodoxy, spelt out, as a true prophet, the
Jewish ethic as it always has been, and that means he demonstrates
how deviant are the exegeses of Jacobovitz, and corroborates the
Archbishop's Commission's interpretation of the traditional Jewish
morality. In a notable essay, contrasting Jewish and Christian ethics,
clearly aware of the 'excessive individualism' of nineteenth-century
Christian preaching which the Archbishop's Commission regrets, he
affirmed the true traditional Jewish approach:[5]

> There is no need to dilate on the familiar truth that Judaism
> conceives its aim not as the salvation of the individual but as the
> well-being and perfection of a group of the Jewish people, and
> ultimately of the whole human race. That is to say, the aim is
> always defined in the terms of a collectivity which has no defined
> and concrete form. In its most fruitful period, that of the prophets
> and the divine revelation, Judaism had as yet no clear ideal of
> personal immortality or of reward and punishment after death.
> Religious and moral inspiration of the Prophets and their disciples
> was derived not from any belief of that kind, but the conviction
> of their belonging to the 'chosen people', which had, according to
> their belief, a divine call to make its national life the embodiment
> of the highest form of religion and morality. Even in later times

when the Babylonian exile had put an end to the free national life of the Jews, and as a result the desire for individual salvation had come to play a part in the Jewish religious consciousness, the highest aim of Judaism still remained a collective aim. For proof of the truth of this statement there is no need to look further than the prayers in our daily and festival prayer books, of which only a minority turn on the personal needs of the individual worshipper, while the majority deal with the concerns of the nation and of the whole human race.

And again, in another influential essay, Ahad Haam stressed how, from the very beginning, the Jewish imperative was collectivism.[6]

. . . early Judaism was not perplexed by the problems of life and death, it knew nothing of the despair which begets the materialistic philosophy of the exaltation of the flesh and of sense-enjoyment as a refuge from the emptiness of life; nor did it turn its gaze upwards, to create in Heaven an eternal habitation for the souls of men. It offered eternal life here on earth. This it did by emphasising the sense of collectivity, by teaching the individual to regard himself not as an isolated unit with an existence bounded by his own birth and death, but as part of a larger and more important whole, as a member of the social body. This conception shifts the centre of personality not from the body to the spirit but from the individual to the community; and concurrently the problem of life is trans-ferred from the individual to the social plane. I live for the sake of the perpetuation and the well-being of the community to which I belong; I die to make way for others, who will remould the community and save it from petrifaction and stagnation. When the individual loves the community as himself, and identifies himself completely with its well-being he has something to live for: he feels his personal hardships less keenly, because he knows the purpose for which he lives and suffers.

This is authentic Judaism, with no linkage with the aberrant doctrines of the Chief Rabbi, ready to preach to his wealthy congre-gants in St John's Wood (as he formerly sermonised to the rich of Manhattan), the comfortable view that 'true contentment' is to be found in economic self-reliance and self-sufficiency; and it is, of course, the antithesis of Thatcher's view that 'there is no such thing as society' and that 'society as such does not exist except as a concept'.

When I entered the Commons in 1958, exactly a hundred years after the first Jew was admitted to the House, I found there a substantial number of Jewish Labour MPs conscious of their intellectual heritage of collectivism. Although mostly secular men, the reverberations of the teachings of Ahad Haam's Judaism could still be heard from them in the Chamber and Committee Rooms of Westminster. That was a time when, just as Welsh MPs, on trooping through the voting lobbies, would talk to each other in Welsh, commenting outrageously on the unwitting colleagues surrounding them, so did many of the Jewish MPs simultaneously talk in Yiddish, using an irony which, if understood, would have devastated many a pompous minister walking alongside.

At that time the politicised Jew neither wished for, nor found, a place in the Tory Party: there were then only two Tory Jewish MPs, both of whom had inherited baronetcies, and such paucity of numbers was due not only to the anti-semitism then prevailing in the Conservative Party but because the Tory philosophy was felt to be alien to the Jewish tradition. This situation continued until 1966 when still only the self-same two Jewish Tory MPs were elected, in contrast to the thirty-eight Jewish Labour MPs who found their way to Westminster. Since the Jews of Britain constitute at most 0.7 per cent of the population, such numbers indicated how committed was most of British Jewry, a generation ago, to the collectivist Party.

But there were other echoes coming from the past that explained the presence of so many Jewish MPs. And, here again, the introduction of personal biography may not be self-indulgent, and may help to explain the singular contribution of yesterday's British Jewry to the Labour Party. If my maternal grandfather introduced me to the spiritual content of Judaism, it was my paternal grandmother who opened up to me the raillery of the nineteenth-century and early twentieth-century secular socialist Jews, mockers of the superstitions and legalisms that had become encrusted upon Britain's conservative Rabbinate.

For I lived my boyhood in many worlds: this belligerent atheist grandmother had come as a young woman to South Wales from Königsberg, which was then in Germany, now in the Soviet Union. Her first language was the dialect of the area (now, as I understand, becoming extinct), and since her husband was a Lithuanian Jew, with his own language, they communicated between themselves in Litvak Yiddish, broken English, and heaven knows what mixture of their first languages. Meantime, my maternal grandmother never learned English and used Yiddish, and a sprinkling of vernacular Welsh, to speak to her grandchildren. I was brought up in a veritable Babel; and since my home and both sets of grandparents were all within a stone's throw of each other, I moved between these worlds almost every day. I would attend synagogue with my grandfather and go three evenings a week, after attendance at my working-class elementary school, to 'Cheder', the classes where I would learn biblical Hebrew, and, in due course, study for my barmitzvah. Then I would be off to my atheistic grandmother, receive my weekly 6d bribe, and be introduced to all the joys of the taboo food of shellfish and bacon, and, more important, hear, without fear, the provocative secular talk that would have terrified my Cheder friends.

In my grandfather's house all was ordered and ritualised; but in my grandmother's home – dishevelled, full of rumbustious uncles, aunts, cousins, and passing Jewish travellers, often little more than pedlars, but by their secularism assured of hospitality – I lived in an open society that was to leave me easily receptive to the tales and disputations of the Jewish socialists, communists, and anarchists, who, three years before my birth, were still bringing hope and *élan* to those being brutally exploited in the sweatshops of London's East End. And yet these swings between my grandparents, both contending for the allegiance of their grandchildren, occasioned me no stress or bewilderment; I accepted it all as normal, even as I saw, as a child, nothing contradictory in playing at Cheder, during the Festival of Purim, the part of Mordecai, thundering against the evil Haman, and then, at my school, on St David's Day, playing the role of Prince Llywelyn, battling against the wicked English. I thought it was all of one piece – as, indeed, I now know it to have been – for both households, though the language and the outward forms differed, defined themselves in terms of the community to which they belonged: they did not repudiate their minority status or attempt to merge into the host society, relishing as they did the special vantage point which those on the periphery always enjoy. And in their several modes they had the capacity to dream of a return to Zion, or of a just, rational society and the brotherhood of man.

But in Thatcher's constituency, which probably has a larger Jewish electorate than anywhere else in Britain, few such dreamers will now be found. Most of these voters, possessed of a vulgar materialism, reached North London from the East End: there they often had grandfathers and grandmothers whose yearnings were not for BMWs, minks, diamonds, cruises, or holidays in Cannes, Florida or Bali. Although the immigrant Jews of the nineteenth- and early twentieth-century lived in squalid hovels, and worked in primitive, stench-ridden sweatshops for a pittance most of the day and half the night, their imaginations were not impoverished. In secular terms they dreamt – no less – of the redemption of all mankind: and believed in its possibility, and worked and sacrificed for its attainment.

Thanks to the historian, William Fishman, much of the story of the radical immigrant Jews of the nineteenth- and early twentieth-century will not be lost.[7] But their grandchildren and great-grandchildren, prosperous entrepreneurs, always numerate, rarely literate, now caricaturing the phenomenon of the embourgeoisement of the working class, would consign the nobility of their immediate ancestors to oblivion. It is a nobility that reproaches them as today, encouraged by their Chief Rabbi and Thatcher, they dedicate themselves to the 'enterprise' culture, and believe they can obtain their individual redemption by bestowing charity which is as munificent as it is ostentatious. Few of them know or practise the Talmudic precept:[8] 'He who gives alms in secret is greater than Moses.' But many of them are supreme practitioners of the active citizenship which Thatcher extols.

Their charitable contributions are their conscience-money, exempting them from the commitment to the societal changes which so many of their grandparents knew were necessary if the disadvantaged were to be emancipated from the indignity of dependence upon the caprices of patronage. They attend the synagogue on the holy days, their wives and daughters encouraged to bedeck themselves to stir their neighbours to envy, not to symbolise their love of God, and mechanically they recite the prayers which tell them of the community values they ignore; and they believe that, when they repeat the ancient supplication, 'Next year in Jerusalem', it suffices to visit the luxury King David Hotel, not struggle in spiritual or secular terms to rebuild a new Zion on this earth.

To the despair of the Israeli Left, they cheered on the generals marching their troops into Beirut from the safety of the heights of Hampstead. When, on the BBC, I denounced the immorality and folly of the invasion of Lebanon, and called upon the young Israeli soldiers to lay down their arms rather than submit to such orders, there were sympathetic resonances in Israel to my condemnation, but the anger here of the leaders of the synagogue-based Jewish Board of Deputies knew no bounds. These 'professional' Jews, by their intemperance and press statements claiming the impossible – that I lacked Jewish credentials – confirmed me in my judgment and, in due course, events left them sulkily chastened. But their initial approbation of that invasion showed how far British Jewry's establishment has severed its moorings, and cut itself adrift both from spiritual Zionism and from the socialist Zionists who, within the Histadrut (their co-operative and trade union movement), and within the kibbutzim, believed they had laid down the ethical pattern upon which the new state would be built. Forty-five years ago, when I was with the RAF in Egypt, I would use my treasured leaves to stay in Palestine, either at the villa which my grandfather had built on Mount Carmel when, at eighty, he quit Cardiff to die in his Holy Land, or within one of the socialist kibbutzim. I was there not two generations ago, but light years away from today's Finchley and Hendon North where, in successive elections, thanks to the Jewish electorate, increasingly these constituencies show a loyalty ratio to the Conservatives markedly higher than the wider electorate's.

The Nobel Prize winner, Elie Weisal, recently said of the Jews:[9] 'Their best characteristic is their desire to remember. No other people has such an obsession with memory.' But establishment British Jewry scorns its most precious inheritance: it is lost precisely because it has lost its memory. The passionate debates in the early twentieth-century Jewish East End between socialist Zionists and those in sympathy with the Bund (the General Labour Union) in Lithuania, Poland, and Russia which were possessed with the heroic ambition to integrate a Jewish revolutionary movement, with its autonomy preserved, into an international framework[10] would be mumbo-jumbo to the great-grandchildren of the original participants. Certainly they would not wish to recall the intellectual jousting between the followers of Marx and those selfless, gentle anarchists who, in the end, happily captured the allegiance of a significant section of the East End Jewish working class, and were capable, as late as 1912, of bringing out, in a famed strike, 13,000 Jewish tailors, backed by the Jewish Union of bakers, plumbers, cigarette makers, cabinet makers and slipper makers, against their largely Jewish employers. Such battles find no echo today in Finchley and St John's Wood where, for too many Jews, the only battles that can command their attention are the takeover struggles of the company boardrooms.

The Jewish anarchists, forebears of many of today's north London yuppie Jews, held a conviction that subverted all dogmatists: rabbinate and Marxist. Their leader once made his declaration of faith in these terms: 'There is never an end to the future, so it can have no final goal. I am an Anarchist not because I believe Anarchism is the final goal, but because I believe there is no such thing as a final goal. Freedom will lead us to continually wider and expanding understanding and to new social forms of life. To think we have reached the end of our progress is to enchain ourselves in dogmas, and that always leads to tyranny.' For these anarchists even the millennium was but a staging post on the onward march of mankind. No wonder such libertarian visions frightened the rabbinate of the day who, in panic, reacted fiercely, using every tactic to sabotage the anarchists' press, eject them from their club premises and denounce them from their pulpits.

The tone of the Chief Rabbi of those days, while faced with a deputation pleading for him to intervene with the employers to mitigate the exploitation of their fellow Jews in the sweatshops, reveals how squarely Lord Jacobovitz stands in the long and dishonourable tradition of the British Chief Rabbinate. *The Times* reported,[11] 'The Chief Rabbi in reply, calling the deputation "fellow working men" said he called them such because he also had to toil from morning until night, and he probably had to work harder than any of those whom they represented . . . no good would be effected by . . . the preaching of doctrines of Anarchism and Nihilism. They could instead utilise the Jewish welfare and charitable institutions. It was outside his jurisdiction to denounce Jewish employers publicly, or allow laymen to do so from his pulpit.' Faced with such provocations, it is not surprising that the more moderate anarchist leaders could never restrain their followers from holding, each Day of Atonement, large balls where, in defiance, the dancing Jewish workers mocked at the humbug of the fasting rabbis in their synagogues. But such events, and others like the marches on the synagogues and their occupation by near starving workers, are erased from the memory of the Jews of the embourgeoisement: today they suffer from a collective amnesia. Within the yuppie world in which they live, they wryly illustrate the old adage that the Jews are like other people, only more so.

The First World War was to see the extinguishment of the Jewish anarchist movement, but growing up as a boy in the South Wales of the 1920s meant they were not for me distant figures; and that was not only because of my mother's tales of some of their legendary activists, but because, curiously, they had established a toe-hold in Wales. Fleeing from police raids in the East End and then later from internment, a handful came, initially to the Swansea Valley, where their Welsh anarcho-syndicalist comrades gave them shelter. In return, the Jewish anarchists, a few of whom were professionally qualified dentists, taught them their skills which meant that for some years the travelling dentists of West Wales, Welsh and Jewish, pulled out the teeth of the miners whilst spreading their gospel. I have relished few evenings in the Commons more than one spent with James Griffiths, not long before his death, as he recounted his uproarious recollections of those dentists, full of divine optimism, who profoundly believed they would bring relief to the ills of society even as they brought an end to the toothaches of the tinplate workers of the Welsh Valleys.

The loss of such pristine minority views is sad for the wider society; but it is suicide for the Jew, for if, while being a participant, he loses his role as a detached observer, he is drained of all intellectual activity. 'Because I was a Jew,' Freud declared, 'I found myself free from many prejudices which restricted others in the use of their intellect: and as a Jew I was prepared to join the Opposition and to do without agreement with the "compact majority".'

Now, reflecting the abandonment of that traditional Jewish stance, in the present Parliament there are only seven Jewish Labour MPs, less than half the number of Jewish Tories, and that is without counting the Conservative MPs who pusillanimously conceal their origins. Meantime Nigel Lawson is reported to be preparing himself for conversion; Leon Brittan, whose father arrived here as a Lithuanian Jew, returns to Europe as an Englishman with only the most tenuous connections with Jewry; and silly Edwina Currie, in haste to belong to the 'compact majority' has long since declared herself a Christian, a claim not conceded by many who have to endure her enthusiastic implementation of Thatcherite policies.

Yet it was as a Jew, mindful of the searing experience so often endured by my people as a minority group in the diaspora, that, exercising my Jewish duty to help another persecuted group, I put an end to the criminality of private adult homosexual conduct. Jacobovitz, however, in a pitiless article published in *The Times*, at a date timed to sway the 1988 Synod into an harassment of homosexual churchmen, asserted that such conduct was 'heinous', deserving of punishment, and so added to his ever-lengthening list of assaults upon disadvantaged minority groups. He has disdained the Church's plea for collective action to assist the blacks in the inner cities, attacked the Warnock recommendations to help the infertile, and resisted, in his attacks upon artificial insemination by donor, the efforts of those of us determined to release the illegitimate from their ambiguous status and give those yearning for parenthood the legal right to describe the children of their families as their own. The *Sunday Times* tells us:[12] 'He condemns sodomy as an abomination and would not tolerate a gay minister. He prohibits sexual relations outside matrimony, abortion for any reason other than the mother's safety, and any tampering with the human foetus. He regards the use of condoms as unacceptable.' Defensively he has said, 'I have never deliberately involved myself in church issues or challenged other religious leaders. But as Jews we have to make this contribution to the moral advancement of society.' It would be more becoming of a claimed proponent of Jewish morality if he desisted from attacking the weak and, like some of the bishops, turned his attention to the abuses of the strong, and made a sustained onslaught upon the vices and current scandals of the City which lamentably have involved so disproportionate a number of his congregants.

But he appears to have other preoccupations. He bewails constantly the increasing inter-marriage occurring within British Jewry, a course now perhaps taken by up to one third of young London Jews. I do not preach inter-marriage, though to my great advantage I have practised it. Marriage between different ethnic and cultural groups can add to the heavy strains that fall today upon a marriage relationship. Within my marriage we celebrate both Christmas and Passover, and we observe no fast. Such happy resolutions and conjunctions are not within the capacity of all. But the real extra threat to Jewish marriages comes from other sources: the divorce rate of London Jews is now higher than the national average, and tells us how low is the threshold of tolerance of so many immature young Jews, overindulgently brought up in vulgar, vapid homes which have long since abandoned learning, and substituted money-making as the ultimate achievement. The Liberal and Reform Synagogue unencumbered by Jacobovitz's intolerant fundamentalism valiantly seek to arrest the moral decline; and, although they have inevitably produced the odd rabbinical starlet twittering on chat shows, most of the male and female rabbis have gravitas and a profound ethical sensibility. They try to overcome the handicap of that part of their history which associated their syna-gogues with that small section of yesterday's Jews who strove in Britain to be overdeterminedly British, and, in Germany, to be over-committed Germans.

The overall picture of British Jewry is one of increasing rootless-ness, and it is from this sadly disintegrating community that Thatcher has recruited such a disproportionate number of her cabinet ministers, her speechwriters and political advisers. The *Spectator*[13] a few years ago ambivalently carried on its front page the headline: 'Thatcher Chooses the Jews'; they could still today make the same jibe. As Keith Joseph leaves the Cabinet, Lord Young and Malcolm Rifkind enter. When Alan Watkins asked 'one of her entourage, not himself a Jew, about her preference he replied: "Simple. No mystery at all. They work jolly hard. There's no nonsense about them. Most of them have made their own way. Broadly they share her approach to life. Above all, they run her constituency for her in Finchley."'

The reply falls far short of explaining Thatcher's fascination with the Jews. The singular temper of East Anglian Methodism, renowned for being the *petit bourgeois* at song,[14] plays its part. In the austere Roberts' home, where fantasy was discouraged, little Maggie found her fairy stories elsewhere: on the Sabbath in between attending morning and evening service she would twice attend Sunday School to be tutored in the legends and tales of the people of the Book. Now, in her adulthood, the journalist Paul Johnson has claimed her favourite bedtime reading is the Old Testament and his *History of the Jews*. During 1988 she read the Old Testament, but not the New, from cover to cover and gave daily reports to her staff about how she was getting on: it was the biblical tales of vengeance that she particularly relished.[15] Meantime the Finchley Jews have continued to be flattered by her idealisations and attentions: she finds in them the same sickly pious celebration of the work ethic which was at the very centre of the smug non-conformity characterising yesterday's East Anglian Methodism. But both Thatcher and her Jews, in their odious stresses on individualism, are in fact casting aside the most valuable elements of their Judao-Christian heritage.

Certainly the support given to Thatcher by these Jews is not that of tepid floating voters. Living within an ahistorical vacuum, they are unaware of how grievous is their violation of the fundamental tenet of the Jewish morality, laying all its stress on the well-being of the group, to which individual self aggrandisement and individual salvation must be subordinated. Once a Jew minimises the significance of the group ethic, and extravagantly emphasises the overwhelming importance of self achievement, he leeches himself away from the Jewish tradition. This is the path down which this Chief Rabbi, teaching that 'true contentment' is to be found in 'self sufficiency', leads his flock. He rails against inter-marriage whilst committing the ultimate apostasy; that of political miscegenation with his favourite 'shiksa', Margaret Thatcher. For me, there is no uglier sight in Britain today.

★

Significantly, Freud's assertion of his Jewishness is made in the preface he wrote for a Hebrew translation of his *Totem and Taboo*, Freud's favourite work. Acknowledging his 'estrangement' from the religion of his father, and describing himself as one who 'cannot take any share in nationalist ideals but who has never repudiated his people', and as one who 'feels he is in his essential nature a Jew who has no desire to alter that nature', he answers the hypothetical question, 'Since you have abandoned all these common characteristics of your countrymen, what then is left that is Jewish?' 'A very great deal,' Freud replies, 'and probably its very essence.'

Paradoxically, although *Totem and Taboo* has implications that shake the foundations of Jewish, and indeed all religious faith, there is indeed no work that reflects the Jewish 'essence' more clearly: for it is in that masterpiece that we are directed to the original source of the collective societal injunctions which gave birth to civilisation and it is there we find spelt out to us how that coercive strength becomes internalised to become part of the commandments of our super-ego.

In the beginning there was the primal horde dominated by the tyrannical father who thwarted his sons' incestuous lust for his women. Then the band of brothers excluded from sexual intercourse formed the group, a fraternity, reinforced by binding homosexual feelings, to perform the act that no one of them dared do as an individual, the slaying of the father. Maybe, as Freud suggests, our ancestors did actually kill the father and, in communion, eat his flesh, for the primitive often proceeds from thought to deed. Maybe it was imagination and they, like neurotics who mistake a wish or a thought for the deed, were stricken with guilt for the crime of parricide which they had fantasised: and then, unable to bear the weight of guilt, as an act of atonement, the renunciation was made and a taboo placed on incest. But out of such incestuous yearnings and real or fantasised parricide our civilisation was born. 'Society was now based', Freud wrote, 'on complicity in the common crime, religion was based on the sense of guilt and the remorse attaching to it; while morality was based partly on the exigencies of this society and partly on the penance demanded.'

These propositions about the historical life of mankind, written in 1913, have inevitably been assaulted by some latter-day anthropologists, like the structuralists, but it is not surprising that, increasingly, one notes contemporary sociologists and anthropologists returning to Freud's thesis which he unrepentantly included in a lengthy summary in his late work, *Moses and Monotheism*, for it has a sinister relevance to the condition of our contemporary society. The Britain of 1989 has been compelled to acknowledge the terrifying and grim fact that incest between fathers and their own young children is widespread: suddenly there has become an awareness that child abuse is taking place, perhaps on an astonishing scale. Certainly now each year, increasing numbers of cases are being investigated. Given Freud's unshakeable conviction that all moral rules derive so much of their strength from the original incest taboo, then if the taboo is weakening and, worse, has ended for many, the bell is indeed tolling for our civilisation.

I am not comforted by those who claim that we have simply become aware of a phenomenon that has always been with us. The Victorians, always searching for sin, never discovered it, and had such confidence in the inviolability of the taboo that incest was not then a criminal offence. When it was made a criminal offence, in

1908, it was not because of a genuine belief that incest had become widespread: the Incest Act reached the statute book only after a prolonged crusade in which the moral entrepreneurs had a wider purpose than the one actually achieved.[16] They were seeking to frighten the government into providing for the working class better housing and improved conditions, holding that those prevailing were responsible for precipitating incest. It was so obvious a symbolic crusade that many of the Tories resisted the passage of the Bill, insisting that 'the evil, though shocking, is of rare occurrence',[17] and expressed the view that to publicise the few cases that occurred may kindle others. Nor can the passage of the Criminal Law Amendment Act of 1885 (which incidentally provided for the prosecution of fathers having sexual intercourse with daughters under the age of sixteen) be cited as evidence that widespread child abuse was always with us: as the Josephine Butler Society has asserted, that Act's prime purpose, which raised the age of consent to sixteen, 'was designed to save women and girls from enticement, abduction or sale into prostitution at home or abroad, where their probable fate would be ill-treatment, disease and early death.' There is much historical evidence of ill-treatment of children in Victorian times. There was considerable child neglect and physical abuse of children among deprived working-class households and many orphaned and destitute children were shipped overseas to Canada and other parts of the Empire to be used as cheap labour: but there is no record of widespread incest between fathers and their young children. I believe we are whistling in the dark if we deny that today's sombre revelations are anything but a specific symptom of the sickness of the 1980s.

The unconscious wish to commit parricide and enjoy incest appears to be an irrevocable part of our archaic heritage; and so far it is through collective ritual and ceremony that we have kept these dark passions in check. Repeatedly, in fellowship, from the earliest form of religion expressed in totemism to the gatherings of Christians to take communion, the original slaying of the father is crudely or symbolically re-enacted. By the sacrifice of the totem animal, a surrogate of the father, which was then eaten by all present, who thus bound themselves together, social cohesion was maintained: the renunciation, by way of repentance, of the parricidal crime and of the lusting after the father's women was reasserted, and the totem clan's rule of exogamy ensured that fraternity should not be destroyed by sexual and incestuous rivalries between the brothers. It is no derogation of Christian communion to point to the origins of the flesh-wafers consumed or the blood-wine drunk, for it is in such collective rites that, as ever, social solidarity is strengthened and morality upheld.

But the bulwarks of these collective rites are crumbling. When *The Times*'s commentator, Ronald Butt,[18] a good man with a genuine concern for the family, asks 'Why is there more child abuse now?' and, 'What is its connection with the wider culture in which the break up of family is taken for normal and taboos are dismantled?' he is asking the right questions, and none could gainsay his accurate comment on his own questions. 'A culture is indivisible and it fashions in one way or another those who belong to it.' But his allegiance to the Conservative Party inhibits him from pursuing his comments to the obvious conclusion. Thatcher preaches to the nation that a society is made up of separate, sovereign, atomistic individuals.[19] 'Society as such does not exist . . . individuals are the real sinews of society. To leave things to society is to run away from real decisions.' The real flight is, however, Thatcher's: she cannot tolerate any doctrine which promotes and blesses mutuality, for, as has been seen, she is possessed by a neurotic fear and hatred of dependency. So maimed, as a prime minister, she has created a culture in which the collective and often unconscious restraints upon anti-social conduct wither. It is a culture which is strewn with detonators exploding taboos even as deeply buried as the ultimate prohibition, the outlawing of incest.

The threat Thatcher poses to the Judaic-Christian values that have evolved out of the totemist religions which first created fraternity is now felt and perceived by the Chapel and by so many churchmen. Methodism, the church into which Thatcher was born, voted overwhelmingly in its 1988 Conference for a 'declaration of outrage' against her policies. The Bishop of Gloucester, Chairman of the Board for Social Responsibility, spoke for many Christians when he made his riposte to Thatcher after she sought unsuccessfully and presumptuously to instruct the General Assembly of the Church of Scotland on the theology of self reliance and independence. 'But,' asked the Bishop, 'can we understand personal responsibility without stressing also the essential social character of human life? Individuals are born into relationships and born into families and communities. The social dimension is fundamental and inescapable.' The Bishop was probing Thatcher's deepest wound: for her whole life is spent denying that she was born into a relationship with her mother and her political, as her theological creed, rests upon that denial.

When the Moderator of the General Assembly of the Church of Scotland, Professor James Whyte, made his considered reply to Thatcher in February 1989,[20] he saw clearly that her philosophy rested upon that denial. 'We are none of us', he chastised her, 'self-made men or women. It is in the family where we are loved and talked to and smiled at, that we learn to love and talk and laugh. Through the family we are introduced to the wider community where we belong.' But Thatcher had no such introduction: to her mother she never talked, and we have learned laughter was as absent in the Roberts' home[21] as it is in her Cabinet. The 'defective view of human nature' which the Moderator correctly attributed to her is the consequence: so desensitised by upbringing she is 'insensitive to the things that are important to us – our sense of community, our sense of belonging'.

That sense of community has in the past been reinforced by collective worship: but now church and chapel attendances drop. Thatcher's cult of individualism has come therefore at a time when the cement of social cohesion, which religion provided, is already badly chipped. Moreover, her assault has come about when a wholly distorted and mistaken view of psychoanalysis has, during recent decades, permeated the general culture. No aspect of Freud's assertion initially aroused greater indignation than his insistence upon the existence of infantile sexuality, a fact which was for so long heavily repressed, not least by parents; the reality of the phenomenon is no longer widely denied but the result, as some psychoanalysts have pointed out,[22] is that 'In place of the denial of infantile sexuality we have the "permissiveness" which, as it were, does not take the drive seriously.'

Twenty years ago these American psychoanalysts were expressing their forebodings, telling that we have a situation where 'It is a difficult task for parents to consciously recognise infantile sexuality without being seduced into the role of a participant. The incest taboo lost its firm ground with the lifting of the parents' repression and is now only half heartedly observed.' Now in some parts of Cleveland it is evidently not observed at all. To blame Freud for these consequences is as absurd as blaming Darwin for having ended literal belief in the Bible, or Einstein for the bomb. Man's discovery of truth cannot be banned, nor can his intellectual curiosity be quenched.

This new awareness and acknowledgment of the strength of infantile cravings presents us with weighty challenges. The instinctual drives are now dangerously at large, lacking the containment that formerly boxed them in. The weakening of religious faith, and the consequent lack of efficacy of ritual-ceremony exuding mutuality, means that political leadership concerned with the survival of our civilisation has an urgent task: an ethos has to be created where fraternity assumes a renewed emphasis. Secular society has to provide the brotherhood which was formerly found at the totem pole and so revitalise the essential taboos which keep a society integrated. Freud saw 'civilised society perpetually threatened with disintegration.'[23] 'Civilisation', he declared, 'has to be defended against the individual and its regulations, institutions and commands are directed to that task.' The expression of mutuality within the ritual of totemistic and later religions dampened down the tempestuous and destructive desires of the individual. Now we have a prime minister who, without conscious intent, inflames them.

The 'think tanks' of the Labour Party have therefore the duty and task to lay down the blue-print which would, in legislative and administrative terms, translate fraternity as an ideal into a fact of our society: preoccupations with liberty and equality are certainly not enough. So far the most eloquent exposition of the need to give priority to the development of a public philosophy of mutual obligation and active citizenship has also come from the ex-Labour MP, Professor David Marquand, whose work *The Unprincipled Society*[24] has been described by Hugo Young as the most coherent and stimulating book of political analysis of the 1980s. Certainly, whatever considerable reservations one may have of Marquand's prescriptions, his analyses take him, although by a very different route, to the emphases urged here. He wants a public philosophy which 'would have at its heart a view of the choosing self of a fundamentally different kind than that which has prevailed in the last 200 years. Instead of seeing the individual as an isolated atom which chooses solitarily, we would see individuals as being the product of the community.'[25]

Marquand himself is the product of a very special community, and his origins are reflected in his vision of the ideal society. His father, a socialist Professor of Industrial Relations at Cardiff, made valiant efforts to relieve the pre-war distress of South Wales and produced an economic blue-print which, in a less heartless world, would have been splendidly ameliorative; and his mother and her family all came from a little village in the Swansea Valley where my mother was born. Marquand's forbears there produced a famed Welsh socialist weekly to which my mother's sister, as a young woman, was a regular contributor. That mining village was infused with the community spirit for which Marquand has such commendable nostalgia.

He should surely take, in political terms, the final step and return to his origins. David Owen, the man whose ramshackle intellectual political structure Marquand, in his book, demolishes, has certainly returned to his; for Owen, who once so dominated Marquand in the

Commons, emerged from a *petit bourgeois* world well known to those of us familiar with the nuances of yesterday's Welsh society, of local doctors, dentists, solicitors, mine and forge managers, and comfortably-off shopkeepers who clustered together to play-act as lords and ladies, fantasising themselves as the aristocracy which Wales lacked, and deliberately disassociating themselves from the overwhelmingly solid proletarian majority which surrounded them: Geoffrey Howe, Michael Heseltine and Kenneth Baker, all born in South Wales within a few miles of each other, sprang from such pretentious backgrounds. In the Owen family, however, there was one man who was out of step: this was his engaging uncle who shared a cell with my uncle in the First World War when they were both conscientious objectors. After a spell in the Communist Party, Owen's uncle joined the Labour Party where, since he lived to a good age, I enjoyed his friendship; but such warmth was not extended to him by his family; they treated him as an outsider. The political fissures between Marquand and Owen, between an emphasis on communality and the presentation of Thatcher's views in a pretty 'social market' package by a pretty face, has a history which tells not a little of the class structure of yesterday's Wales.

The split in the Alliance Party stems from the conflict of political philosophies represented by these two men: but the internal struggles of their peripheral political parties are but side-shows.

On a wider front, a battle is now waging and has to be fought to the end by all who believe no man is an island. It is not dewy-eyed to assert that only a society informed by fraternity and comradeship can arrest the disintegration with which we are threatened. Thatcher and her guru, Chief Rabbi Jacobovitz, have laid down their positions, and against their reductionist individualism the war must be waged. And if we doubt that victory will be ours, let us remind ourselves that we have enlisted under the banner of Eros, the 'Heavenly Power', as Freud named the life instinct, which has as its goal the binding together of men into society and is for ever engaged in the struggle with the other 'Heavenly Power', the destructive instinct, Thanatos, ever attempting to atomise society.

When, in 1931, the menace of Hitler was already beginning to be apparent, Freud wrote, 'And now it is to be expected that the other of the two "Heavenly Powers" eternal Eros, will make an effort to assert himself in his struggle with his equally immortal adversary. But who can foresee with what success and with what result.'[26]

Given the nature of Nazism, it is not surprising that Freud left the issue open. But in the end, after appalling carnage, Eros did not fail him. Nor, if we become the gods' allies, will Eros fail us.

14

Secrets

THE anxiety which has been noted as the societal condition which assisted Thatcher to power in 1979 has, despite her promises, not dissipated: it has increased. The novelist Margaret Drabble in 1988 accurately depicted our condition.[1]

A new tyranny of fear has been born from today's unequal society. Britain, we are repeatedly told by the press and the politicians, is richer under Thatcherite monetarism, with the newly released competitive energies of the market place, than it has been for decades. How odd, then, if this is so, that we should be so nervous, so alarmist, so frightened of walking the streets at night or taking public transport of an evening. Should we not feel safer, more protected in the citadel of our money? We are not, we know, and we know although we do not admit it, that we live in a society so unjust and unequal that groups within it declare unofficial war upon other groups . . . What are our growth industries now? They are the offspring of fear. Private health insurance, private hospitals, burglar alarms, barbed wire, guard dogs, fortress architecture – these are the fruits of our profit and progress, as is the garbage which litters our streets.

Anxiety can spring from threats felt to exist in a changing environment or it can be invoked by the stirring of forces within the self with the changes science and technology are provoking unmetabolised in our increasingly unequal society; the consequent fears that are abroad need the containment of a political leadership able to allay the desperate feelings of insecurity that the imaginative novelist sees cannot be bought off with money and consumer goods. Such a political leadership cannot be supplied by Thatcher for, yet again, she cannot give what she does not possess; the basic trust which would have endowed her with emotional security is not part of her inheritance.

According to Erik Erikson,[2] the psychoanalyst whose divinations often have the vision of a great artist rather than a scientist, there is buried in all of us a nuclear conflict of basic trust and mistrust which meets its crucial test during the rages of the teething stage, when the teeth cause pain from within and when one of the few ways the baby has of obtaining relief is by biting the nipple which is, as a consequence, withdrawn from him. Teething seems to have a prototypal significance: if comfort and security are not felt by the child, if social trust is not established in the baby in the ease of his feeding, if the outer goodness of the succouring mother has not become an inner certainty, then the pain of teething, the inner harm, is intensely experienced as an external one and is projected upon those nearest to him. This is a mechanism which, in adulthood, in acute crises of confidence can often characterise irrational attitudes of mistrust towards friends and adversaries alike. Whatever the validity of Erikson's hypothesis, we are clearly formed in our mothers' arms as well as in her womb. And if the baby has been deprived of basic trust, if adult ineptitude has made the unavoidable imposition of outer controls upon an infant appear as intolerable prohibition, then the basis may be laid down for a vengeful adult personality.

In the crisis of the 1987 election when Thatcher felt Labour's electoral propaganda machine could overwhelm her, all the syndromes of a woman deprived of basic trust came to the fore. She turned upon her closest ally, Norman Tebbit, and the mistrust she displayed during those days has led to Tebbit leaving the Cabinet and biding his time preparing for the coming leadership struggle. But her mother's incapacity to give her the base upon which social trust could be built has more serious consequences. As head of our security services a prime minister has, by the conventions of our constitution, a special role untrammelled by any monitoring body of legislators. With the security services answerable in political terms only to the prime minister, they have in Thatcher a woman who will corroborate, not challenge, all their worst features.

Those lacking inner security grasp at external security, but they are chasing shadows. To reclaim even part of the loss of efficient parenting requires a painful reconstruction of the psyche; but Thatcher is not the woman to be found on the couch gaining the insights which may assist her in such a quest. She takes the easy but spurious option of demanding that the external environment gives her what she lacks. We have a fundamentally insecure woman in charge of our security service: and it has proved a combustible combination.

Under her regime, prosecutions for offences against the Official Secrets Act have proliferated, the explanation always being that

Britain's security demands absolute secrecy. It is this stance which led to Sarah Tisdall being sent to prison for alerting the *Guardian* to the arrival of cruise missiles at Greenham Common, and to the trial of Clive Ponting for communicating to an MP information uncomfortable to Thatcher about the sinking of the *Belgrano*. Her insistence against all advice on banning the trade unions at GCHQ at Cheltenham, even though they offered a no-strike agreement, her assaults upon both the BBC and the IBA for daring to impugn and reveal the activities of the security services, the intemperate and absurd pursuit of the egregious Peter Wright for publishing *Spycatcher*, and her refusal to countenance any substantial modification of the obsolescent Official Secrets Act, all reveal her passion for secrecy: without it she affirms Britain would be insecure. What is far more self evident is that without it *she* cannot feel secure.

However, the threat to democratic government does not simply arise from Thatcher's temperament. The activities of some sections of the security services who, during Wilson's premiership, deliberately attempted to destabilise the government, illustrate how menacing are some of the influences within our society. The continued troubles in Ireland and the ever pervasive fear of nuclear war gives the paranoid new opportunities to demand, in the name of national security, restrictions and censorship which severely encroach upon our civil liberties, while the public's extraordinary fascination with the feared spy can be exploited to justify the need for an increasingly secret and censored society. Security debates have always been part of the Westminster scene, but never until recent Thatcher years have they been so sustained; and the battle between those claiming to be protecting the national interest and the libertarians is often uneven, for those gripped by what Margaret Drabble calls the 'tyranny of fear' are easily stampeded.

Lamentably, Thatcher's distemper adds to the fever within our society. Yet only if we are sufficiently emancipated from these neurotic fears will the search for national security not subvert our liberties: the enemy is within us, raising false and distorted alarms. A glance at some of the unconscious motivations which cause us to over-value secrecy and so make us the easy victims of alarmists may be more than an intellectual exercise; it may be a necessity if we are to armour ourselves against those who would rob us of our liberties. And, no less, every attempt to demythologise our contemporary spy culture may act as insulation against those who tell us we are so surrounded by dangerous enemies that our freedom of expression and our liberties are luxuries we cannot afford. The traditional vigilance to preserve those liberties has never been more needed now when we have a prime minister incapacitated by her upbringing to protect us against those who would use the national security as a bludgeon to concuss our open democratic society.

When Thatcher is protecting and defending the secret services, no organisation or individual is sacred, as she showed when she raged against Thames TV for presenting an award-winning programme which, in defence of the rule of law, queried the shooting down of IRA terrorists in Gibraltar. The assault upon freedom of expression in Britain requires us to use all our armoury against the censors who, unassailed, would bring to us the premises and values of Eastern Europe.

★

The redoubtable Dr Samuel Johnson understood the nature of secrets. He observed that 'Secrets are so seldom kept that it may be with some reason doubted whether the quality of retention be generally bestowed, and whether a secret has not some subtle volatility by which it escapes imperceptibly, at the smallest event, or some power of fermentation by which it expands itself, so as to burst the heart which will not give it way.' Dr Johnson anticipated the psychoanalyst for, less elegantly, one psychoanalyst has described the temptation of secrets and the dilemma posed by our wish to keep them whilst bursting to tell them: 'The secret tempts its owner both to surrender its content and to retain it or, to put it in psychoanalytic terms, the secret pushes its owner into the familiar ambivalence conflict between expulsion and retention. This leads us to ask whether there is not in our unconscious a complete identity between the secret on the one hand and the body excretions on the other.'[3]

This psychoanalyst is prompting us to direct our attention to our early defaecations. The child prohibited from enjoying the sexual pleasure of retaining faeces; rigidly commanded to relinquish them; given no approval for her obedience; and then deprived by an enthusiastic mother of pride in her production, is the child who desperately wants to emancipate herself from dependence on her parents for the defaecatory function. She wants to control it herself and seeks to exclude the mother from the process so that she can treat it as a secret, as does everyone else. Early dissonances between the child, forced by the provocations of an unresponsive mother into a premature battle for a right to privacy, continue into adulthood; and I doubt if we can fully understand Thatcher's determined erosion of the independence of the Attorney General's Office and her absurd attempts to maintain obsolescent secrets even unto the antipodes without taking into account this facet of the wretchedness of her infancy.

However, her continued efforts to maintain secrecy are futile, for the same unconscious forces that propel her into chronic clandestinity will, given different mothering and toilet training, compel others to prattle lest, as Dr Johnson has it, their hearts burst; and the law will not silence them for the unconscious does not hold Her Majesty's judges in awe.

All of us, of course, strive to keep secrets about our personal lives and not only to keep them from the outside world: we keep our darkest secrets even from ourselves, for so often we dare not acknowledge our unconscious wishes and fantasies. Our fear of disclosure is inevitably heightened if the extravagant, unrealisable desires which possess us in infancy still remain unmodified, embedded within us, in adulthood. And whilst all children keep secrets, the greatest significance of secret-keeping is to the Oedipal child.[4] The child's sexual desire for the parent of the opposite sex and aggressive feelings towards the other parent must be kept secret or the wrath of the parent-rival will be incurred.[5] If the rival mother, despite the destructive secret wishes of the infant, nevertheless continues to respond with love and reassurance, the infant can move forward and renounce the impossible desire; but if the child is left bereft of a protective mother or care-taker who provides comfort and who shows a loving constancy, despite the secret destructiveness of the infant, then the child's fear that the terrible secret will come out mounts and that fear will cling to her right through to adulthood. She will never have the security which would help to diminish her anxiety that the wrath of the mother will fall upon her; she will be fated as a grown-up to walk not only in fear but in loneliness.

That tragic loneliness will come about because the mother is feared as enemy, not embraced as ally. When the mother is felt to be good she can be encapsulated, introjected, and thus internalised, can be with us to the grave giving us confidence and solace in our life struggles. When we lack such internalised supportive figures then, never having had the initial comfort, as John Bowlby in his magisterial work *Attachment and Loss* has so richly illustrated, the world is found to be comfortless and the adult's response to that world is to wage unceasing war upon it.[6] In that war the secret must always be sustained by the isolated adult, from herself and others, that the ultimate source of her belligerency is to be found in unabated incestuous rivalry. When we find those who are passionate and extravagant in their affirmations of the need to protect state secrets we must look to the personal secrets they are so desperate to hide from themselves.

All this should be borne in mind when we find Thatcher, more than any public figure, so insistently declaring her allegiance to her father without any acknowledgment of the existence of her mother. As the years go on, the adulation of her father becomes more and more extravagant. In a revealing interview with Brian Walden in May 1988 she went completely over the top.[7] The grocer's ultimate apotheosis was delivered. 'Her eyes shone as she delivered it,' Walden tells us and then, swooning romantically (as becomes so total an anchorite), he asked, 'Was any man better loved by his daughter?' Breathlessly she poured out her tributes, 'he had great breadth of wisdom', 'he was a very clever man', 'I would talk to him about the great financial matters of the country', 'he understood the fundamentals'. Walden, overcome by her fervour – and no doubt recounting, as is his wont, what she wished to have recorded – concludes that 'all her ideas are inherited from her father as is her courage and strength of character.' I knew one other public woman who constantly spoke to me in similar terms of her father: Lady Megan Lloyd George. But then her father was Lloyd George, not the tinpot Alderman Alfred Roberts of Grantham.

Yet after that interview even Walden was left with certain misgivings about his heroine. In the Commons smoke rooms or bars I often observed this supreme schmoozer flattering colleagues and massaging their egos whilst masking his ironic mockery of their weaknesses, and on this occasion, too, his dubious detachment did not desert him. He began to think Thatcher had a secret. 'I claim to understand Margaret Thatcher but I wonder if I do? I wonder if anybody does? How much does this passionate, repressed woman keep to herself? Is the certain sound of the trumpet a necessary outer protection for a deep loneliness within?' The interrogator had boobed. If he had asked about her mother he would not have had to ask himself those questions, he would have discovered the secret and known the answers.

Daughters making exaggerated claims for their fathers was a phenomenon explored by Freud as long ago as 1913. In his essay, 'Two lies told by children', he tells of a daughter whose unusually strong attachment to her father was destined to wreck her happiness in life. Freud describes how when the child could no longer escape the discovery that her beloved father was not as great a personage as she was inclined to think him, she could not put up with this departure from her ideal, so she continued to boast of his attributes to her school friends. These deceptions, Freud tells us, arose from 'the sense of guilt which was attached to her excessive fondness for her father': to have made an admission of her deceit was impossible, for 'it would have inevitably been an admission of her incestuous love.'

Therefore when we examine Thatcher's fierce attachment to the need for secrecy we ought to bear in mind the imbalance in her relationship with her father and her banished mother, her intemperate declarations of fealty to her father, and the loneliness about which Walden speculated, and which I believe is her lot because she is bereft of the internalised, comforting mother.

More, we should remain on enquiry wondering whether there are additional secrets concerning her father which move her to so ostentatiously defend his memory. We now know that when Margaret Roberts was a schoolgirl of eleven a satire on the town of Grantham entitled *Rotten Borough* was written by a local journalist.[8] Because of its scandalous nature, under threat of libel actions, it was withdrawn after circulating for some weeks. However, before its suppression, the *Grantham Journal* had reported: 'Grantham is agog. Not for years has that respectable town been so excited. Grantham thinks it recognises itself as the "Rotten Borough" in the book . . . it thinks it recognises some of its most eminent burghers in the story . . . ' Among those fictional characters was a local councillor who ran a corner grocer's shop, not unlike the one where Margaret Thatcher was born and reared. That fictional character is depicted as a humbug, with wandering eyes and hands. The *Guardian* correspondent who revealed the existence of the novel and made a trawl in Grantham to investigate the background, tells us he was told that Alfred Roberts had 'a reputation for behaviour somewhat like that of the fictional character in Rotten Borough'.[9] And, understandably, he asks whether there is any connection between Thatcher's banning of *Spycatcher* and the suppression of *Rotten Borough*. 'When Margaret Hilda Thatcher went to school did the other girls giggle because they had been reading *Rotten Borough* (it sold like hot cakes in Grantham)? And if Daddy and his friends could get a book banned why shouldn't she?'

There are other speculations too that suggest themselves. Is she forgiving her father's sexual skirmishes when she is so indulgent to those of her ministers? What is certain is that sometimes she can, seemingly wholly out of character, be determinedly non-judgmental on the follies of the previous generation. There is a curious paragraph in one of her speeches which begins predictably enough but then suddenly changes direction: ' . . . it is arrogant to claim that our generation is any wiser than previous generations. We are here they are gone. We can stand on their shoulders as I hope succeeding generations will be able to stand on ours. But we should not be too hasty in judging them . . . because to judge requires so much knowledge, such an effort of imagination to put ourselves into their shoes, which could well be spent – barring the professional historian

– on understanding our own pressing problems.' 'It may not be going too far to see this', Graham Little has shrewdly observed, 'as a personal comment that shows how Thatcher has dealt with that fraught period in her childhood before she entered the groove she now recalls . . . '[10] Thatcher frequently has said that she is not affected by attacks on her but that her hurts come when her family is attacked. Is she referring to her living family or her dead one? In almost all families there are skeletons in the cupboard; one is left feeling the Roberts family had more than their share and that, in turn, the young Margaret had more than her share of dilemmas. The poignancy of her early predicaments must not however so enlist our sympathy when we debate the issues of national security that we fail to discount the private nexus upon which her prejudices on secrecy issues rest.

There are some, like the Kohutian self-psychoanalysts, who conceptualise an irrational demand for secrecy in somewhat different terms from Freud but do so in a manner which should put us no less on guard when Thatcher defends her stance on security issues. These psychoanalysts, using the term 'self' to mean the organisation of experiences that – in combination with inborn givens – have shaped one's individual and unique psyche, say that the importance of keeping something secret about oneself increases with one's sense of the vulnerability and fragility of one's self. They claim there is no greater danger to one's person than of losing the coherence and continued viability of one's self. The more fragile this organisation of experiences, this self, the more anxious one feels and the more one will try to protect this self against its vulnerability being exposed; for exposure means that one's real or imagined adversaries will find a chink in one's armour and exploit it to one's destruction.[11]

Secrecy thus not only protects against dangers from the outside, but in an even more compelling fashion keeps hidden one's weaknesses from oneself because an acknowledgment would be so shattering to one's self esteem as to be unbearable: rather act self-destructively than admit a shortcoming. None of us are completely free from this dangerous need to lie to ourselves but there are certainly some who have a more fragile self and those so stricken can be extraordinarily self-deceiving. I believe Thatcher never had the early corroboration which would have given her a cohesive self, and that her fears of disintegration consequently limit her capacity for openness. The fervour with which she seeks to enforce secrecy in our public affairs betrays the source: it is not founded on a cool, objective assessment of the balance between freedom of investigation and right to information on the one hand and national security on the other.

It stems from Thatcher's need to convert her fear of her innermost secrets being revealed to herself into a fevered terror of freedom of information in the public sphere.

Indeed, it is difficult not to be drawn to the surmise that Thatcher, when resisting freedom of information in the public sphere, moves involuntarily in a waking dream. There is clinical evidence that ablators – those attempting to obliterate a parental image – often dream about espionage and double agents, for it is not possible to exclude from consciousness one's own mother without the consequence, the sense of betrayal of a parent, finding some outlet; and it is in the dream, when the internal censor is somnambulent, that the truth, however distorted and condensed, emerges.

The psychoanalyst, Charles Rycroft, telling of the sense of betrayal felt by his ablating patients, has written, 'This underlying sense of betraying something, even and indeed especially when they feel they are being creative, explains, I think, why such people not infrequently dream about espionage and double agents, since the world of espionage is one in which every action is ambiguous, in which physical courage may be linked with moral cowardice and in which the hero and the traitor may be one and the same person.'[12] But just as the psychoanalysts find that ablators people their dreams with spies and counterspies, so we find Thatcher engaged in a similar exercise in the public domain. Dreams, Freud has told us, may be a necessity to enable us to sleep. Thatcher, however, sleeps but a little; and I suspect she acts out what other ablators mediate in their dreams. Her vain bid for psychic discontinuity results in a projection outwards and, in her trance, she conjures up for us a world full of menacing infiltrators who can be overcome only by security measures which would stifle our freedoms.

We may regard her plight as piteous – such were the misunderstandings between her mother and herself sixty-four years ago that now, to avoid deepening her pain and wishing to maintain the delusory caesura in her biography, she would deny us a more open society. But if we value our liberties we must temper our sympathy for her in her predicament. Because if we believe we have some understanding of the causes of the weakness, we cannot allow her to wreak her havoc. If, sadly, she was so disadvantaged that she was faulted at the start, we cannot relieve her of her individual neurosis by permitting it to become the collective neurosis of the nation.

*

On Kim Philby's death the *Guardian* editorial affirmed 'In a furtively governed country the morbid fixation on spies is insatiable.' It is a fixation which can be a bane to defenders of civil liberties and a boon to Thatcher. The editorial writer has perceptively seen the conjunction of Thatcher's compulsive need for secrecy with the nation's resistance to demythologising the spy. It was no editorial extravagance when the *Guardian* added, 'Those, if any, who understand why Kim Philby held a nation in thrall for a quarter of a century and inspired a whole library of fantasy (much of it passed off as a fact) are probably as close to the soul of modern Britain as any one is likely to get.'

The sickness is indeed within the soul: the insistence in Christian cultures upon the Virgin Birth stands witness to our deep sense of betrayal. It is not only Thatcher who would fantasise that she is a parthenogenetic product, appropriating for herself the uniqueness of the immaculately conceived Virgin Mary. All resent their own conception. The denial in the Christ myth of the intervention of the human father reveals the true agony of us all: Judas was our scapegoat. Upon him we projected all our repudiated anger against the parents who dared to love exclusively.

Now Christian faith totters in Britain and Judas has become geriatric, unable to bear our burdens. No longer can the edicts of the Catholic Church, carrying with them our subterranean fury, act as a prophylactic: the injunction imposed by the sons of God upon parents, forbidding them to revel without thought of children, has lost its force. We are consequently desperate for alternatives, drugs that will give us the relief of amnesia and blot out our parents' sexuality. With a prime minister whose needs are in concordance with her electorate, the spy culture is the cocaine which contemporary Britain has chosen.

The betrayal theme has always haunted Christian culture. On the Cross, Christ accuses God the Father of betraying him: the cock – an uncomfortably explicit sexual symbol – crowing thrice to herald Peter's foreshadowed betrayal of Christ is, some would say, one of the most significant leitmotifs of the Testament. But today that theme is no longer worked through by believers in a reading of the Epistles; the abreaction is attempted in a shallow culture of contemporary espionage fables. But the tale of the spy, the voyeur, seeking and reviewing the secrets of the State, is only our cover story. It is hiding our buried wish to see and discover the secrets of our coupling parents and then to have them punished for their licentiousness.

When early in the century Joseph Conrad[13] wrote the unsurpassed espionage tale, *The Secret Agent*, telling all to be known of the tragic emptiness, futility and nihilism of the game, he was compelled to apologise to the reading public for presenting so sordid a theme. He would not have needed to excuse himself today. Now a ceaseless flow of television spy tales and tedious outpourings of cold war novels are eagerly consumed. The spies are endowed with beauty, evil, heroism and cunning, but all their compulsive symptoms are smudged. Yet the fictions leave the viewers and readers unassuaged. Still the aching heart yearns for vengeance, spies from the real world are demanded and these heroes and villains, all part of ourselves, must triumph and then suffer. Fearful lest otherwise we will not hold ourselves in check, we demand that doom always follows their success: and the wages of their sins must be death or imprisonment. Only thus can we dare to enjoy, second-hand, the betrayal of the betrayers. Our personal emotional security demands both that there are spies and that we must pursue and harry them. Thatcher and the security services, for their own sakes and for the sake of the panting electorate, liberally supply the raw material and the required harassment.

Not since the days of repression in Britain occasioned by the Establishment's fear of the French Revolution has there been such a paranoiac era. Pitt and Lord Liverpool could at least, however, have claimed that the realities justified their vigilance, given the turbulence abroad and the restlessness and agitation among the working classes. Thatcher has no such fig leaf; yet, under her premiership, spies and their pursuit have been the subject matter of hours of Parliamentary debates and television series and of acres of newsprint. Her interest in spies is no new phenomenon: her schoolgirl contemporaries[14] still vividly recall the fourth former's persistent and over-eager questioning of a visiting lecturer known for his spy tales and biographies: spies light her up. Morbid excitements which should be dampened are stirred up and often provoked by Thatcher herself. Healthy leadership, contrariwise, would *deglamorise* the spy, strip him down to his pathetic psychopathology, and so, elliptically, woo a nation away from its childish arrest to discover the secrets of the parents' bedroom and help it to accept, without fear, that parents too are sexual beings.

Certainly when spies are viewed clinically, their fascination vanishes. By a curious combination of circumstances in my political and professional life I have been compelled to ponder on the psychopathology of a number of major spies, either because I have met them, or because their activities have impinged upon a field of endeavour such as penal or homosexual law reform in which I have been involved. Their case histories are so repetitive, so explicit, and indeed so monotonous, that one has to conclude that they would never have been allowed to enter and penetrate our security services – which contain many of high intelligence – if it were not that too many of those who man our services and screen the new entries bury the unconscious motivations which cause them to choose their odd career. To weed out their enemies would require a self scrutiny which they cannot face: if they understood themselves, they would understand and identify those who seek to subvert.

The secretive Prime Minister has in her eye her own special mote which obscures her vision. Way back in 1981, raising the issue not for the first or last time, I pressed her:[15]

Mr Leo Abse (Pontypool): Is there not a clear need to strengthen still further the rigours of the Security Service selection board which was introduced in 1977, so that the motivation of candidates is probed in depth? The dangers are increasing. We face dangers in admitting those whose private heterosexual infidelities bear witness to their incapacity for loyalty, or those whose disturbed homosexuality – following a long line of spies from Marlowe, to Casement, to Burgess and Blunt – means that they are compulsively disloyal. Surely it is time that we sophisticated our procedures and brought in psychoanalysts and psychiatrists to be attached to the board, so that we do not use out-of-date old-fashioned, rule-of-thumb methods of selection. If the Prime Minister is looking to the future as she says, surely it is time that we made certain that our selection procedures were worthy of the twentieth century not the nineteenth century.

The Prime Minister: That is exactly what the terms of reference will enable the commission to do, among other things. The terms of reference are: 'To review the security procedures and practices currently followed in the public service and to consider what, if any, changes are required.' What the Hon. Gentleman said will be within the terms of reference.

Within the terms of reference it undoubtedly was but commissions – as the truncated reports which they issue so often illustrate – prefer to sail in shallower waters, and the lessons to be gained by a close study of the early lives of those who have betrayed the nation remain unlearned. Yet even a perfunctory glance, as I now propose, at some of our notorious spies, surely illustrates the high price we pay for the refusal of the Prime Minister, the security commissions and the security services to use the available armoury of contemporary depth psychology.

*

I have an especial grudge against those who so naively recruited George Blake, the double, perhaps treble, agent who inflicted more damage on the British security services than any other man in this century; caused the death of scores of British agents on Soviet territories; and upon whom the Lord Chief Justice inflicted a sentence of forty-two years, the longest determinate sentence ever meted out in recent legal history. His escape after a short period in prison, with considerable resources, and ultimately with Soviet aid, scandalised a nation. Following upon the escape I was appointed to a small committee of the Home Office Advisory Committee on Penal Reform and charged with the task of reviewing regimes for maximum security prisons. I found it no easy task to hold back the reaction against liberal penal reform that Blake's return to Russia precipitated; for the demands which were made for greater security in prison could only be achieved at the expense of the constructive and rehabilitative elements which feebly struggled to gain a place within the regime. To have weakly responded to the clamour in the House and the country would have meant that our prisons would have become still more primitive, still more destructive and, in the long view, still more used. But the nation was certainly not then in the mood to hear – as I had often been told by RAF prisoner-of-war friends of mine – men can only live in a prison if they believe there is some hope of escape. Blake's escape still continues to hinder the acceptance by the House of Commons that we cannot indefinitely continue to expand the prison population when prison sentences neither deter nor reform those who receive them. Wanting vengeance, the nation resists the alternative (for those who are not dangerously violent), of a rapid build-up of strong supportive services within the community, services which are designed to rehabilitate criminals in a non-custodial setting. The hopes of those of us proposing such reforms were dashed by the furore caused by Blake's escape. In a nauseating self-righteous book published in April 1989[16] the authors boast, that with a convicted paederast and the supply of funds from an unidentified source, they assisted Blake to reach East Germany: unconvincingly they seek to exculpate themselves from any responsibility for defeats suffered by penal reformers as a result of their self-proclaimed humanitarianism. In fact, as a consequence of their adolescent romanticism, the Russians triumphed over the penal reformers; and, by a rare irony, the thousands of men who today rot three to a stinking cell in our jails can lay not a small part of the responsibility for their grim fate upon Kosygin's hirelings and dupes.

It required no special prescience to identify Blake as far too vulnerable a man to be employed in our Intelligence services. His whole early life was punctuated by events calculated to make him, at least unconsciously, yearn for revenge upon Britain. His father, Behar, an Egyptian Jew holding a British passport and living in Holland, was an ostentatious British patriot who probably acted as a British Intelligence agent in the First World War. In honour of George V, young Blake was burdened by his Christian name and, like everything else that was to associate him with his determinedly British father, it was to bring him little but misfortune. His father was poisoned by German phosgene gas in the First World War, and died when George was only thirteen. Children irrationally interpret the death of a parent as a desertion; George's father's death also meant that the boy was summarily wrenched away from his mother (a Lutheran Protestant), from his sister, from his ambition to be a priest, and from his settled home. For Behar had left a fiat, submitted to by his wife, that on his death his son had to be sent to an uncle in Egypt. It needs no special imagination to relate to the feelings of the young adolescent who found the consequences of his Egyptian father's love for Britain was to make him an orphan, exiled in a strange land.

Worse was to follow. When eventually George Blake returned to Holland, the tenuous British connection was to precipitate the break-up of the family home, with the Dutch mother and daughter compelled to flee to Britain and with the British George arrested by the Gestapo. When the young man did finally succeed in making his getaway he came to a Britain where his foreign descent barred him from ever feeling fully accepted. Certainly holding a British passport was no blessing but a curse for George Blake. With a father who had betrayed him by his choice of nationality, by his unnecessary death condemning him to exile, and whose allegiances had provoked his son's arrest in Holland and alienation in Britain, it would indeed be astonishing if the son's deep resentment was not to be worked out against his father's first love. Only our secret service could have been so accommodating as to provide full facilities for George Blake to attack his father's land and so to commit posthumous parricide. Yet the scantiest psychiatric screening by the Intelligence service would have saved Blake from himself; scores of our agents from falling into Russian hands; and penal reformers in Britain from a tragic setback.

Those in the spy industry, anxious, like many in the security service, to protect their territory, dismiss such psychologising; it deromanticises the glamorous characters who people their books, for they know their readers want to read of heroes and resourceful bold villains, not maimed, immature men, all suffering lonely exiled lives.

One of the doyens of the industry, the journalist Phillip Knightley, quoting a *Times* article of mine in which I sought to diagnose Blake's predicament, has angrily attacked me in his book[17] and affirms the facts about Blake to be quite otherwise and quite simple. Blake, he tells us, was a committed communist from his youth and acted throughout in accordance with his principles. But it is very naive to imagine that professional spies choose their roles out of ideological passion alone, and Blake was certainly no exception to the rule. To justify his conclusion, Knightley tells us that as a youngster in Cairo, Blake was influenced by his cousin, a founder member of the Egyptian Communist Party, but he revealingly adds that Blake has said that 'early in his life he had thought of becoming a Roman Catholic priest but chose instead the alternative faith of the communist world.' Despite Knightley's assiduous collection of facts, on this recounting he will never be a successful hacker, able to decipher the code of the spy. The oscillation of the young Blake between the infallibilities of an authoritarian-toned religion, and a party of anti-clerical atheism presages the future switch of loyalties which made him the supreme double agent. The ambiguities and doubts of those youthful commitments were but reflections of the struggles being waged within his psyche, conflicts which were never to be resolved, but were acted out throughout his life. Knightley's understanding of Blake falls far short of the insight of the fellow prisoner, a psychopathic attempted murderer, who masterminded the spy's escape and later joined him in Moscow. He said of Blake 'he is a born traitor. Blake does not betray for ideals; he betrays because he *needs* to betray. If Blake had been born a Russian he would have betrayed the KGB to the British. That's how he's made.'[18]

The same wearisome syndromes to be observed in Blake were presented to me when I met the spy Peter Kroger in prison where he was serving a twenty-year sentence after his raided house had revealed a treasure trove of Soviet-made espionage paraphernalia: a short-wave transmitter, false passports and concealed bundles of a variety of currencies. In gaol he had insulated himself from his severe surroundings and from his long sentence by play-acting a part in a debased Dostoevsky story. It was an easy role for him to assume. He was a half educated man with embarrassing literary pretensions and a self-conscious love of books and, despite the absurd press glamorisation of this spy – as of every spy – the only identity he was capable of attaining was of a second-rate hero in a shabby novel. The stilted literary language and the vulgar brummagem of sentiment in which he artificially described to me his predicament trivialised the real tragedy of his position. Yet, from the interstices of the droll and over gentle lines he had assigned to himself, there welled up a great hatred of authority.

He shared, with all the murderers and violent robbers by whom he was surrounded, a hatred and fear of all the parent-surrogates – from the Home Secretary to the prison governor responsible for containing him in the maximum security block. He was clearly at home with all these rejected men and, with barely concealed conceit, used his slightly superior intelligence to act as priest-confessor to them and become a presiding chairman between the rival gang groupings within the security block. The game became him. He could empathise with his outcast prison colleagues and at the same time play the father: simultaneously he was betrayer and betrayed, and although the fear of dying in the prison sometimes overwhelmed him, the satisfaction to be obtained from his fantasy as a gaoled romantic hero shored him up.

Kroger bristled as I sought unobtrusively to move to a discussion on his relationship with his parents. His defences were alerted and determinedly he redirected the conversation and discussed his wife Helen, telling me of his love for her in embarrassingly novelettish terms. She had been separately jailed, and I found his opportuning, asking me to intervene and obtain for him the right to meet her periodically, couched in adolescent terms. He addressed me not as man to man: he seemed to be more concerned to assert his rights under the prison regulations, and persuade me of the tyranny of the authorities, than to meet his woman. The shadow of assertive antagonistic parents, thwarting his claims, enshrouded him.

Kroger's fellow spy, the Russian masquerading as Gordon Lonsdale, has given us even more explicit documentation of his motivation. Whatever ambiguity there may be about his birthplace, it is established that Lonsdale's parents' marriage broke up and the deserted mother, living in Russia, unable or unwilling to keep the twelve-year old boy, sent him far away to a state institution school. Lonsdale has explained the position in a letter discovered in Kroger's bungalow. 'I did not wish it and I did not seek it; but it turned out to be. I have thought very much about it – why all this? The answer is it all started in 1932 when mother decided to send me to the nether regions. At that time she could not imagine all the consequences of this step. I do not blame her.' His protest that his mother did not bear any responsibility may be too much, but the significant lack of acquittal of his deserting, betraying father cannot be denied: in all his life he worked out his revenge by creating a life totally dedicated to betrayal.

Sometimes these unhappy men, who, as Lonsdale poignantly

declared, do not freely seek their fate, are propelled a little off the more usual spy trail. There is a character type that originates in a childhood picture of the father as a figure of almost unlimited power who sets a problem in loyalty because the child does not know how to dispose of the hostility which grows up together with his strong feelings of love. This ambivalence is sometimes imperfectly resolved by distinguishing between a good father who is loved and a bad father who is repressed and displaced. In adult life, the less integrated may recreate a representative of the good father as the head of the country: and the bad figure as the world outside. Out of such material can spring blind patriotism and great hatred of alien authorities. But sometimes the primal loyalty of the child to a father who was himself an outsider causes a reversal in the pattern.[19]

Kim Philby was the son of such an outsider. His singular father, St John Philby, had played the part of an Arabist *éminence grise* to the oil chiefs of the desert, receiving much honour outside Britain but little or none within, and his resentment of such lack of recognition consumed him. His hostility to Britain was so fierce that it was felt safer during the last war to imprison him. It was incredible folly on the part of the security services to have elevated to a key position the fractured son of such a man and so give that son full opportunity to act out his unresolved Oedipal problems.

In Kim Philby's case, the original love bond had prompted an alliance between the son and his father in the wilderness. In his alienation from Britain the fractured son was following his father's example. When Kim Philby said, 'To betray, you must first belong', he was announcing the fact that he was always estranged from Britain: his communism was but a vehicle for his hate. In Britain he found only his bad father: Russia was his good father and it was his bad father who was, deservedly in his eyes, to be punished by him. For his wretched work he was to receive full praise from his good father and he was buried in Moscow in 1988 amidst paeans of appreciation from the Kremlin. Those in our security services who were so blind as to let him wreak his vengeance would, before he was lowered into his honoured grave, have been deserving bearers of his coffin. Those who prompted him not only lacked insight; they lacked any sense of history, for there is no novelty in the role or psychopathology of Kim Philby. He had followed the same course as had been precariously walked by many alienated Englishmen who, in other days, eulogised Napoleon and loathed the British Government.[20]

Philby of course had conquered them with his extraordinary charm, an essentially feminine quality, to which those in our security service responsible for his advancement yielded so bounteously. Men who never accept their homosexual component, and are forever rigorously repressing it, are particularly vulnerable to charm of Philby's order. In such company, they can release an imperfectly repressed element in their nature in socially acceptable form. How dangerous and how extravagant and blinding such repression can be is only too obviously revealed in the ease with which the most blatant and disturbed homosexuals have, to their discomfort and the nation's, been granted clearance by our security invigilators.

The spy, Vassall, provides an obvious example of the self deceit of those who direct our Intelligence services. An agent for the Russians for seven years, he was positively vetted by the security service before being sent to Moscow and again positively vetted before being attached to the Naval Intelligence Division. Yet he is as obvious a passive homosexual as I have ever encountered. A few minutes' conversation with such a man, and an awareness of his style of speech, manner and posture, would surely have alerted any worldly person, unless of course the interviewer was so anxiously trying to obscure his own homosexual component that he was oblivious to its appearance in anyone else.

The worthy judges and lawyers who conducted the Vassall inquiry and came to the conclusion that no one could be held responsible for failing to detect Vassall's homosexuality as a security risk, and, further, that the senior members of our Moscow Embassy could not be blamed for failing to notice his effeminacy were, however, bound to record that the more robust members of the junior embassy staff referred to Vassall amongst themselves as 'Vera'. And whatever assessments our ambassadors, the under secretaries of state for Scotland, and security chiefs may make, I have no doubt he would have been so described by any group of factory workers within my former constituency if he had spent ten minutes with them.

I am entitled to suspect the fastidiousness that fails to recognise a homosexual after months of associating with him. Those who have come to terms with their own homosexual component, possessed as it is by every man and woman, are not terrified to see and sympathise with a man whose homosexuality has overwhelmed him and left him emasculated. For many years the wretched Vassall languished in his cell after being thrust into roles by men of superior rank and intelligence that, given his character, provoked his nemesis. The over-civilised Radcliffe Tribunal acquitted his superiors of responsibility for the resulting breaches of security; but I doubt that any of his superiors are entirely without responsibility for this miserable man having found himself in a maximum-security prison.

There was within the Radcliffe Report, as in the later Diplock

Security Commission Report, an assumption that the real danger to our national security comes from a homosexual's vulnerability to exposure and prosecution, not from his homosexuality. Indeed, the Diplock Commission justified their policy of barring anyone discovered by positive vetting to be homosexual from the diplomatic services – and from any government or civil service post which might involve an overseas posting – by explaining that 'adult homosexual relationships between consenting male adults are still offences against the criminal law of foreign states to which persons serving in the diplomatic service are liable to be posted, and these include the USSR and other states in the Soviet bloc.'[21] This is an extraordinarily jejune view; the antics of heterosexuals have been used as blackmail by the Russians with equal effect, as they have used the conduct of homosexuals. The Commissioners appeared to have an inability to face the real problem which is only too clearly spelt out in the spy stories strewn across British history.

From James I – of whom it was said he gave his money to his favourites and the secrets of state to everyone – down to Guy Burgess, treachery is uncomfortably linked with disturbed homosexuals who are unable to come to terms with their sexual destiny. This is a harsh judgment, but from Elizabethan times until today the names of notorious homosexual traitors and spies ring out. Vassall, Burgess and Blunt are but the end of a long line stretching back to Lord Henry Howard, Francis Bacon, Christopher Marlowe and Antonio Pérez. In this century two of the most notorious traitors, the Austrian Colonel Redl and the tragic Roger Casement, were compulsive and bizarre homosexuals. This correspondence between irreconciled homosexuality and treachery is not surprising. In so many cases a contributory cause of homosexuality is a hostile father, or one who is felt to be hostile; who takes away the manhood of the son. It would be more surprising if such an emasculated son did *not* grow up feeling compelled to seek revenge upon the State, the symbol of all authoritarian and interfering paternalistic qualities.

So obvious was Vassall's frailty that to fail to keep him away from security matters was inexcusable. But an Intelligence service with a serious and sophisticated capacity to invigilate those they recruit would have also disqualified Anthony Blunt – and that was not only because of his past public commitment to Marxism or because of his homosexuality, activities which were also recklessly ignored. There are other factors which could have placed informed recruiters on enquiry; for the reputation which was later to lead Blunt to become the Keeper of the Queen's pictures had become well established before he had been recruited. Art critic to the *Spectator*, lecturer at the Warburg Institute, reader in the History of Art at the University of London, and deputy director of the Courtauld Institute of Art, were all part of his CV by the time, in his early thirties, he entered the secret service. As his revelatory and sparkling books show, he had the gift of vision, and a penetrating mind: he was, in short, the supreme voyeur. But our security services were not alert enough when faced with such a disturbed homosexual to recall the warning jingle, 'I spy, I spy with my little eye, said the spider to the fly.' We can learn much from our nursery rhymes if we recall them in adulthood: they have endured because of the truth they tell. The spy, it can be learned, enjoys the considerable pleasure of the eye.

No man who has been given the glad eye by a flirtatious woman will be surprised to learn that in a child's early development the eye can act as an erotogenic zone in the same way as other bodily areas, such as the skin, mouth, anus and genitals. Freud said, 'The eyes perceive not only alterations in the external world which are important for the preservation of life but also characteristics of objects which lead to their being chosen as objects of love – their charms.'[22] The vicissitudes of development which an erotogenic zone and its accompanying instinctual processes may undergo apply to the eye and seeing. I have in my time defended too many peeping toms in the magistrates' courts not to have become aware how compulsive scopophilia (the eroticisation of the wish to look) can be; and how that early urge to look will persist in a most dangerous form in adult life if it has been frustrated and denied adequate expression because of lack of response by a nursing mother. Blunt's scopophilia clearly persisted; its singular libidinal vitality made him a good art critic but it also made him a compulsive viewer, a course which gave him the same sexual release as was obtained by my wretched clients who were compulsively driven to spy upon couples petting or copulating.

At first I had treated the conduct of my clients as mere peccadillos and pleaded for them on that basis. I did not fully appreciate that their sexual perversions were the living out of pieces of infantile sexual behaviour which had been retained in the personality in order to hold in check other, more undesirable, elements.[23] For the clinicians have pointed out that the scopophiliac impulse also regularly includes an element of sadism.[24] I was to discover that highly developed voyeurist perversions did not always act as a sufficient guard to protect the afflicted men from the sadism welling up inside them. Sometimes, happily infrequently, the defence breaks down and I then saw those whom I had originally defended on a minor offence were now facing serious charges of grievous bodily harm, sexual assault and, indeed, of murder.

Blunt's sadism almost certainly was not adequately held back by his scopophilic guard: it burst out in a determined prolonged assault on the nation's security. His massive intellectual ability gave him the capacity to rationalise his behaviour as a political commitment, but the source of his treachery lay not in his Marxism but in his perversions. He may have been able to deceive himself, but he should not have been able to deceive the security services. Those like Professor George Steiner who, in a coruscating essay on Blunt in the *New Yorker*, appear to suggest there is a perplexing dichotomy between the man as great art critic and traitor are wholly mistaken. He was, tragically, all of one piece.

Similarly, there was no paradox in the many lives led by Tom Driberg, one of the most delightful and stimulating of my Commons colleagues. His wit and erudition enlivened for me many a dreary hour in the Commons Smoke Room as, during all-night sittings, we awaited the division bell to release us from our captivity. Now a whole gaggle of spy writers heap their obloquy upon him, claiming that, as an MI5 agent, he spied on the Communist Party and on his Parliamentary colleagues. They allege our secret services used him as a means of colluding with Burgess in Moscow, thereby ensuring that the book Burgess was publishing would whitewash MI5; and Chapman Pincher, never loath to yield to a paranoid elaboration, claims too that Driberg was a double agent.[25]

Notoriously, indeed deliciously, indiscreet, he was an odd choice for MI5: I believe it is more likely he hooked MI5 into recruiting *him*. All his life he walked on a tight-rope and gained his thrills by a never ending series of public and private adventures, courageously and foolhardily oscillating from one role to another almost every day of his life. Distinguished journalist, grammarian and churchman, he would be as punctilious about ecclesiastical ritual or a semi-colon as he was obsessional in his trawl of the 'cottages' of Britain – his fastidiousness was never extended to the unkempt, delinquent youngsters who, in his prowling, he compulsively pursued. Driberg doubtless played the part of a spy with superb skill. The MI5 officers who ineptly recruited him would never have been able to use Tom; Tom would have had an especial pleasure in making fools of them. And, knowing him, I have no doubt he would have told his credulous controllers Bible stories they would never have heard before: it must have been a glorious send up. Surely such a debunker of the secret-service myth deserved the peerage bestowed upon him.

Tom Driberg's activities in MI5 were probably little more than harmless fooling showing in a very less acute form the symptoms of traitors like Blunt and Burgess. They belong to the group of disturbed homosexuals with a long and dishonourable tradition. Did not Judas kiss and embrace Christ as he betrayed him? It unhappily cannot be disputed that there is an association between irreconciled homosexuality and a propensity for spying and often, in addition, for treachery.

★

The roll-call of those afflicted with the Judas syndrome drearily continues here and in the United States. The announcement by Thatcher in April 1987 that the one-time head of MI6, Sir Maurice Oldfield, who became security co-ordinator in Northern Ireland, was dismissed because of his homosexuality had an ominously familiar ring. And in the USA the syndrome manifests itself repeatedly. Thanks to retrieval under the Freedom of Information Act, we have learned that Whittaker Chambers, whose role as informer precipitated the notorious Alger Hiss spy-trial, was an active homosexual; and since my meeting with the attractive and formidably intelligent Alger Hiss left me unpersuaded of his innocence, my judgment on the sorry affair is that Chambers is a familiar case of the betrayer of the betrayer. Other ironies drift across to us from the other side of the Atlantic. Few who remember the persecution of liberals in the McCarthy era failed to note that Roy Cohn, one of those principally responsible for rooting out homosexuals whom he claimed were grave security risks, has himself recently died of AIDS.

The link between these disturbed homosexuals and treachery is in their childhood inability to reconcile their hatred and love of their fathers. Whatever multiple factors contribute to the aetiology of homosexuality, all the psychoanalytical data shows how the child's fear of the father, when he is perceived as dangerous, and when the child fears his own dangerous impulses towards the father, play a considerable part. If one is not able to face the predicament caused by such a vision of the father, there remain only two alternatives and they are not necessarily mutually exclusive: either to submit to the father or to ally oneself to the dangerous forces by way of the psychological mechanisms of acceptance and identification. Ernest Jones's wartime lecture on quislings[26] – in which he anticipated Mussolini's submission to Hitler – posited acceptance as the characteristic of the passive homosexual, and identification as the characteristic of the active one. If some of these insights were applied, and if it were understood how easily the State can unconsciously be regarded as a surrogate father, then there would be little possibility of a Vassall, whose mien showed him to be a passive homosexual, being positively vetted by Intelligence and then thrust into roles by men of superior rank, which, given his character, provoked his nemesis; nor would a rampant, active, disturbed homosexual like Burgess have been allowed to charm his way through the Foreign Office. The incapacity, which I believe to be endemic to the role of the invigilators within the security services, to use the available insights has too often allowed our espionage and counter-espionage departments to be fairgrounds where intelligent but immature men, compulsively disloyal, enjoy an interlude from frenetic heterosexual or homosexual infidelities.

The gay press, perplexed that someone who has campaigned vigorously against disabilities endured by homosexuals should so brutally stress the association of irreconciled homosexuality with a proclivity to spy and betray, have understandably reproached me. I have not helped my defence by tactlessly pointing out to my critics that it was a homosexual double agent who unwittingly played a major part in bringing about the reform of our homosexual laws. Though it was not publicly known at the time, when Sir John Wolfenden made his recommendations, which after years of Parliamentary struggle I was to implement, he was influenced by his knowledge that his son was a homosexual: that son was to become a double agent whose work for MI6 and the KGB only ended with his suicide. But the rebukes I have received from the gay world have come not primarily from my lack of tact but from my failure to emphasise sufficiently what is the quiddity of the issue: my concern is with the consequences of having many in our secret service who, in their desperate anxiety to deny their own homosexual component, blot out any sign of their buried lives in anyone else. The astigmatism, which has permitted so many traitors to continue in their treachery unnoticed, is but one symptom of repressed homosexuality. There is a far more terrible sickness that can arise from such deeply buried drives, and that is paranoia; and there can be no greater danger to a democratic country than a paranoid secret service.

Freud's monumental contribution to an understanding of the aetiology of paranoia came from his scrutiny of the extraordinary delusions of a German politician-lawyer.[27] Although in recent years it has been suggested Freud misled himself about the facts of the lawyer's life, I doubt whether Freud's hypothesis has been fundamentally invalidated. Freud concluded that the man's faulty attempt to repudiate his homosexuality and his failure to sublimate his homosexual component was the source of the delusions. Freud has put the view that there comes a time in the development of the child when he unifies his sexual impulses which have hitherto been engaged in auto-erotic activities in order to obtain a love object: and he begins by taking himself, his own body, as his love object and only subsequently recedes from this to the choice of some person other than himself, first choosing a similar person – that is a homosexual object choice – and then proceeding on to heterosexuality.

Freud, always insisting upon the bisexuality of all men and women, believed that a residual homosexual component remained within us all. That homosexual component of our emotional life may be disposed of in our friendships, in the circumscribed *esprit de corps* of an organisation, in measured comradeship, in our membership of some political or sporting organisation, in a love of mankind – or indeed this homosexual erotic element, its sexual aim inhibited, may luxuriantly bathe our social and working relationships. And often, happily, it is deployed so that it brings, through identification, a sensitive appreciation and understanding of one's partner within a heterosexual relationship.

Those, however, who do not move on, from the earlier stage of self love to the homosexual one, are exposed to particular dangers; these are men whose emotional retardation is shown by their blatant exhibitionism – as displayed by many a politician and actor – or is shown by the inadequately mortified scopophilia of many a spy catcher. The particular hazard these men face is that some unusually intense wave of libido may well up and, unable to find a narcissistic outlet, it surges forward to sexualise their social impulses. Thus recharged, the homosexual component threatens to overwhelm them and these men may no longer be able to sublimate the component in social, political or working relations. Now they face the terror that their homosexuality may become overt.

With their homosexual impulses running too strongly to be contained, to protect themselves from the dangerous sexualisation of their social instinctual cathexes, a remedy, however desperate, has to be found. Freud explained the remedy is paranoia. The man not daring to face the true proposition of 'I love him', declares 'I do not love him – I hate him', and then justifies this assertion by saying, 'I do not love him, I hate him because he persecutes me.'

This paranoid technique I saw operating every day in Westminster. The party system depends to a large extent on its continuance. Within the essentially male-club ambience of the House of Commons, the MP can disperse much of the homosexual component in his nature: but much remains. Those whose narcissism is greatest have the greatest need for the party game. The accusations these party players level against their opponents – the delusions of persecution or exploitation they fluently rationalise – all protect the weak spot in their development which, according to Freud's assumption, lies somewhere between the stage of auto-erotic narcissism and homosexuality. Party politics under the influence of such personalities can, at its worst, degenerate into institutionalised paranoia.

However, in the Commons the irrational persecutory and delusionary elements which pervade party conflict usually lack the strength to totally distort decision-making. The openness of the discussions, the critical evaluations made by the protagonists, the assessments of the media, all act as checks to prevent the emergence of a Stalin who, seeing conspiracies everywhere, made millions victims of his paranoia. No such checks, however, are imposed on the secret services which, by their very nature, attract paranoid personalities. There, as the literature of ex-members of the service illustrates, clandestine internecine warfare between sections of the services is incessant; rival groupings abound, and the higher the rank of the individual, as the case of Sir Roger Hollis illustrates, the more exotic will be the allegations made against him. It is a murky, conspiratorial world, and out of its foetid atmosphere there arose the unbounded presumption that attempted to destabilise Wilson's elected government.

It is always chilling when political leadership emerges – as in the case of Andropov, who was head of the KBG, and Bush who was head of the CIA – which has been conditioned by the Byzantine environment of a secret service. Thatcher needs no such conditioning to become an uncritical ally of her security services; her emotional handicaps ensure she needs them and will protect them, and thus the intactness of her self, to the utmost. On no occasion was this partisanship, and her desperation, more blatantly revealed than in her frantic efforts to suppress the publication of *Spycatcher*. In pursuit of her goal, she had no hesitation in throwing to the wolves her pliant 'economical with the truth' Cabinet Secretary: but far more sinister, and revelatory of the dangers her temperament brings to our liberties, was her usurpation of the Attorney General's role to ensure the proceedings were commenced, and then relentlessly pursued. The insulation of the Attorney General from political pressures is an imperative of our constitutional conventions: indeed, on the last occasion it is believed to have been seriously breached it led to the fall of a Labour government. But Thatcher, totally out of control, flouted the constitutional conventions and imposed her will on Michael Havers, the Attorney General. Reluctantly, for we enjoyed in the House a warm personal relationship, I was compelled to assail his surrender.[28]

Mr Abse: Does the Attorney General agree that when all the spy froth has disappeared, the important fact is whether his office remains inviolate and is not dominated by the Prime Minister or any so-called collective decision?

On what basis and on what precedent does he base the view that he is able to have instructions on civil matters, such as are taking place in Australia . . . clearly on information coming from Number 10? On what basis does he rest the view that he can take instructions from the Cabinet to commence proceedings? Does he not realise there is widespread concern at the Bar . . . and among all within the legal profession, and among all libertarians, that his office is being assailed and that he is being manipulated by a Prime Minister who is dominating the whole of these proceedings.

The Attorney General was understandably taken aback by my assault and could only irrelevantly protest his long relationship with me and then, lamely, plead he was bound by the decision of the Thatcher Cabinet.

The Attorney General: I am surprised at the Hon. Gentleman whom I have known for many years. I am quite able to look after my independence and I always have. The Hon. Gentleman must realise . . . that this was a Government decision and, of course, like my fellow Ministers I accept collective responsibility.

Eighteen months later the *Observer* lobby correspondent, Adam Raphael, noting the continuing fanaticism on the subject of secrecy, appears to have sensed, as increasingly others do, that we are dealing with a psychological rather than a political issue.[29] 'Mrs Thatcher is determined to use and, if necessary bludgeon, her huge majority in the Commons to make sure she is not embarrassed ever again by such leaks of official information. The collapse of the prosecution of Clive Ponting, the Ministry of Defence civil servant who leaked documents about the sinking of the *Belgrano* and the . . . world-wide legal saga to prevent the publication of *Spycatcher* by the former MI5 officer Peter Wright, are humiliations which have etched deep into the Downing Street psyche.'

She cannot tolerate the humiliations for they could cause her psyche to crumble. So frightened is she to acknowledge her deep-seated personal secrets that rather than confront and, with insight, overcome their terrors, she would prefer to confront her Cabinet, the press, her dissident backbenchers and the whole opposition. It is easier to confront others than ourselves. Blind to the unconscious forces that have taken her over, she runs away from herself in a frenzy, lashing at all who would obstruct her. The spectacle is indeed piteous but we must not in compassion retreat and abandon all our personal liberties on the battlefield she has created. Nietzsche's adage needs to be recalled: 'Beware of Pity'.

15

Woman to Woman: The Dark Continent

FREUD completed his famed lecture on 'Femininity'[1] with an ac-knowledgment that what he had to say on the subject was incomplete and fragmentary; and then, after warning that women's nature is not only determined by their sexual function, he bade us, if we wished to know more about femininity, to enquire from our own experiences of life and from the poets. A politician living through the Thatcherite era should, unless he is wilfully blind or obtuse, have his own particular experiences to contribute to the more coherent assembly of information which Freud hoped would one day come into existence to help to resolve some of the riddles of feminin-ity. What is certain is that it will be to the male politician's electoral peril if he ignores the singular and complex relationship which exists between the women voters and Thatcher, and fails to differentiate it from that existing between Thatcher and the male electorate. Difficult and indeed frightening though it may be, the male politician in Thatcher's Britain has therefore to be ready to explore what Freud has described as the dark continent of femininity. In despair and perplexity Freud asked, *'Was will das Weib?'* – 'What does Woman want?' The politician in a democracy has a duty to attempt to find some of the answers and to discover what are the real needs of half his electorate. It is one of the beneficial side effects of Thatcher's reign that the male politician has to overcome his chauvinism, and to acknowledge that his women voters, as women and not as append-ages, exist.

The Labour politician will receive a dusty answer if he turns to the militant, campaigning feminists and asks them to encode the relationship between Thatcher and the woman voter. There are women like Beatrix Campbell[2] and Juliet Mitchell[3] ready to contrib-ute notable elucidations: but they are exceptions. More usually, the Marxist and neo-Marxist feminists are so locked into their preoccupations with the consequences and nuances of what they perceive as the continuing class struggle, they have nothing to tell us about a Tory prime minister who is the granddaughter of a railway cloakroom attendant and the daughter of a seamstress. Just as their Marxist male counterparts behave as hypnotised rabbits when confronted with the dominant personality traits of Thatcher, so too Marxist women freeze up when they address the Thatcher phenomenon.[4] Their learned essays do not even refer to her by name; for Thatcher is a taboo word in their convoluted vocabulary. They are ready to discuss all the consequences of her government's policies on women, but never the woman herself. Women Marxists have of course placed themselves in an impossible situation, for they, like Margaret Thatcher (and for the same unconscious reasons) must smudge the differentiation between man and woman; and thus, denying biology, commonsense, and the differing developmental schedules of boys and girls, they dare not examine the relationship between Thatcher the woman, and the woman voter. Such a scrutiny could lead them to the uncongenial view that men and women do not have similar psychological bio-graphies; a conclusion which would subvert so many of their spurious assumptions. We can expect no aid in our quest from these intelligent but soul-blind women. Too often they demean themselves and become mirror images of the dotty Edwina Currie, who has declaimed, 'I'm not a woman. I'm a Conservative.'

The male politician, therefore, must turn to his own limited resource; and for my part, acknowledging that limitation, I am conscious of how tentative and slight must be my conclusions. But it would be cowardice not to make the attempt, even though the effort may be labelled a sign of masculine hubris. Let me declare my sources: they are threefold. First, when canvassing the electorate I have been exposed, in election after election, to the never neutral reaction of so many women to Thatcher. I have too the happy benefit of, if I may dare so coldly describe it, the domestic clinical material of my wife and daughter, and I have therefore noted the reactions of two generations of women to Thatcher's intrusions, which none escape but which are particularly persistent in a politician's home. I have also perhaps a special vantage point, whilst practising as a divorce lawyer, of having placed myself over so many years into the heart of controversies which have raged around legislation which supremely concerns women. It is impossible to have assumed prime responsibility for three Divorce Acts; to have precipitated a Select Committee on abortion and vainly sponsored bills seeking to modify the existing abortion laws; to have sponsored the first Family Planning Act; to have fought for the right of the infertile to have a child; to have lightened the legal burdens of the child of the unmarried mother; and to have presumptuously through agitation and legislation adjudicated between a natural and adopting mother, without having drawn upon all the anguishes of the modern woman. For decades during my Parliamentary life I was forever besieged by women's lobbies and by individual women, sometimes heaping upon me much opprobrium and sometimes a little praise, resenting or welcoming the male legislator acting as an interloper seeking to make laws which so intruded into affairs of the heart, their special domain.

All my interventions have, to a greater or lesser extent, left me seared: it cannot be otherwise. Around the world the most commonly oppressed group is woman, and Britain, with its churlish and half hearted acknowledgment of women's rights, is no trail-blazer in the fight for women's emancipation. The battle is not half won. Although the oppressive relative status of male and female has lost its old definitions, and husband and wife are no longer assigned rigid roles, the woman, cut adrift from the old intolerable moorings, has a quest but no certain destination. I have learned that all the floating, suspended anxiety of women suffering a crisis of identity, and all the stored up legitimate grievances against the impositions of the male culture, will be targeted against any male legislator who dares to put his head above the parapet and tries to view, with empathy, their cruel predicaments.

To suggest that women's predicaments are more onerous than those suffered by men; that they are not all culturally induced, and that their impact may be lessened by positive discrimination, may be treated as the observations of a patronising male: yet the reality is that from the outset, the little girl is faced with ordeals the boy is spared. All infants turn to the mother, the fount of life, the source of nourishment, and, if the child is fortunate, the source of care and tenderness. However, the increasing impingement of the father, gradually ceasing to be an abstract figure, means the child has to say goodbye to Eden and painfully accept paradise is lost and monopoly-control of the mother must cease. The boy has his agonies as he works through this Oedipal phase but the boy's psychological work is less onerous than his sister's. His mother can remain the love of his life even if the harsh realities of the family constellation compel his desire for her to undergo drastic retrenchment. The girl cannot loosen the spell of the mother in like manner. She is fated to pay a heavier price if she is to end the powerful attachment to the mother, a price that *must* be paid if the girl is to advance to a resolved womanhood.

The little girl, Freud always insisted, was no mere passive creature easily able to switch her attachment from mother to father, from a female to a male. On the contrary the girl's sexual aims with regard to the mother are active as well as passive and contain a wish to give her a baby as well as to bear her one. The women psychoanalysts, like Lampl de-Groot[5] and Enid Balint,[6] have presented clinical material illustrating the immense difficulties a little girl has in giving up her possession of her mother and changing from possessing her to having her solely as a loved one with whom she can identify. They do not find it surprising that there should be such difficulties; the girl has to painfully face the fact of the physical impossibility of her possessing her mother, 'The little girl feels that the possession of her mother can only be maintained if she, the girl, is not castrated, that is if she has a penis'.[7] The discovery that she has no penis and that her genitals are invisible leaves, the Freudians tell us, lasting deposits in her mind. Indeed the traumas associated with the discovery are so fateful that it led Freud to affirm, 'Anatomy is destiny'.

Such a psychodynamic formulation may help to bring conceptual order but it can lead to misinterpretation, and to the chauvinist and offensive view that woman is 'mutilated'; a castrated male. Too often the blessings of a woman's anatomy are consequently ignored: although unfortunately in public life there are few such women, there are many women who bestow fullness, warmth and generosity, the psychic analogues to the woman's pregnancy, childbirth, lactation and to the richly convex part of her anatomy. Nevertheless it cannot be gainsaid that the sense of incompleteness, which is the lot of all human beings, is painfully and visibly anatomically corroborated to a woman.

Heinz Kohut has taught us that if the child is to survive psychologically, he must be born into an empathic-responsive human milieu, just as he must be born into an atmosphere that contains an optimal amount of oxygen if he is to survive physically. His nascent self 'expects' – to use an inappropriately anthropomorphic but nevertheless evocative term – an empathic environment which is in tune with his psychological need-wishes with the same unquestioning certitude as the respiratory apparatus of the newborn infant may be said to 'expect' oxygen to be contained in the surroundings.[8] And those need-wishes remain with us throughout our lives. We cannot live our lives in solitary confinement; we need to be responded to by others, and our need-wishes are boundless and the threat of loneliness ever present. It is the emphasis which the Kohutian psychoanalysts place upon the impossibilities of our ever gaining the completeness for which we yearn and our despair that so often we are condemned to walk alone, that has caused them to declare Homo sapiens to be

Tragic Man; and to argue that Freud's Guilty Man – man in conflict, burdened by the shame of his sinful thoughts and desires – is only a part of the story of man on earth. But what of Tragic Woman?

She is disadvantaged, physically less well equipped, to attempt, as man so often does, to deny the tragic imperative. He can bluff himself by regarding his penis, and declaring he is whole; the 'mutilated' woman has not that option and feels herself only a fragment. Under the guise of macho conduct the man affects his need of woman is limited to the satisfaction of his sexual appetite. Mistaking sexuality for genitality he can turn confidence trickster and maintain the pretence that he is self sufficient even though his real needs are far more profound than to ejaculate. Woman, by her very anatomy, has a self image which denies her the disguise the man assumes. She both knows and sees her dependence on the other, and, as if to taunt her still further, the evolutionary process has imposed upon woman a manifestly unfair share of the reproductive cycle. Oppressed by her periodicity and the pain of childbirth, it is not surprising that modern woman, now torn by all the conflicts which her role within the social mores provokes, can be replete with discontents. She is the true *dolorosa*: full of sorrows. An illusionist woman leader who presents herself as an exemplar, 'strong', able to walk alone and, in a role reversal, is surrounded by men dependent upon her – not she on them – can have a fatal attractiveness. Thatcher's assertiveness and triumphal marches, and, above all, her mask of total self-sufficiency – her indifference to and independence of all and sundry – holds out to many a woman the delusionary hope that relief is possible, that escape from the constant fear of aloneness can be attained.

When life rains blows upon women, that terrible fear becomes awesome. And so many crises can arise in a woman's life when that fear can become overwhelming. The utter desolation of the late-middle-aged wife; deserted by her husband, feeling that her physical charms have faded, and wrongfully interpreting the ageing husband's failing libido as a consequence of her decay, is a piteous spectacle. The unmarried mother who, under social and parental pressure, reluctantly hands over her child for adoption, riven with guilt, is forever wounded. And the woman who endures an abortion can be left, while she mourns for her unborn child, with a depressing emptiness unknown to a man. Life is not easily lived by any of us, man or woman. In the face of life's hostility, man too can suffer rejections which corroborate for him his essential aloneness, an isolation that is mitigated but never totally vanquished by relationships with another; and all of us, willy-nilly, are doomed to die alone. Woman's travail along life's journey can be of a different order to a man's. In the past she could turn to religion and bind herself in prayer to a god in a bid to obtain a completeness she lacked; but in our secular society that is a therapy which for many has lost its ancient efficacy.

The allure of a leadership offering completeness has always been present and it has been remarked upon by psychoanalysts long before the advent of Thatcher. Now, with a woman leader and a woman electorate stripped of old certitudes and not yet the possessor of new ones, the comments of those psychoanalysts on the attractions of hermaphrodite leadership have acquired a special relevance. More than twenty-five years ago, two psychoanalysts wrote of the characteristics which a male leader has to possess if he is to be regarded as charismatic by his followers:[9]

> His main weapon (and armour) is charm. His charm conveys not only his magic power but all his delicate need for love and protection. He yearns to be not only a man, but a woman at the same time; his inner balance is precarious because of the concurrence of active domineering and submissive seductive strivings. It is an eternal wish of mankind expressed in the mythic idea that once man and woman were one . . . The biological basis of charm and the modes of mutual attraction, shared by bodily characters in the male and female of the human species are relevant to the psychological characteristics of the charismatic leader. For he fascinates by a display of both male and female qualities, simultaneously or more often in more or less rapid alternation, just as in some hypnotic procedures.

The yearning of the leader and the masses to be both male and female continues: but now it exists where there is a sexual ambiguity abroad, when the old stereotypes of male and female identities are dissolving, the male becoming feminised, the female masculinised, and where there is a growing acknowledgment of the great plasticity in the human capacity to develop and sustain differing patternings of sex roles. This can lead to our developing new, more relaxed and happier configurations of our roles but it can also lead to confusions finding ominous expressions, not least in our divorce rate; and it can lead to a desperate and over-eager perception of Thatcher as the charismatic leader who can free woman from her fragmented separateness. Such a perception is of course false, for Thatcher is offering salvation on terms that still leave the woman painfully dependent; Thatcher's hermaphrodite leadership counsels continued subordination, not manumission. Beatrix Campbell, in her sparkling contribution, 'To be or not to be a woman',[10] sees clearly the trap Thatcher sets.

Thatcher is a model neither of traditional femininity nor feminism, but something else altogether – she embodies female power which unites patriarchal and feminine discourses. She has brought qualities of ruggedness and ruthlessness to femininity which perhaps only men hadn't noticed before in women. She has not feminised politics, however, but she has offered feminine endorsements to patriarchal power and principles.

Not all women are ready to fall into the trap. On the doorstep, I have met so many women who fiercely react against Thatcher, and their emotionally charged response reveals it is not founded on their policy preferences, on their concerns for peace and for protection of the health and social services. These are women who resent being lectured to by a woman who constantly tells them of the importance of the housewife, that the family is the centre of the universe, and the home the centre of the woman's life, when they sense or know that her whole life belies her declared commitment. And they are not appeased by being told 'It is possible to carry on working, taking a short leave of absence when families arrive and returning later. The idea that the family suffers is, I believe, quite mistaken.'[11] They know the stresses placed on the working mother and feel Thatcher's comment to be humbug, as it is. The polls tell us that Labour's greatest support among women is with young working mothers:[12] these young women know that Thatcher's assured comment comes because Denis Thatcher's money was always available. Thatcher could afford a living-in nanny-cum-housekeeper until the children went off to boarding school. While the twins were toddlers in middle-class Farnborough, tea was cooked by the nanny who 'took over management of both children and house', while Margaret Thatcher travelled into Chambers at Lincoln's Inn. After they went to boarding school the nanny returned during the school holidays.[13] The women who attack her so fiercely see her as a wealthy, cosseted wife, not as a magic, charismatic hermaphrodite leader. Indeed, very often maternity has given such women a proximate completeness which leaves them less inclined to embark on a fevered search for such a leader.

But for many other women there is a different response and it is one known to all Labour MPs. Even as they assure us of their votes, they feel compelled to qualify their support by telling us how strong Thatcher is, how wonderful is her courage and how extraordinary is her stamina. When one hears these comments it is not difficult to divine some of the reasons for the voting gender gap which, although now fading, has worked in the past to Thatcher's advantage. There are women who wish to believe in Thatcher's fearlessness. By identifying with Thatcher they hope to escape from the undercurrent of fear with which they live. No penal reformer can be unaware of how constant is this fear, for it is woman's fear which emotionally ignites all the debates on law and order, an issue which Thatcher so sedulously exploits. In such debates the fundamental fear is undisguisedly re-vealed: the woman is afraid of walking the streets alone, afraid of letting her child return alone from school, afraid of a breakdown on the anonymous motorway while she is driving alone. It is the fear of abandonment: it is the fear of which Ernest Jones appeared to have been writing when he introduced the Greek term of aphanisis into psychoanalysis.[14] He insisted that the common denominator in the sexuality of boys and girls has to be sought at a more fundamental level than the castration complex, that the fear of castration is but a concrete expression of the more general fear of aphanisis. Aphanisis is total and permanent extinction: and it is in the fear of separation from the loved object that the fear of aphanisis is to be discerned in woman.

All of us, men and women, walk through the valley of the shadow of death but man, intoxicated by his phallic potion, boastfully swaggers along, cocksure, knowing that he has awaiting him the consolatory advantage of a woman in his mother's image who may yet bless him with intimations of the lost paradise. The woman, thanks to her anatomy and her decreed procreative role, is barred from such reassurances and consolations: if all of us are fated to be victims, she is the particular victim. The penal reformer can see this with blinding clarity for he knows how highly sexualised is the public discourse on the causes of crime and its prevention. Always there is a gendered dialogue, always a sexual subtext to the debate. The growth in the incidence of crime, with women the worst victims, inflames the pre-existing condition. The wounds inflicted upon her in the early days of her psychological biography are reopened, and all the associated feelings of panic are evoked. In such seasons, she is particularly vulnerable to Thatcher's siren calls.

There is an irony in Thatcher's appeal to such women for, in truth, their very acknowledgment of their predicament, their desire to be healed of their wounds, is a tribute to their refusal to take the regressive course of manic denial of their hurts and fears. It reveals how more psychologically mature they are than Thatcher whose much acclaimed political courage, strength and stamina, lack authenticity. There is a hollowness and, inevitably, a strained quality about the attributes conventionally granted to her, for they are an overdetermined creation of a woman so uncomfortable in her body that she denies her sexuality. The sharp eye of Beatrix Campbell has seen how severe is that denial.[15] 'Her body language is "womanly" – as she speaks into the glass screens scrolling up her speeches at party conferences she tilts her head in that gesture which is placatory but superior, her stride is stiff from the waist down, she makes her point in the nuanced tilt of her shoulders and her bosom, which manoeuvres sexuality into vision. Her gender is unmistakeable, her power is manifest, but her sexuality . . . ?'

There is an absolute adherence to the appearance of femininity even as she is engaged in both a flight from it and from the world of women. Her attempts to blot out, in political terms, her sexual identity can astonish her advisers. Her admirer and colleague, Patrick Cosgrave, who worked for her, had short shrift when he put forward the suggestion that a private opinion poll should be conducted to see how Thatcher could be presented to women. He has reported, 'Since, however, my draft idea for a poll depended upon an emphasis upon her sexual identity, she turned the scheme down flat.'[16] Those women who, subliminally, visualise Thatcher as a liberator, a super-real human being, whole, unfractured, transcending masculinity and femininity, beyond the partitions and limitations of gender, are, although the illusion may comfort them, seeing a mirage. She is more diminished than they are, for they are struggling honestly with their lot but she defies the commandment, refuses to honour both father and mother, and attempts to edit her mother out of her life, a task not within the capacity of anyone born of woman.

Once more we should look at the relationship between the child Maggie and her mother if we are to understand the passion behind this attempt of Thatcher's to annihilate Beatrice Roberts, an attempt which has had such grave political consequences for Britain.

*

The husband, as the stock mother-in-law jokes reveal, well knows that his most significant rival is not his father-in-law or any other male rival. It is his mother-in-law, alive or dead, with whom he competes for the love and attention of his wife. A woman may appear to have chosen her husband on the model of her father but the wise husband knows better; in reality he becomes the inheritor of her relationship to her mother, and, if his marriage is to succeed, he must learn not only to receive the love his wife once gave to her mother but also to contain the hate which was part of her primal relationship.[17]

Thatcher's protestation of a primary allegiance to her father should not deceive us. In her adult life it is woman's inexorable destiny, as Freud gradually learned, to hear and hearken to the echoes that come from a woman's first relationship with her mother, a determinate relationship which comes into existence before the father, within the confusions and resolutions of the girl's Oedipal stage, attains significance. Juliet Mitchell has succinctly emphasised its primacy:[18]

> The father, so crucial for the development of femininity, and the men that follow him, so essential for the preservation of 'normal' womanhood, are only secondary figures for pride of place as love objects is taken by the mother – for both sexes . . .
>
> *Preceding* any rivalry the little girl might feel for the mother in her demands for the father in the positive Oedipal stage, there is already considerable hostility to be found in her attitude. A generalised rivalry with siblings and father certainly causes a good deal of the jealousy and resentment, but this primary hostility is something else again. It would seem to arise from the fact that there is no bottom, none, to a child's boundless love and demand for love, there is *no* satisfaction possible and the inevitable frustration can cause violent feelings. The mother simply cannot give the baby enough. And then, of course, finally, there is the situation in which the girl blames her mother for the fact that she is a girl and therefore without a penis . . .

Mitchell, in drawing attention to the 'violent feelings' that can accompany the realisation that the girl cannot possess the mother, is corroborating the views of an earlier generation of women psychoanalysts, Lampl de-Groot, Helene Deutsch, Balint. All of them saw the entanglements that can result when the anxious little girl, overcome by hostility, fumbles in her attempts to loosen her passionate emotional ties with the mother. At its most extreme, the girl can totally deny her incapacity to be the possessor, firmly refuses to give up her masculine position; a stance that can contribute to her becoming a lesbian. Or, less radically, she may not deny entirely her incapacity, and seeks compensation for her bodily 'inferiority' on some plane other than the sexual; in her work, in her profession. She represses sexual desire, remains sexually unmoved. 'I may not and cannot love my love and so I must give up any further attempt at all.'[19] Her unconscious belief in the possession of a penis has then been shifted to the intellectual sphere: there the woman can be masculine and compete with the men. Or again, when these women psychoanalysts treat women with problems of frigidity, they tell us that a woman may form relationships with a man but yet remain inwardly attached to the first object of her love – her mother – and her sexual disabilities arise because she does not desire the man and still wants her mother.

Many and various are the consequences for the little girl of a botch-up in her pre-Oedipal phase; whether, later, she has more grievous burdens to carry than most of us in our adult lives, depends, so unfairly, on the nature of the mothering she received at that vital time. And if that mothering is unempathic, if it lacks love and affection, and is unable to receive and contain the hostility which every little girl has to release, then the pent up rage of the little girl persists. Then, instead of entering the 'Oedipus situation as though into a haven of refuge', as Freud put it, she arrives there furiously resistant. She has no wish to identify with her hated mother, she has no wish to become the mother, receive the father, and thus prepare the way for herself to become wife and mother.

Beatrice Roberts, subordinate to her husband, and under the domination of her martinet mother, was drained of affect: she could not prepare the way for her child to leave her, stoically ready to move on to the next rite of passage. The daughter's disappointment was bitter; her defeated mother was unable to temper the pain of the child's discovery that she could never possess her. Such cruel indifference called for revenge, the revenge of the rejected lover. It is a revenge that explicitly surfaces in her put-down of her mother. Beatrice, she tells us, was 'the Martha rather than the Mary.'[20] Thatcher is of course identifying with Mary: she was the favoured one chosen to anoint her father and wipe his feet with her hair. Beatrice, like Martha, is relegated to the chores:[21] this ex-Methodist remembers her Sunday School teaching a little too well. But the revengeful depreciation of her mother moved beyond the private domain: it echoes throughout all Thatcher's political policies. Her relentless assault upon the welfare state – the caring mother imago – and her contempt for the feminists' demands, are both vengeful. If she had been able to move forward less burdened, it would have been otherwise; but never able to identify with her own mother, never able to take her mother's side, she could never be a champion of women's causes. The beleaguered women who hoped a woman prime minister would remedy their grievances have waited and will continue to wait in vain: she is there to take revenge not give relief.

Such revenge has been considered by many women psychoanalysts, and, perhaps a little surprisingly to men, they pinpoint the source of the vengefulness within the fantasies of prostitution indulged in by so many women. Lampl de-Groot has told us, 'Now these considerations place in a different light the fantasies of prostitution so common among women. According to this view they would be an act of revenge, not so much against the father, as against the mother. The fact that prostitutes are so often manifest or disguised homosexuals might be explained in analogous fashion as follows: the prostitute turns to men out of revenge against the mother, but her attitude is not that of passive feminine surrender but of masculine activity: she captures the man on the street, castrates him by taking his money, and thus makes herself the masculine and him the feminine partner in the sexual act.'[22]

Such couplings are more suited to the brothel than the public stage. When revenge of this order is translated into public policy it can have menacing consequences. And when we wonder at the fierceness, fury and persistence of Thatcher we should ponder on its sources; then we will be less inclined to extend admiration, and more likely to understand that her vibrant vengeance bodes ill for both men and women.

The emotional needs of the women who have been drawn to Thatcher are real. It would be shallow political opportunism to attempt to disabuse them of their illusions; hope their votes will follow their disenchantment; and still leave them without solace. There is substance in the feminists' charge that the Labour Movement has, in the past, been curmudgeonly in its attitudes to women's demands. The allegation that the Labour Government of 1945 ended women's brief wartime encounter with economic and personal independence, abandoned social child care, and failed to attempt to 'reorganise working time which would have integrated women into the culture of workplace politics and men into the culture of the child care and community'[23], cannot be dismissed, even if it is overstated. The affirmation by the TUC in 1947, when taking up a negative attitude to day nurseries, that 'the home is one of the most important spheres for a woman worker and it would be doing a grave injury to the life of the nation if women were persuaded or forced to neglect their domestic duties in order to enter industry,' was too informed by misogyny to be regarded as an expression of a genuine concern for family life; and the attitude embedded in the TUC statement has for too long determined priorities in Labour's policy-making.

It does not help us to redefine future policies if we burden ourselves with myths about the past structure of working-class family life. My experience of family life in South Wales in the 1950s taught me how many micro-cultures could exist almost side by side. The formulation that we have advanced, and must advance further, from an authoritarian family system to an egalitarian one, to the obvious benefit of women, is too simplistic: it can lead to the creation of imbalances which will benefit no one, man, woman or child. When I first came to my constituency, any miner who permitted his wife to work outside the home was despised by his peers and by the community; when I laid down my trusteeship in 1987, I was forever being lobbied to bring more work for women into the valley. The zealous feminists may regard this change as part of women's emancipation. In fact the change has brought her disadvantages as well as benefits, and not all the disadvantages the woman worker suffers are due to the State's refusal to assist her to be both mother and worker.

The typical miner's wife was certainly not 'oppressed'. When the miner came home on pay day, his money went in her apron and she gave him his pocket money. In the house she was queen and received deference: he ruled in miners' lodge, miners' institute and on the local council. She worked hard, even scrubbing the steps and pavement outside the house, washing and mangling all the clothes on Mondays and ironing them on Tuesdays, helping – before the pit baths were installed – to wash down the grime-laden husband in the zinc bath, often without the help of a hot water supply, and doing all the cooking. But parenthood was shared: whilst the miner was off shift and his wife was about the chores he would take the baby out and, until the days came when a pram was financially possible, the father would wrap the child in a shawl and carry him 'Welsh fashion' so that the child was held fast while the man stood with his butties on the street corners, discussing the merits of their greyhounds and whippets and much else. The famed Welsh valley 'Mam' was not a satrap but a ruler with mighty influence in the family, and the husband was no tyrant but one who formed delicate relationships with his children: the adult son would kiss his father goodbye regularly, sealing the affection between them. Even if such a recounting does not fit feminist folklore of yesterday's family, an understanding of the balances and checks within such working families should be noted, and lessons learned.

I do not wish to make an idyll of yesterday's working-class family life; on the contrary, sombre lives were indeed endured by many working-class women. Only a few miles from the South Wales valleys, in Cardiff, on the coast where steelworks sprawled, there was a different culture, shapeless and disorganised. The children of the immigrants from Ireland and elsewhere who had built the docks continued to live essentially displaced lives, their working lives so often punctuated only by drink, gambling and brutality towards their wives. Every Monday in the early days of my solicitor's practice, my waiting-room would be full of bruised and battered wives, bearing the marks of their husbands' weekend revels. In those days I spent much of my time in the courts seeking to obtain persistent-cruelty maintenance orders which could give these women and their children a little relief, trying to wrest for them a meagre allowance and the blessing of separation. The advances that have since been made are real and not a little credit for such changes go to campaigning feminists.

Though there is still much to be done, the assaults women politicians launch upon the male culture are often conducted with such hostility that they arouse fear and become counter-productive. There are many public women in and out of the Commons who, like Thatcher, are at odds with their own womanhood and, as a consequence, can be extraordinarily vigorous and destructive. They are continuously in a state of outrage, and although their protests, often directed against real evils, result in needed changes, the shrill persistence of some women politicians, their ceaseless and humourless challenges and their exaggerated, impatient demands, can be absurdly disproportionate to the wrong they seek to command the House to remedy. Too often they lambast the House; they demand of the House; they complain and harangue; but surprisingly, they rarely woo the House. The splendid exceptions, women like Eirene White and Lena Jeger – now both in the Lords – and Peggy Jay, all of whom I have co-operated with in many a past campaign, illustrate by their achievements how more resolved women can enlist support.

For many women in public life the extra battle a woman has to reach the top confirms, even as she is resisting it, the extra anguish suffered by one half of the tragic human race. The backlash against the feminists comes from many men who equate the feminists with Thatcher; both are seen as Alice in Wonderland Queens sending out the command, 'Off with his head' and, ever fearful of castration, these men join with the women who feel their confusions are being confounded, not resolved, by the militant feminists.

The discontents which precipitate these confusions will certainly not be relieved by a policy of tokenism. The appointment of a woman to act as Labour's shadow spokesperson charged with supervising women's affairs is a puny and cosmetic response to profound needs. The belated pledge made in November 1988 by the Shadow Cabinet that women's perspective on political issues will in future be given a new emphasis must be regarded with high seriousness by all Labour male activists, for if there is to be a change in gender perception – reflected in legislation and social policy – it must be accomplished by men as well as women. It will fall, above all, upon the new generation of Labour MPs to act as exemplars to their constituency parties and electorates and bring about the change. Their task is not easy. It involves not only self-scrutiny but also a scrutiny of the prejudices of many of their women voters. These prejudices can overcome dislike of Thatcher's policies, as is well illustrated in the response given to Anthony Howard, the sophisticated journalist and subtle biographer, when he counselled a meeting of distinguished writers forming an anti-Thatcherite group. Antonia Fraser, telling of the 'thrill' she remembered at seeing Margaret Thatcher outside No. 10 replied, 'Personally I am prejudiced in favour of Margaret Thatcher. Any woman who is interested in the history of women, as I am, must admire what she has battled through, in spite of her attitudes to feminism, which she shares with Queen Victoria. Her policies are another matter.'[24] In Antonia Fraser's case, she overcomes her pro-Thatcher prejudice, but many women do not.

The Labour MPs, at a time when they are realistically reassessing their allegiances to past doctrines, could well follow the Russian example by examining past condemnation of ideological 'errors' said to have been made by leaders now long-since dead. The founding father of the Labour Party and first Chairman of the Parliamentary Party, Keir Hardie, was bundled out of his office and probably driven to his death by his misogynist colleagues, furious at his insistent commitment to the feminist movement at the beginning of this century. They could not tolerate his belief that the suffragettes should have as much of his time as the Parliamentary Party;[25] but Keir Hardie had the right sense of priorities. His cynical colleagues attributed his feminist commitment to his love affair with Sylvia Pankhurst, the suffragette leader, but, then, Keir Hardie liked women, unlike not a few of his colleagues who, I suspect, only lusted after them.

Our young Labour MPs should recall that they owe to Keir Hardie much of their present freedom of action. It was because he defied the 1907 Labour Party Conference, telling them he would resign his leadership rather than submit to their resolution[26] ordering Labour MPs not to vote for a Women's Enfranchisement Bill, that we have today the rule that no simple majority at the Labour Party conference can make enforceable Party policy; and the conscience clause which keeps the Whips away from Labour MPs on many sensitive questions stems again from Keir Hardie's determination not to be bound by the majority vote of his colleagues on the feminist issue.

As Labour MPs leave the Chamber to enter their dining-room, they pass a commemorative bronze head of Keir Hardie: they would be wise to pause at the corner where he gazes upon them, recall his empathy with the women of his time, vow to follow his example and transmute their understanding into a commitment to relevant economic and social policy. When their women electors feel their concerns for them, then they will be less likely, in their painful bewilderments, to continue in the vain hope that one day Thatcher will be on their side.

Epilogue

And what of the future? Two of my political contemporaries who are still in Parliament, both aware that I was completing this essay, separately and unknown to each other, urged upon me that I should conclude with a call for faith in the future; for hope.

There were good reasons for these veteran Parliamentarians wanting me to conclude optimistically. Despite their confidence in the Parliamentary Labour Party, where there is a cadre of young MPs well equipped to be cabinet ministers, so many of their younger colleagues, reflecting a mood which has prevailed for some years in the wider Labour Movement, were stricken with melancholia and lacked the firm hope that there would ever be another Labour Cabinet. Many of them belong to the 'now' generation whose members wilt under the strain of delayed expectation. The European elections of June 1989 have now raised their morale: but my experienced colleagues believing the general election may be nearly three years away requested a firmly founded rallying call, for they know that even as one considerable gain can temporarily boost hope, so one setback can shatter a faith tenuously dependent upon a mid-term poll.

Unwittingly, however, their request contained a warning, not only to younger Labour MPs but one directed at me, for an observer seeking to apply psychoanalysis to current politics can become his own victim. He is in danger of using tools that have a retrospective pathological bias: for I have, in this scrutiny of Thatcher, presumed to borrow the tools which a psychoanalyst may necessarily have to use to assist the patient to recall the difficulties of the past and, thus, by explaining the present in terms of the past, can lazily fall into a habit of mind which excludes consideration of the potentialities of the present for the future. Such an approach would indeed be an abuse of psychoanalysis, for it is improbable that a healing art, so often dependent upon dream interpretation, has nothing to tell us of political dejection and political optimism, particularly since political leaders are forever dealing in dreams; some as misshapen as Hitler's, and some as Utopian as the glorious dream of Martin Luther King.

Freud has written 'The ancient belief that dreams reveal the future is not entirely devoid of truth. By representing a wish as fulfilled, the dreaming certainly leads us into the future'.[1] The political leader who cannot dream of a better future will equally certainly never lead his followers to the promised land. Daydreams may be a mirage, but anticipatory dreams, as Jung has described them,[2] are not to be dismissed as hallucinatory gratifications of repressed wishes. While asleep, nearer to our unconscious, we may unravel problems, and envisage the possible outcomes of our concerns, and then, in our waking life, having listened to our unconscious, make the option which will determine the future.

It is not, therefore, unreasonable to ask that a psycho-biography, written by a politician claiming to use the insights provided by depth psychology, should not only provide a diagnosis but should also venture towards treatment and prognosis. I could perhaps excuse myself this almost impossible task, and plead that here diagnosis is part of the cure; the effect of deglamorising Thatcher may itself contribute to ending her inimical spell over sections of the public. But it cannot be the role of a self-respecting politician simply to be a nihilist, stripping down illusions and leaving an electorate naked.

There is a readiness to believe in happy forecasts in order to seek recompense for past disappointments; and when the blighting of early days of promise in childhood has been keenly felt, the assurance of the politician that all is – and will be – well can be fatally seductive. George Bush, within the traditional, but now shallow, optimistic culture of the USA, was able to exploit this yearning for a future solace capable of healing past wounds in his Presidential Campaign of 1988. His opponent, Dukakis, emphasising the fragility of the American economy, suffered the fate of so many messengers of bad tidings.

The abuse of optimism by manipulative politicians, as in Bush's campaign, increases my reluctance to attempt to mobilise it. Such diffidence may, it is conceded, be a temperamental prejudice; every biographer tells of himself as well as of his subject. But an agnostic stand is surely justified. In recent British history there are too many illustrations of the temptations and hazards of political optimism – as there are of political pessimism. We have seen chancellors of the exchequer – from the ascetic Stafford Cripps to the self-indulgent Nigel Lawson – steer the British economy, by their depressive or manic moods, on to the rocks. From such débâcles, the lesson to be learned by the wise politician is to exercise restraint in prediction. Recalling the adage, '*Pour trouver la verité il faut travailler contre soi-*

même', the politician worthy of his role should always strive against his temperament, sanguine or gloom-ridden, for only then will his proposed remedies be likely to be authentically prophylactic.

Although political optimism and pessimism are so suspect, the response to the mood Thatcher has brought to the land is certainly not stoicism; endurance too easily becomes resignation, and political defeatism takes over. Like optimism, with its stress on the future, such passive waiting empties the present. The acquiescent, and the political fantasist, wait in vain for the golden future to be bestowed; but the mature, adult, political activist has available a resource which, if deeply mined – hard though the quarrying may be – can give him the *élan* to overcome. That resource is hope, an affect necessarily contingent, but one having an energic potential never to be gained from shallow optimism. And, since this is a politician's psycho-biographical essay and the habits of a long lifetime cannot be sloughed off, it is concluded with a manifesto, the only manifesto worth writing: it is the manifesto of hope.

★

Spurious optimism has a close relative, an impostor masquerading as hope. Variously described by analysts as pseudo hope[3] or magic hope,[4] this confidence trickster, although seductive and plausible, will find no place here. One psychoanalytically-orientated political scientist has described the wares this huckster peddles as 'empty, grandiose, viciously enervating and selfish':[5] the goods offered are all privatised, lacking the hallmark of the social matrix. They are geegaws which the impoverished imagination of Thatcher conjures up as the signs of success, and she would stir within us a longing to acquire them; but it is a shoddy aspiration and, essentially, a desperate one, for it is a useless stratagem to deal with the repressed despair of which it is the symptom.

The wish for a Barratt house in Dulwich, for the Porsche and the yacht and yet more skiing holidays, lacks all generosity; its fulfilment is posited upon the disappointment and failure of others. A top would not be worth reaching if there was room on it for everyone. Sometimes the disguise of this pseudo hope slips and it is then explicitly revealed, as in Thatcher's aspiration, 'Let our children grow tall, but some taller than others'.[6] To be envied is the quiddity of this genre of pseudo hope; and the ugly response of the less tall, thus provoked, is predictable. Sensing the mood of Thatcher's Britain, the gutter press has consequently never been more avid in ferreting out, for the pleasure of their envious readers, the misfortunes and scandals of the famous.

There is another distinguishing feature of this cheating hope, and it is one which betrays its impersonation. Unlike genuine hope, it cannot look the present in the face. Some time ago, conscious of how all-pervading was its presence among too many of my Parliamentary colleagues, I wrote, 'The greatest tragedy of the professional politician is his incapacity to enjoy the present: he lives to become a candidate and then dreams of entering the House where, dream fulfilled, he yearns for a Junior Ministership. His compulsions enforce him to resent being a Minister without Cabinet status, and, that achieved, even as a Chancellor of the Exchequer, he wishes to be Prime Minister at which level, it will not have escaped notice, frequently there are visible traces of the assumption of the role of a Deity, against whom, doubtless, envious feelings are focused.'[7] (If I had made those comments today, with Thatcher as the Premier, I would, of course, have interposed the Queen as a focus of envy between the Premier and the Deity.)

It is, however, not only professional politicians who so frequently lack joy in the present. The condition is seen in its most ironical mode among those who Thatcher would hold up as exemplars to us all. I have encountered no greater joylessness than among some of my entrepreneurial millionaire clients, frenetically working around the clock for a future that will grant yet more millions to bring them to the top of the league. It is not greed that devours their 'now'. Their present wilts because it lacks the oxygen of social hope. To visit them on their vulgar yachts, as they cruise along the Riviera, is to appreciate that despite all the sophisticated equipment aboard to keep them in touch with their offices, their minions and brokers, nevertheless they are isolated. The multi-millionaire's spurious, private brand of hope necessarily requires that he is alone, singled out, that destiny will favour him above others, that he is the lucky one. Even on his yacht he does not commune with the environment; he does not see the sparkle of the sea or the wondrous light.

In the last century, Tocqueville observed the same condition as he viewed the emergent America. He commented, 'Each person, withdrawn into himself, behaves as though he is a stranger to the destiny of all others . . . As for his transactions with his fellow citizens, he may mix among them, but he sees them not; he touches them, but does not feel them; he exists only in himself and for himself alone. And . . . there no longer remains a sense of society.'[8] He understood hope needs a present as well as a future, and, moreover, since hope is the emotional relationship between present and future, it can only become meaningful when it is perceived as part of a web of social relations rather than the lonely inexpressive end of individualism.[9]

When hope is privatised, when a man does not link his future destiny to others and becomes a 'stranger', then he suffers the emptiness of which Pascal has written: 'We never take hold of the present. We anticipate the future as though it were too slow in coming and we want it to hasten its arrival . . . The present never is our goal: the past and the present are our means; only the future is our end. Thus, we never live, we only hope to live; and, in awaiting and preparing ourselves for happiness we inevitably never are happy.'[10]

Thatcher would trap us into such a dismaying lifestyle, one essentially lacking a social matrix. That matrix is absent because it was not Thatcher's endowment to have a mothering which instilled the belief that the world is good, and that it will be good. For her, the world was hostile, to be conquered, triumphed over; because there was no initial reciprocity, she was not attuned to have the conviction that if she gave, she would receive. She was not granted the faith that reciprocity is available and enriching; so unfairly excluded from such a faith, she has never understood that this reciprocal mood should pervade societal relations. The conclusion of the psychoanalyst, Charles Rycroft, that 'Hope is in fact something that circulates within that total wider system of relationships we call society'[11] is meaningless to a woman who denies the existence of society. Thatcher has said, 'There is no such thing as society. There are individual men and women and there are families.' For her, hope must be directed towards personal fame, personal success, to achievements like her own. There is an irony in her call to us to follow her example, for we see before us the spectacle of a woman forever in a fury, never at peace, tossed around by anger, bitter of tongue, still at war with the world she never felt, as a baby, to be benevolent. She strives for the ultimate privatisation, that of hope. But seeing the torn woman before us, we learn that hope privatised cancels itself out.

The emphasis placed on the social quality of hope by psychoanalysts was especially meaningful during the Second World War. The bombing and hardships suffered by the civilian population and the dangers and separations of those of us serving abroad, never brought demoralisation. Hope is compounded of desire and expectation: we had both. Even in the darkest days, our hope was certain because it was firmly based on our sense of community. We lived through a time when there has never been less selfishness; neighbourliness in the civilian population and comradeship in the services provided the ethos within which hope thrived. The mood was carried forward to the post-war years; despite the austerity and rationing, the sense of sharing meant the energic potential of hope was realised and found its expression in the creation of the Welfare State. And, unlike private hope, marked by its meanness, the genuine hope did not place boundaries on its generosity; it willingly gave independence, even to far-flung colonies that had not demanded it. When the era ended in 1951, the Labour Party received more votes than ever before in its history; the Attlee government fell not because hope was exhausted in the electorate, but because its ageing leadership was clapped out.

Those remarkable years illustrate that a nation moved by hope responds in a similar fashion to that observed by psychoanalysts in their patients. The American analyst, Ernest Schachtel, long ago saw how wondrously therapeutic hope can be. 'Hope is based on the attempt to understand the concrete conditions of reality, to see one's own role in it realistically, and to engage in such efforts of thoughtful action as might be expected to bring about the hoped-for change. The affect of hope, in this case, has an activating effect. It helps in the mobilisation of the energies needed for activity. By activity I mean not only motor activity but also the activity of thought or of relenting to another person in an attitude of loving concern.'

When optimistic changes are put forward by a political party, an audit is needed. An assessment of their realism; their freedom from millenarian pseudo-hope, is clearly required but, more important, they must also be tested to see whether they will generate the activity-affect of realistic hope even as the changes are fought for, or are being carried out. Only thus, as in immediate post-war Britain, is social cohesion not only maintained but strengthened.

So what are we to do about it? A singularly heavy burden falls today on a responsible political party seeking government. It has to declare a preparedness at a difficult time, when paternalism is often irrationally attacked and irreverence is lauded, to accept a substantial portion of the responsibility of maintaining social cohesion, a responsibility which was formerly carried by Church and Crown: for those institutions – despite all their negative aspects – by inspiring faith, giving hope, and distributing charity, were the mortar keeping society together. Without these two forces a vacuum is left.

The religious Christian believes God is the source and the end of hope: there is no hope in Heaven where its object, the Beatific Vision, has already been attained, and there is no hope in Hell where its object is irretrievably lost. But in the meantime, here on this earth, hope, despite all disappointments, could be sustained. The Crown contributed to keeping society intact by distributing hope. Charles II, held to have the royal therapeutic power, touched 100,000 people for the King's Evil, scrofula, and a form of service for touching was included in the Book of Common Prayer until the eighteenth century. Today, however, most would regard the idea that our Queen is infused with Divine Grace, because of her anointment with oil at her Coronation, as an engaging fiction, not as fact. Neither genealogy nor faith has the capacity to provide contemporary Britain with the hope needed to bind us together in community, and Thatcher, denied by her upbringing the enjoyment of social hope, assails such capacity as they still possess: she obliterates the aristocracy in her own Party, attacks the archbishops, and puts herself at odds with the Queen.

Moreover, while Thatcher continues in her attempts to plug the sources of hope, we must not be distracted by other unhelpful campaigners from the task of replenishing it. There are well-meaning liberals who will always give their signatures but usually not their selves; they publish calls for constitutional changes which by way of a new Magna Carta will relieve all the ills of society.[12] And, more perniciously, there are the modern Marxists, the darlings of right-wing publicists and editors,[13] whose solution for the future lies in ending 'the pyramid of power' by modern technology. We are told 'on a video-tex network like Minitel in France or Compuserve in the United States, activists can very quickly link together on a campaign, sharing ideas, research and best practices without the need to meet together or establish a formal institution with Committees, standing orders and officials: the "virtual" campaign comes to stand alongside the "virtual" classroom and the "virtual" laboratory, existing in electronic space rather than the formal physical space of meetings and structures, its structures instantly formed or dissolved'.[14] Human contact can thus be avoided, emotion can be eliminated. The computer will take us to a new age where, authority denied, the adolescent wish to overcome the parental-surrogate of the State will be fulfilled and each of us, alone, protected against any of the hazards of flesh and blood relationships, will sit by our videos, dreaming of the future.

The characteristic of these tepid campaigners, liberal and Marxist, is the limit most of them impose upon their engagement. But creative hope will not come into existence by signing a declaration; nor can it exist in 'electronic' space. It is essentially an activity-affect needing personal commitment and ceaseless perseverance; it is important but not sufficient for the policy statements of my Party to be constantly monitored to ensure they always encourage a sense of community. A socialist party, containing within its designation the affirmation of its preoccupation with the social dimension, cannot through its individual members simply be a purveyor of hope, for hope cannot be bought or sold. Only from relatedness does hope spring.

It is actualised in the relationship that can be established between the good MP and the committed local councillor, and their constituents. It can emerge in the stillness of the consulting room when psychiatrist and patient silently sit together. It is present in the rapport established between the sensitive social worker and her client; and sometimes it can overcome despair as the harassed probation officer finds a reciprocity with an outcast delinquent.

Its prototype is to be found within the whole yet separate relationship between mother and child. The paediatrician, Donald Winnicott, once exclaimed, 'There is no such thing as a baby', meaning the infant cannot be considered as an isolate; it is from a dyad that the human being has developed, and his or her fate so substantially determined.

To attribute, as I have, such a baleful influence upon contemporary Britain to the lack of affect of Beatrice Roberts, will be resented by those who wish to give grand sociological, economic, or technological explanations to our present predicaments. Yet the self-mortifying Beatrice casts a shadow on us all. Margaret Thatcher is certainly no exception to the rule that our mothers significantly shape our characters. And the nearer one is to the centre of political decision-making, the greater is the certainty that character, not principle, is the determinant.

This strength of character can be used for good or ill. John Biffen, whose wit and talent made him so splendid a Leader of the House of Commons, and unerringly marked him down to be a victim of Thatcher, recently wished for a modern Trollope who would portray politics in terms of personality rather than principles. 'I am certain', he wrote, 'there is a legitimate role for the interpretation of public life as a struggle of individuals involving the noble and the base, as well as the great clash of ideologies and principles.'[15]

In British politics the protagonists are rarely wicked, and are only noble in exceptional cases. Nevertheless, the assertion that the politician can debase or elevate society rings true. Nowhere is that seen more vividly than when we contrast the enervating negativism of Thatcher, bringing a mood of hopelessness and defeat to so many, from dons to nurses to young unemployed, with the hope that Gorbachev inspires. Whether Gorbachev, in his interaction with many groups in the Soviet Union, will be blessed with sufficient feedback to create a vigorous hope, powerful enough to overcome the appalling demoralisation and depression within Soviet society, remains uncertain. In Britain, although the task of mobilising hope is considerable, it is not of the same order and is, more certainly, as has been proved before, capable of achievement.

In the task, the politician who, by conduct and by creed, spreads brotherliness, has an ally. Just as private hope is marked by joylessness, so social hope in its ongoing activity is spurred on by joy. It is the emotion celebrated by Schiller in his renowned *An die Freude* – *Ode to Joy* where he describes the connection between joy and the feeling of brotherliness. It is the activity-affect consisting of continuing acts in the present of turning towards the world; it is not hypo-manic or impatient and, in its highest form, Schachtel[16] has told us is based on openness towards, and affirmation of others. It will always be present when the politician-preacher is offering, and receiving from, his congregants genuine hope. Such energetic hope can effect the transition away from Thatcher's present cultural dominance. This way the imbalance can be ended between the social and individual domain which now so overburdens the intimate zone, leaving it oppressed and joyless.

This is not a romantic declaration; it is a restatement, in the language of secular politics, of the traditional theological virtues of faith, hope and charity: their established chronology, as their conjunction, is meaningful. Faith comes first, strong or weak, depending upon the quality of trust established by the mother ministering to the infant's needs; without faith, based on past trust, there can be little hope, for, denied experience of good relationships in the past, there can be small expectation of a benign future, and, no less, without the experience of primal reciprocity, true charity – translated in the modern Bible as love – which gives, and hence receives, cannot be evoked.

These were the virtues which informed the early socialists who founded the British Labour, Trade Union and Co-operative movements; and these virtues are neither quaint, out of date, nor anachronistic. Their inspirational strengths remain available to those with the courage to ignore the raillery of those who would expel affect from politics. So often fearful of their own emotions, the mockers would command that attention be given only to the ideational crusts of politics. Their resultant discourses, with the emotions ebbed, high and dry, become doctrine or clichés. The politics of passion are of another order; and those who dare to practise them know that social movements take their whole shape and force, as the Labour Movement historically has done, from their constitutive and binding affects.

If we can now kindle these unifying emotions, the joyless dirge of Thatcher need no longer dispirit us. We have another song to sing. Beethoven's affirmative Ninth Symphony provides us with the music and Schiller's *Ode*, which furnishes the text of the last Movement, provides us with the words. Let the cynics and the over-sophisticated scoff at our naivety; we know the strength of our innocence. It is time for us to rejoin the choir.

> Oh friends no more these sounds!
> Let us sing more cheerful songs more full of joy!
> Joy, bright spark of divinity,
> Daughter of Elysium,
> Fire-inspired we tread thy sanctuary.
> Thy magic power re-unites
> All that custom has divided,
> All men become brothers
> Under the sway of thy gentle wings.

Notes

Apologia

1 *Guardian*, 3 June 1987.
2 A. F. Davies, *Skills, Outlooks and Passions*, Cambridge University Press, 1980.
  Graham Little, *Political Ensembles*, Oxford University Press, 1985.
  Graham Little, *Strong Leadership*, Oxford University Press, 1988.
  A. F. Davies, *The Human Element*, Gribble/Penguin, 1988.
3 Paul Roazen, *Freud, Political and Social Thought*, Hogarth Press, p. 39, 1969.
4 Jeremy Waldron, *The Times Literary Supplement*, 22 January 1988.
5 Michael Shepherd, 'The Psycho-Historians', *Encounter*, March 1979.
6 Catherine Clement, *The Weary Sons of Freud*, Verso, 1987.
7 Robert S. Steele, 'Psychoanalysis and Hermeneutics', *International Review of Psychoanalysis*, Vol. 6, p. 389.
8 Robert S. Wallestein, Presidential Address at 35th International Psychoanalytical Congress.
9 Yiannis Gabriel, 'The Psychoanalytic Contribution to the Sociology of Suffering', *International Review of Psychoanalysis*, Vol. II, 1984.
  Hanna Segal, 'Silence is the Real Crime', *International Review of Psychoanalysis*, Vol. 14, Part 1, 1987.
  Malcolm Pines, 'Stepchildren of Vienna', paper delivered, Buenos Aires, August 1985.
10 C. R. Badcock, *Madness and Modernity*, Basil Blackwell, pp. 89–134, 1983.
11 Carl E. Schorske, *Fin-de-Siècle Vienna*, Cambridge University Press, 1981.
12 Ernest Jones, *Sigmund Freud: Life and Work*, Vol. I, Hogarth Press, p. 48, 1953.
13 Letter from Freud to Julia Braun-Vogelstein 1927, telling of Freud accompanying his close friend Heinrich Braun, father of the late Prussian Prime Minister, Otto Braun, and brother-in-law of Victor Adler, to Victor Adler's home, 'It strikes me as strange this took place in the same rooms as those in which I have been living for the past 36 years.'
14 Mark E. Baum, *The Austro-Marxists 1890/1918*, University Press of Kentucky, 1985.
15 Arnold A. Rogow, 'Dora's Brother', *International Review of Psychoanalysis*, Vol. 6, p. 239.
16 Jaap van Ginneken, 'The Killing of the Father', paper, International Society of Political Psychology, 1983.
17 Eugene Weber, *The Times Literary Supplement*, 5 January 1988.
18 Michel Bruguière, *Questionnaires et Profiteurs de la Révolution*, Orban, Paris, 1987.

19 *Sunday Times*, 25 November 1973.
20 Bion, 'Group Dynamics', *New Directions in Psychoanalysis*, ed. M. Pines.
21 Edna O'Shaughnessy, *International Review of Psychoanalysis*, Part 1, Vol. 14, p. 133, 1987.
22 John Bowlby, *Attachment and Loss*, Hogarth Press, Vol. 2, p. xi, 1973.
    Joseph Weiss, 'Testing Hypotheses about Unconscious Mental Functioning', *International Journal of Psychoanalysis*, 1988.
23 Ernest Jones, *Sigmund Freud: Life and Work*, Vol. 2, Hogarth Press, 1955.
24 Friedrich Nietzsche, *Ecce Homo*, Vintage Books, 1969.

1 Tory MPs in the Crèche

1 Leo Abse, *Private Member*, Macdonald, 1973.
2 Peter Jenkins, *Mrs Thatcher's Revolution*, Jonathan Cape, 1987.
3 Ben Pimlott, *The Times*, 20 December 1987.
4 D. Wilfred Abse and Lucie Jessner, 'The Psychodynamic Aspects of Leadership', in *Excellence and Leadership in a Democracy*, ed. Stephen R. Graubard and Gerald Holton, Columbia University Press, 1962.

2 Phallic Woman

1 Sigmund Freud, *Collected Works*, Hogarth Press Standard Edition, Vol. XIX, p. 145.
2 Marina Warner, *Monuments and Maidens*, Picador Books, 1987.
3 Wilhelm Reich, *Character Analysis*, Vision Press, 1969.

3 Margaret at the Breast

1 Robert Harris, *Observer*, 3 January 1988.
2 Hugo Young and Ann Sloman, *The Thatcher Phenomenon*, BBC Books, 1986, p. 16.
3 Charles Rycroft, *Psychoanalysis and Beyond*, Chatto & Windus, 1985.
4 David Cooper, *The Death of the Family*, Allen Lane, 1971.
5 *Sunday Times*, 13 December 1987.
6 Interview with Terry Coleman, *Guardian*, 24 July 1985.
7 Patricia Murray, *Margaret Thatcher*, W. H. Allen, 1978.
8 Broadcast, Radio London, January 1987.
9 Alan J. Mayer, *Madam Prime Minister: Margaret Thatcher*, Newsweek Books, 1979.
10 Geoffrey Smith, *The Times*, 28 January 1987.
11 D. W. Winnicott, *The Maturational Processes and the Facilitating Environment*, Hogarth Press, 1965.
    D. W. Winnicott, 'Through Paediatrics to Psychoanalysis', *Collected Papers*, Tavistock Publications, 1958.
12 Jeremy Seabrook, *Guardian*, 16 November 1984.
    Jeremy Seabrook and Trevor Blackwell, 'Mrs Thatcher's Religious Pilgrimage', *Granta 6*, Cambridge 1983.
13 *Sunday Times*, 8 May 1988.
14 Kohut and Ernest Wolf, 'The Disorders of the Self and their Treatment', *International Journal of Psychoanalysis*, 1959, pp. 413–25.
15 Hugo Young and Ann Sloman, *The Thatcher Phenomenon*, BBC Books, 1986.

16 Elliott Jaques, *The Measurement of Responsibility*, Tavistock Publications, 1956.
17 Melanie Klein, 'A Study of Envy and Gratitude', paper delivered to the International Psychoanalytic Congress, 1955.
18 As note 9.
19 As note 15.
20 *Guardian*, 10 May 1988.
21 Peter Gay, *Freud for Historians*, Oxford University Press, 1985.
22 Peter Jenkins, *Mrs Thatcher's Revolution*, Jonathan Cape, 1987.
23 Sigmund Freud, *The Acquisition and Control of Fire*, Hogarth Press Standard Edition, Vol. XXII.
24 Sigmund Freud, 'Anxiety and Instinctual Life', *New Introductory Lectures on Psychoanalysis*, Hogarth Press Standard Edition, Vol. XXII.
25 Karl Abraham, 'Oral Eroticism and Character', in *Selected Papers on Psychoanalysis*, Hogarth Press, 1954.
   Edward Glover, 'Notes on Oral Character Formation', in *International Journal of Psychoanalysis*, Vol. 6, 1925, pp. 131–53.
26 Heinz Kohut, *Restoration of the Self*, International Universities Press, 1977.
   Heinz Kohut, *The Analysis of the Self*, Hogarth Press and Institute of Psycho-analysis, 1971.
   Heinz Kohut, *Self Psychology and the Humanities*, W. W. Norton & Co., Inc., 1985.
27 Melanie Klein, *Envy and Gratitude*, Tavistock Publications, 1957.
28 Donald Winnicott, 'Psychoses and Child Care', *Collected Papers*, Tavistock Publications, 1958.
29 Hanna Segal, *Introduction to the Work of Melanie Klein*, Hogarth Press, 1973, p. 52.
30 As note 27.

4 On the Pot

1 Frieda Goldman-Eisler, 'Breast Feeding and Character Formation', *Symposium on the Healthy Personality*, ed. Milton J. E. Senn, Josiah Macy Foundation, 1950.
2 Karl Abraham, 'Oral Eroticism and Character', *Selected Papers on Psychoanalysis*, Hogarth Press, 1954.
3 Sigmund Freud, *Collected Works*, Hogarth Press Standard Edition, Vol. XII, p. 187.
4 *Observer*, 12 January 1986.
5 *Observer*, 18 May 1986.
6 *The Times*, 15 October 1987.
7 *Guardian*, 26 November 1984.
8 Elvio Fachinelli, 'Anal Money-time', *The Psychology of Gambling*, ed. Jon Halliday and Peter Fuller, Allen Lane, 1974.
9 Romans, 6, v. 15.
10 E. Benson Perkins, *Gambling in English Life*, Epworth Press.
11 Sigmund Freud, *Dostoevsky and Parricide*, Hogarth Press Standard Edition, Vol. XXI.
12 *Hansard*, 16 November 1959.
13 Peter Fuller, 'Gambling: A Secular Religion for the Obsessional Neurotic', as note 8.
14 Edmund Hergler, *The Psychology of Gambling*, International Universities Press, New York, 1970.
15 J. M. Keynes, *Essays in Persuasion*, Macmillan, 1972.
16 William Keegan, *Observer*, 18 September 1988.

17 Karl Marx, *Selected Writings in Sociology and Social Philosophy*, ed. Tom Bottomore, Penguin, 1970.
18 Reimut Reiche, *Sexuality and the Class Struggle*, NLB, 1970.
19 As note 17.
20 A. and E. Newsom, *Four-year-olds in an Urban Community*, Penguin Books, 1970.
21 Ronald Fletcher, *The Shaking of the Foundations*, Routledge, 1988.
22 Graham Little, 'Ambivalence, Dilemma and Paradox', Sixth Annual Conference, International Society of Political Psychology.
23 Patricia Murray, *Margaret Thatcher*, W. H. Allen, 1978.
24 Simon Hoggart, *Punch*, 14 March 1984.
25 Carol Thatcher, *Diary of an Election*, Sidgwick & Jackson, 1983.
26 Penny Junor, *Margaret Thatcher: Wife, Mother, Politician*, Sidgwick & Jackson, 1983, p. 178.
27 As note 26, p. 179.
28 Leo Abse, *Private Member*, Macdonald, 1973, pp. 19–20.
29 Ernest Jones, 'Anal Erotic Traits', *Papers on Psychoanalysis*, Baillière Tindall & Cox, 1927.
30 Allan C. Elms, *Personality in Politics*, Harcourt Brace Jovanovich, 1976.
31 *Spectator*, 20 April 1985.
32 Peter Hennessy, 'The Prime Minister, the Cabinet, and the Thatcher Personality', in *Thatcherism: Personality and Politics*, ed. Kenneth Minogue and Michael Biddiss, Macmillan, 1987.
33 Matrimonial Proceedings Bill, 1982.
   Matrimonial and Family Proceedings Act, 1984.
34 Report of the Conciliation Project Unit to the Lord Chancellor, 1989.
35 Lord Mackay, Joseph Jackson Memorial Lecture, 1989.

5 Oedipal Rivalries

1 Interview with BBC, 28 February 1984.
2 William H. Gillespie, 'Woman and Her Discontents: A Reassessment of Freud's Views on Female Sexuality', in *The British School of Psychoanalysis*, ed. Gregorio Kohon, Free Association Books, 1986.
3 Alfred Adler, *The Family Constellation*.
   J. C. Flugel, *The Psychoanalytic Study of the Family*, Hogarth Press, 1939.
4 World in Action, 'Now We Are Ten', ITV, 8 May 1989.
5 Simon Hoggart, *Tatler*, January 1984.
6 Alan J. Mayer, *Madam Prime Minister: Margaret Thatcher*, Newsweek Books, 1979.
7 Graham Little, 'Why Thatcher has no feel for the Commonwealth', *The Age*, Australia, 22 July 1986.
8 Hugo Young, *One of Us*, Macmillan, 1989, p. 324.
9 Lord Hailsham, *Evening Standard*, 6 April 1989.
10 *Sunday Times*, 20 July 1986.
11 *Spectator*, 20 April 1985.
12 Robert Harris, *Observer*, 3 January 1988.
13 *Sunday Telegraph*, 13 July 1986.
14 *Hansard*, 18 June 1986.
15 Address to Belgian Institute of International Relations, 16 March 1987.
16 *Hansard*, 15 April 1986.
17 As note 6.
18 Graham Little, 'Ronald Reagan's Dorian Gray Complex', *Ageing and Political*

Leadership, ed. A. P. McIntyre, Oxford University Press/State University New York Press, 1988.

19 J. Laplanche and J. B. Pontalis, *The Language of Psychoanalysis*, Hogarth Press, 1973.

20 Charles Rycroft, *A Critical Dictionary of Psychoanalysis*, Nelson, 1968.

21 As note 18.

22 Ronald Reagan, *Where's the Rest of Me?*, Karta Publishers, 1981.

23 Robert Dallek in *Ronald Reagan: The Politics of Symbolism*, ed. G. G. Hamilton and N. W. Pickard, Harvard University Press.

6   Burying Beatrice

1   Melanie Klein, *Contributions to Psychoanalysis 1921–45*, Hogarth Press, 1948.

2   Elliott Jaques, 'Social Systems as Defence against Persecutory and Depressive Anxiety', in Klein et al., *New Directions in Psychoanalysis*, Tavistock Publications, 1955.

3   Franco Fornari, *The Psychoanalysis of War*, Anchor, 1966.

4   Gaston Bouthoul, *Les Guerres: et le mentir de polémologie*.

5   As note 3.

6   Revd Peter Mullen, 'The New Babel', *Observer*, 19 April 1987.

7   Melanie Klein, 'On Identification', in Klein et al, *New Directions in Psychoanalysis*, Tavistock Publications, 1955.

8   *Guardian*, 1 June 1987.

9   *Guardian*, 8 March 1989.

10 BBC Broadcast, 26 May 1985, quoted in Hugo Young and Ann Sloman, *The Thatcher Phenomenon*, BBC Books, 1986.

11 As note 10.

12 Penny Junor, *Margaret Thatcher: Wife, Mother, Politician*, Sidgwick & Jackson, 1983.

13 *Mail on Sunday*, 23 April 1989.

14 Ignazio Silone, *Uscita di Sicurezza*, Mondadori.

15 Anthony Barnett, *Iron Britannia*, Allison & Busby, 1982.

16 As note 15.

17 *Hansard*, 20 May 1982.

18 Hugo Young, *One of Us*, Macmillan, 1989, p. 9.

19 As note 15.

20 *Guardian*, 22 May 1982.

21 Robert Waelder, 'Psychoanalysis and History', in *The Psychoanalytical Interpretation of History*, ed. Benjamin B. Wolman, Basic Books, 1971.

22 *Hansard*, 27 October 1971.

23 The Fortunate Isle is always carefully positioned in the West, as in the Hereford map of the thirteenth century; the twelfth-century map of the world in Corpus Christi College, Cambridge; and the one made by Floridus in the Bibliothèque Nationale in Paris.

24 Martin Wiener, *English Culture and the Decline of the Industrial Spirit, 1850 to 1980*, Cambridge University Press, 1981.

25 Ernest Jones, 'The Island of Ireland', a paper read before the British Psychoanalytical Society, 1922, published in Ernest Jones, *Psychomyth, Psychohistory*, Hillstone, 1974.

26 *Hansard*, 22 November 1974.

27 *Hansard*, 18 May 1979.

28 Hugo Young, *One of Us*, Macmillan, 1989, p. 277.

29 Letter to author, May 1985.

30 Heinz Kohut, *The Restoration of the Self*, International Universities Press, New York, 1977.

7 Sounding Brass

1 Sigmund Freud, *Group Psychology and the Analysis of the Ego*, Hogarth Press Standard Edition, Vol. XVIII (quoting 1 Corinthians, 13, v. 1).
2 Ernest S. Wolf, 'Basic Concepts of Self-Psychology', working paper of the Centre for Psycho-Social Studies, Chicago.
3 *Observer*, 5 July 1987.
4 Karl Marx and Friedrich Engels, *The Communist Manifesto*, Penguin, 1967.
5 Yiannis Gabriel, *International Review of Psychoanalysis*, Vol. II, Part 4, 1984.
6 Herbert Marcuse, *One Dimensional Man*, Sphere, 1968.
7 Elliott Jaques, *The Changing Culture of the Factory*, Tavistock Publications, 1951.
8 Melanie Klein, *Envy and Gratitude*, Tavistock Publications, 1957.
9 Hanna Segal, *Introduction to the Work of Melanie Klein*, Hogarth Press, 1973.
10 As note 1.
11 *The Times*, 29 July 1987.

8 *Les Trahisons des Clercs*: Academic Perfidy

1 Penny Junor, *Margaret Thatcher: Wife, Mother, Politician*, Sidgwick & Jackson, 1983.
2 Patricia Murray, *Margaret Thatcher*, W. H. Allen, 1978.
3 Edward Pearce, *Sunday Times*, 5 March 1989.
4 As note 1.
5 Interview with Kenneth Harris.
6 Dennis Kavanagh, *Thatcherism and British Politics*, Oxford University Press, 1987.
7 Hanna Segal, *Introduction to the Work of Melanie Klein*, Hogarth Press, 1973.
8 As note 7.
9 As note 1.
10 *Thatcherism: Personality and Politics*, ed. Kenneth Minogue and Michael Biddiss, Macmillan, 1987.
11 Sandor Ferenczi, *Final Contributions to the Problems and Methods of Psychoanalysis*, Hogarth Press, 1955.
12 Robert Waelder, *Progress and Revolution*, International Universities Press, New York.
13 As note 6.
14 Leo Abse, *Private Member*, Macdonald, 1973, p. 162.

9 Back to the Womb

1 *The Times* Diary [during] September 1987.
2 Harold E. Lasswell, *Psychopathology and Politics*, Viking Press, 1960.
3 *Hansard*, 2 December 1977.
4 *Hansard*, 22 March 1978.
5 Leo Abse, 'The Windscale Dilemma', *Spectator*, 4 February 1978.
6 Trevor Blackwell and Jeremy Seabrook, *The Politics of Hope*, Faber, 1988.
7 J. G. Flugel, *Psychoanalytical Study of the Family*, Hogarth Press, 1939.
8 John Turner, 'Wordsworth and Winnicott', *International Review of Psychoanalysis*, Vol. 15, Part 4, 1988.

9 Speech delivered at The Royal Society, 27 September 1988.
10 Charles Rycroft, *A Critical Dictionary of Psychoanalysis*, Nelson, 1968.
11 *The Times*, 26 October 1988.
12 *Guardian*, 28 September 1987.

10 Miss Flag

1 D. W. Abse, *Hysteria and Related Mental Disorder*, Wright Bristol, second edition, 1987.
2 Published by Sermons Secretary, St Mary's, Cambridge, 1984.
3 Bishop of Durham and Archbishop of Canterbury, *The Times*, 27 March 1989.
4 Lenin, *Ueber Religion*, p. 65, quoted in Wilhelm Reich, *The Mass Psychology of Fascism*, Penguin, 1975, p. 58.
5 Hitler, *Mein Kampf*, Reynal & Hitchcock, 1939.
6 Wilhelm Reich, *The Mass Psychology of Fascism*, Penguin, 1975.
7 Bob Jessop, Kevin Bonnett, Simon Bromley and Tom Ling, 'Popular Capitalism, Flexible Accumulation and Left Strategy', *New Left Review* 165, September–October 1987. Reprinted together with other essays putting forward an economistic 'Two Nations' interpretation of Thatcherism in Bob Jessop, Kevin Bonnett, Simon Bromley and Tom Ling, *Thatcherism: A Tale of Two Nations*, Polity Press, Cambridge, 1988.
8 Graham Wallas, *Human Nature in Politics*, 1908.
9 Lewis Namier, *Personalities and Powers*, Hamish Hamilton, 1955.
10 Eric Hobsbawm, 'The Forward March of Labour Halted?', in Eric Hobsbawm et al., *The Forward March of Labour Halted?*, ed. Martin Jacques and Francis Mulhern, Verso, in association with *Marxism Today*, 1981. Hobsbawm has now collected all his recent essays arguing for a Popular Front against Thatcherism in Eric Hobsbawm, *Politics for a Rational Left*, Verso, 1989; the epilogue of which reiterates his defeatist call for an anti-Tory electoral pact.
11 Ed. Stuart Hall and Martin Jacques, *The Politics of Thatcherism*, Lawrence & Wishart in association with *Marxism Today*, London, 1983. Hall has recently collected everything he has ever written with even the vaguest bearing on Thatcherism in Stuart Hall, *The Hard Road to Renewal: Thatcherism and the Crisis of the Left*, Verso, 1988.
12 'The Great Moving Right Show', *The Politics of Thatcherism*, as note 11.
13 Antonio Gramsci, *Selections from Political Writings 1921–26*, Lawrence & Wishart, 1978, p. 47.
14 Andrew Gamble, *The Free Economy and the Strong State*, Macmillan, 1988, p. 210.
15 Leon Trotsky, *The Struggle Against Fascism in Germany*, Penguin, 1975, p. 406.
16 *Observer*, 29 November 1987.
17 *Sunday Times*, 27 December 1987.
18 Anna Freud, *The Ego and the Mechanisms of Defence*, Hogarth Press, 1939.
19 Articles in *The Times* and *Spectator*, 26 October 1981.
20 Ernest Jones, 'The Psychology of Quislingism', *International Journal of Psychoanalysis*, January 1941.
21 Woodrow Wyatt, *Confessions of an Optimist*, Collins, 1985.
22 Sigmund Freud, *Beyond the Pleasure Principle*, Hogarth Press Standard Edition, Vol. XVIII.
23 Leo Abse, *Private Member*, Macdonald, 1973, pp. 211–16.
24 As note 23, pp. 62–8.

11 The Harbingers: Keith Joseph and Enoch Powell

1   Michael Grant, *St Paul*, Weidenfeld & Nicolson, 1976.
2   Hyam Maccoby, *The Myth Maker: Paul and the Invention of Christianity*, Weidenfeld & Nicolson, 1986.
3   Romans 7:18; 1 Corinthians 9:27; 2 Corinthians 5:2,5,6,4,7. As quoted in note 1.
4   John Maxwell Atkinson, *Our Masters' Voice*, Methuen, 1984.
5   Angela Carter, *New Statesman*, 3 June 1983.
6   C. G. Jung, *Psychological Types or The Psychology of Individuation*, Kegan Paul, 1923.
7   Hugo Young, *One of Us*, Macmillan, 1989, p. 84.
8   Elliott Jaques, 'Death and Mid-Life Crisis', *International Journal of Psychoanalysis*, Vol. 46, 1965, p. 506.
9   Michael Allingham, *Unconscious Contracts*, Routledge & Kegan Paul, 1987.
10   Speech at Birmingham, 19 October 1974.
11   Peter Jenkins, *Mrs Thatcher's Revolution*, Jonathan Cape, 1987.
12   Cecil Roth, *A Short History of the Jewish People*, Horovitz Publishing Company, 1959.
13   David Marquand, *The Unprincipled Society*, Jonathan Cape, 1988.
14   Leo Abse, *Private Member*, Macdonald, 1973, p. 267.
15   Michael Foot, *Loyalists and Loners*, Collins, 1986.
16   J. C. Flugel, *Psychoanalytical Study of the Family*, Hogarth Press, 1939.
17   Sigmund Freud, *Moses and Monetheism*, Hogarth Press Standard Edition, Vol. XXIII.
18   R. D. Laing, *The Facts of Life*, Allen Lane, 1976.
19   *The Times*, 19 April 1988.
20   Roy Lewis, *Enoch Powell*, Cassell.
21   Andrew Roth, 'Enoch Powell', *Tory Tribune*, 1970.
22   Interview with Robin Day, BBC Radio 4, 21 October 1974.
23   R. A. Butler, *The Art of the Possible*, Hamish Hamilton, 1971.
24   Patrick Cosgrave, *The Lives of Enoch Powell*, Bodley Head, 1989.
25   *Spectator*, 13 September 1968.
26   Leo Abse, *Private Member*, Macdonald, 1973, pp. 243–7.
27   As note 26.
28   Statutory Instruments Committee, 26 July 1978.
29   Leo Abse, 'The Politics of In Vitro Fertilisation', *In Vitro Fertilisation: Past, Present and Future*, ed. Fishel and Symonds, IRL Press, 1986.

12 St Michael and the Dragon

1   Harry Guntrip, *Schizoid Phenomena, Object Relations and the Self*, Hogarth Press, 1968.
2   Patricia Murray, *Margaret Thatcher*, W. H. Allen, 1978.
3   Anthony Storr, *The School of Genius*, André Deutsch, 1988.
4   BBC Broadcast, 9 June 1985, quoted in Hugo Young and Ann Sloman, *The Thatcher Phenomenon*, BBC Books, 1986.
5   Robin Oakley, *The Times*, 2 August 1988.
6   Dr Thomas Stuttaford, *The Times*, 28 November 1987.
7   *The Times*, 24 September 1987.
8   *Hansard*, 29 October 1986.
9   Tam Dalyell, *Misrule*, Hamish Hamilton, 1987.
10   Julian Critchley, *Heseltine*, Hodder & Stoughton, 1988, p. 136.
11   J. C. Flugel, *The Psychoanalytic Study of the Family*, Hogarth Press, 1939.

13   Margaret Thatcher's Jews

1   Letter, Chief Rabbi to author, 12 February 1986.
2   Immanuel Jacobovitz, *If only my people* . . . , Weidenfeld & Nicolson, 1984.
3   Immanuel Jacobovitz, *From Doom to Hope*, Office of the Chief Rabbi, 1986.
4   'Faith in the City', The Report of the Archbishop of Canterbury's Commission on Urban Priority Areas, 1985.
5   Ahad Haam, 'Jewish and Christian Ethics', *Essays, Letters, Memoirs*, Phaidon Press, 1946.
6   Ahad Haam, 'Judaism and Asceticism', as note 5.
7   William Fishman, *East End Jewish Radicals, 1875–1914*, Duckworth, 1975.
8   Talmud: Baba Bathra, 9b.
9   *Daily Mail*, 15 July 1988.
10 Jonathan Frankel, *Prophecy and Politics: Socialism, Nationalism and the Russian Jews, 1869 to 1917*, Cambridge University Press, 1981.
11 *The Times*, 15 November 1892.
12 *Sunday Times*, 3 January 1988.
13 *Spectator*, 24 November 1984.
14 Peter Jenkins, *Mrs Thatcher's Revolution*, Jonathan Cape, 1987, p. 83.
15 Hugo Young, *One of Us*, Macmillan, 1989, p. 425.
16 James Morton, 'The Incest Act, 1908 – Was it ever relevant?', *The New Law Journal*, 29 January 1988.
17 [Quoted in] as note 16.
18 Ronald Butt, 'In Defence of Children', *The Times*, 1988.
19 Authorised Downing Street statement, *Sunday Times*, 10 July 1988.
20 *The Times*, 18 February 1989.
21 Margaret Wickstead, BBC Broadcast, 5 May 1985.
22 H. and Y. Lowenfeld, 'Our Permissive Society and the Super Ego', *Psychoanalytic Quarterly* 39, 1970.
23 Sigmund Freud, *Future of an Illusion*, Hogarth Press Standard Edition, Vol. XXI.
24 David Marquand, *The Unprincipled Society*, Jonathan Cape, 1988.
25 David Marquand, *New Democrat*, Vol. VI, 1988.
26 Sigmund Freud, *Civilisation and its Discontents*, Hogarth Press Standard Edition, Vol. XXI.

14   Secrets

1   *The Times*, 19 April 1988.
2   Erik Erikson, *Identity: Youth and Crisis*, Faber, 1968.
    Erik Erikson, *Childhood and Society*, Penguin, 1965.
3   A. Gross, *Bulletin Menninger Clinic 15*.
4   Sigmund Freud, *Two Lies Told by Children*, Hogarth Press Standard Edition, Vol. XII.
5   Gerald Margolis, *International Review of Psychoanalysis*, Vol. 1, 1974, p. 292.
6   John Bowlby, 'Separation, Anxiety and Anger', *Attachment and Loss*, Hogarth Press, 1973, Vol. 2, p. 208.
7   *Sunday Times*, 8 May 1987.
8   Oliver Anderson, *Rotten Borough*, Fourth Estate, reissued 1989.
9   Richard Boston, 'In Search of Rotten Links', *Guardian*, 9 July 1988.
10 Graham Little, *Strong Leadership*, Oxford University Press, 1988.
11 Correspondence between the author and Ernest Wolf of Chicago.
12 Charles Rycroft, *Psychoanalysis and Beyond*, Chatto & Windus, 1985, p. 222.

13 Joseph Conrad, 'Author's note', *Secret Agent*, Gresham Publishing Company, 1920.
14 Margaret Wickstead, BBC Broadcast, 5 May 1985.
15 *Hansard*, 26 March 1981.
16 Michael Randle and Pat Pottle, *The Blake Escape*, Harrap, 1989.
17 Phillip Knightley, *The Second Oldest Profession*, André Deutsch, 1986.
18 Sean Bourke, *The Springing of Blake*, Cassell, 1970.
19 Leo Abse, *Private Member*, Macdonald, 1973, pp. 118–19.
20 Tangye Lean, *The Napoleonites*, Oxford University Press, 1970.
21 'Statement on the recommendations of the Security Commission', May 1982.
22 Sigmund Freud, *The Psychoanalytic View of Psychodelic Psychogenic Disturbance of Vision*, Hogarth Press Standard Edition, Vol. XI.
23 Ismond Rosen, 'Exhibitionism and Voyeurism', in *Sexual Behaviour and the Law*, ed. Ralph Slovenko, Charles C. Thomas, 1965.
24 Otto Fenichel, 'The Scoptophilic Instinct and Identification', *International Journal of Psychoanalysis*, Vol. XVIII, 1937.
25 Chapman Pincher, *Too Secret, Too Long*, Sidgwick & Jackson, 1984.
26 Ernest Jones, 'The Psychology of Quislingism', *International Journal of Psychoanalysis*, Vol. XXII.
27 Sigmund Freud, *Psychoanalytic Notes on an Autobiographical Account of a Case of Paranoia*, Hogarth Press Standard Edition, Vol. XII.
28 *Hansard*, 1 December 1986.
29 Adam Raphael, *Observer*, 19 June 1988.

15   Woman to Woman: The Dark Continent

1 Sigmund Freud, 'Femininity', *New Introductory Lectures on Psychoanalysis*, Hogarth Press Standard Edition, Vol. XXII.
2 Beatrix Campbell, *Iron Ladies*, Virago, 1987.
3 Juliet Mitchell, *Psychoanalysis and Feminism*, Penguin, 1975.
4 Lynne Segal, 'The Heat in the Kitchen' and Jean Gardiner, 'Women, Recession and the Tories', in *The Politics of Thatcherism*, ed. Hall and Jacques, Lawrence & Wishart, 1983.
5 Lampl de-Groot, 'The Evolution of the Oedipus Complex in Women', *International Journal of Psychoanalysis*, Vol. 9, pp. 332–49.
6 Enid Balint, 'Technical Problems Found in the Analysis of Women by a Woman Analyst: A Contribution to the Question "What Does a Woman Want?"', *The British School of Psychoanalysis*, ed. Gregorio Kohen, Free Association Books, 1986.
7 As note 6, p. 332.
8 Heinz Kohut, *The Restoration of the Self*, International Universities Press, New York, 1977.
9 D. Wilfred Abse and Lucie Jessner, 'The Psychodynamic Aspects of Leadership', in *Excellence and Leadership in a Democracy*, ed. Stephen R. Graubard and Gerald Holton, Columbia University Press, 1962.
10 As note 2.
11 Melanie Phillips, 'Maggie's Family Policy', *Cosmopolitan*, May 1983.
12 Edwina Currie, BBC, 9 April 1989.
13 Penny Junor, *Margaret Thatcher: Wife, Mother, Politician*, Sidgwick & Jackson, 1983.
14 Ernest Jones, Early Development of Female Sexuality', in *Papers on Psychoanalysis*, Baillière, Tindall & Cox, 1927; and J. Laplanche and J. B. Pontallis, *The Language of Psychoanalysis*, Hogarth Press, 1973.

15 As note 2.
16 Patrick Cosgrave, *Thatcher: The First Term*, Bodley Head, 1985.
17 Sigmund Freud, *Female Sexuality*, 1931, Hogarth Press Standard Edition, Vol. XXI.
18 As note 3.
19 As note 5.
20 'Talking Politics', BBC Radio 4, 31 August 1974.
21 St John 12, v.2.
22 As note 5.
23 As note 2.
24 *Observer*, 10 July 1988.
25 Kenneth O. Morgan, *Keir Hardie*, Weidenfeld & Nicolson, 1975.
26 *Report of the 7th Annual Conference of the Labour Party*, 1907.

Epilogue

1   Sigmund Freud, *The Interpretation of Dreams*, Hogarth Press Standard Edition, Vols IV and V.
2   C. G. Jung, *Collected Works*, Vol. III, Routledge, 1978.
3   Charles Rycroft, 'Steps to an Ecology of Hope', in *The Sources of Hope*, ed. Ross Fitzgerald, Pergamon, 1979.
4   Ernest G. Schachtel, *Metamorphosis*, Basic Books, 1959.
5   A. F. Davies, 'Varieties of Hope', as note 3.
6   *Guardian*, 12 October 1988.
7   Leo Abse, *Private Member*, Macdonald, 1973, p. 72.
8   Alexis de Tocqueville, *Democracy in America*, Vol. 2 (ed. H. S. Commager, trans. Reeve), 1961.
9   Richard Sennett, *The Fall of Public Man*, Cambridge University Press, 1977.
10 Pascal, *Pensées, Oeuvres Complètes*, Librairie Gallimard, Paris, p. 1131–2.
11 As note 3.
12 Charter '88.
13 Brian Walden, *Sunday Times*, 4 December 1988.
14 Geoff Mulgan, *Guardian*, 20 November 1988.
15 John Biffen, *Sunday Times*, 27 March 1988.
16 As note 4.

Index